WATCHING
SEX

WITHDRAWN

WATCHING
SEX

How Men Really Respond
to Pornography

DAVID LOFTUS

THUNDER'S MOUTH PRESS
NEW YORK

WATCHING SEX: *How Men Really Respond to Pornography*

© 2002 by David Loftus

Published by
Thunder's Mouth Press
An Imprint of Avalon Publishing Group Incorporated
161 William Street, 16th Floor
New York, NY 10038

Library of Congress Control Number: 2001097335

ISBN 1-56025-360-6

9 8 7 6 5 4 3 2 1

Designed by Kathleen Lake, Neuwirth & Associates, Inc.
Printed in the United States of America
Distributed by Publishers Group West

Contents

Masculine sexuality has been under siege by feminism for its very real abuses, and has often been forced into a cringing and unproductive *mea culpa* for its aggressive fantasies. Yet if, as I have tried to argue here and elsewhere, pornography is not the monolithic expression of phallic misogyny that it has been stigmatised as being, then there is good reason even for heterosexual men to explore the pleasures of the genre without having to admit too many *mea culpas*.

—Linda Williams
"Second Thoughts on *Hard Core*"

Whatever goes on in the mind of pornography's consumer matters tremendously.

—Catharine MacKinnon,
Feminism Unbound

Miss Manners believes that the true value in people is not what is in their murky psyches, which many keep in as shocking a state as their bureau drawers, but in how they treat one another.

—Judith Martin,
*Miss Manners' Guide to
Excruciatingly Correct Behavior*

Introduction

In a much-quoted 1974 essay, Robin Morgan launched one of the most famous salvos against pornography when she declared: "Pornography is the theory, rape the practice." Within seven years, Laura Lederer's *Take Back the Night: Women on Pornography*, Andrea Dworkin's *Pornography: Men Possessing Women*, and Susan Griffin's *Pornography and Silence: Culture's Revolt Against Nature* had all been published. Much of what the authors said—that pornography reflected male contempt for and power over women, incited men to treat women badly, and fostered violence—was persuasive. In the years that followed, Diana E.H. Russell, Catharine MacKinnon, Susan G. Cole, Sheila Jeffreys, Dorchen Leidholdt, and Catherine Itzin joined the cause with their books and essays.

Dworkin and MacKinnon crafted civil rights legislation that empowered individual women to sue the makers, retailers, and users of pornography. The proposal passed in the cities of Minneapolis and Indianapolis but a mayor vetoed the one and a judge struck down the other. Dworkin and MacKinnon's theory became law in Canada, however, when the Supreme Court of that nation adopted their language in *Butler v. Her Majesty the Queen*. In 1986, when the U.S. Presidential Commission on Pornography headed by Attorney General Edwin Meese held its hearings, Dworkin testified as a "friendly" witness, which led to the peculiar circumstance of a radical feminist lesbian being published with approval by Phyllis Schlafly in her book of excerpts from commission testimony called *Pornography's Victims*.

There was something *un*-feminist about all this. The women's movement had correctly championed the notion that the individual has the right to define reality for herself. It sought to correct millennia of men defining women's reality. But some women turned around and committed the same offense against men. Their books were filled with peremptory assertions about what happened to men who look at porn, and none of it was good. "Pornography is often more sexually compelling than the realities it presents, more sexually real than reality," wrote MacKinnon. Sooner or later, all men want to live out the fantasies depicted in pornography, she asserted. But how could she know this? Where was her evidence?

It is one thing to say, "I feel this way when pornography is around; this hurts me." It is quite another to say, "This is what it does to *men's* values and feelings, this is what it makes *them* do." The personal is political, feminism kept repeating. Fair enough. But where was men's personal reality in these theorists' equations? When would men get their chance to say, "This is what *we* feel and think"?

Within the last decade, the public debate has shifted. Feminist scholars such as Lynne Segal, Linda Williams, Lynn Hunt, Alison Assiter, Avedon Carol, and Laura Kipnis have supported pornography and explored its history. National ACLU president Nadine Strossen published *Defending Pornography*, and Canadian activist Wendy McElroy authored *XXX: A Woman's Right to Pornography*. Feminist performance artists and writers such as Susie Bright, Pat Califia, Candida Royalle, and Annie Sprinkle produced their own porn as well as declared their support for it and championed the practice of sado-masochistic sex. Lisa Palac, once an antiporn feminist at the University of Minnesota in Minneapolis, when Dworkin and MacKinnon taught there, went on to edit *Future Sex* magazine and declare, "The censorship of pornography is unfeminist." Camille Paglia, an "anti-feminist feminist," has written: "Pornography cannot be separated from art. . . ."

What's wrong with this picture?

There are still no men in it.

A few men have spoken on the subject of pornography, but almost never from a personal perspective. Researchers such as Edward Donnerstein, a professor of psychology at Florida State University, and his colleagues have studied possible links between pornography and violence. The late Robert Stoller, a psychoanalyst, interviewed and profiled men and women who work in pornography and other sex trades. A 1990 collection entitled *Men Confront Pornography* attempted to address the issue from all sides, but most of the essays were theoretical and analytical, not direct and personal. Even the title suggested the writers were examining something outside themselves, a threat or enticement that was somehow separate from the male consumer and his feelings and self-image. Women writers found the book lacking. Anne McClintock said it had a tone of "male insecurity and sexual distress," and she grew impatient with "a cloying self-pity indulged in by some of the contributors." Linda Williams agreed that *Men Confront Pornography* was "interesting but guilt-ridden, even self-pitying."

Virtually none of the millions of men who were exposed to pornography as youths and annually shell out most of the billions that sustain the industry, have contributed anything to the public discussion. How do men feel about pornography? What do they think it does to their value systems and attitudes toward women?

I decided to find out by doing something no one had ever done: ask the men themselves. I talked to nearly 150 men, some in person, some on the Internet. Their answers might surprise you. Among other things, they said:

1. They would like to see more plot and romance in pornography.
2. They do not particularly enjoy closeups of genitals.
3. They not only do *not* find violence against women or domination of women sexy, they are specifically turned off by such behavior on the rare occasions they see it in pornography, and most haven't even seen any.
4. Though they enjoy looking at women having sex with women, they don't believe the women pictured are actually lesbians.
5. They have not sought ever more vivid, kinky, and violent pornography, but have either stuck with what they liked from the first, investigated wilder content and returned to what they preferred, or lost interest altogether.
6. They don't like the way men are portrayed in pornography.
7. They are against making it available to children, even though many of them were exposed to pornographic stories and images before the age of 12 and don't feel the worse for it.

I talked to men for whom some of the above is not true. I talked to others for whom none or all of it is true. But whatever the antiporn activists and experts have said about men and pornography—whatever you think *you* know about the subject—is not the whole truth. Maybe not even most of it. Even men in the survey voiced assumptions about what other men think and do . . . and were wrong.

In this book you will hear the voices of men sharing aspects of themselves—their experiences, their thoughts and feelings—which they have not shared with any other person, not even the most important people in their lives. You will hear about their fears, their fantasies, and how they view the choices they have made and expect to make. You will learn about their most secret desires and wishes, and whether they expect to see them ever fulfilled.

You will meet male virgins in their 20s and 30s, and men whose only sex partners have been prostitutes . . . but you will also meet men who have been happily married for decades to the only sex partner they've ever known, men with small daughters and men with grown children, men who are widowed and divorced, men who are gay or bisexual, men who are gay or bisexual *and* married to women. You will meet gay and heterosexual men with little sex experience and men with long histories of romance and casual sex, young men just out of high school and men in their 60s, a few men who fit the antiporn caricature of the porn user in many ways and others who do not.

I tried to speak to men from as many different backgrounds and perspectives as I could find who would talk to me: men who grew up fundamentalist Christians and men with no religious background, men who stopped looking at porn after a few years and others who produce it, men who loathe pornography as well as those who love it. They came from all over the United States as well as Canada and Britain. A few grew up in Australia, New Zealand, France, Norway, Finland, Switzerland, Spain, and the Netherlands.

This is not a scientific survey. It will not introduce you to "the average American male" or tell you what he thinks and does. The men in this book chose in advance to participate in the project—they "self-selected" as the social scientists put it—so they do not constitute a random sample.

Because I met most of them on the Internet, they clearly did not represent a cross section of American males. They're more educated than the average, for one thing. Those who did earn an income—who were not full-time students in undergraduate or graduate programs—had a higher income than the typical American male. Many had advanced degrees; in fact, some taught at universities around the nation or overseas. Others were researchers or librarians. Many worked in the private computer industry, or as computer specialists for public institutions. There were more single men and more gays than one would find in a random sample of the general population.

But do self-selected participants in an unrepresentative sample make a survey "so flawed and unreliable as to be useless," as the authors of the 1994 study *Sex in America* described such predecessors as *The Hite Report,* the Redbook survey, and the Janus Report? Not necessarily, I would argue.

The answer depends on what you seek to prove. It is probably fair to say that those surveys were "methodologically flawed, making their data unreliable," as the authors of *Sex in America* claimed, but only if they purported to offer a statistically representative picture of American sexual behavior. The authors of those surveys may have massaged their numbers and overstepped the bounds of scientific accuracy when they claimed to know "what Americans do in bed," but the mere act of speaking publicly about such matters undoubtedly made a positive difference.

The first Hite Report on female sexuality unquestionably did a world of good for many of the women (and men) who read it. They learned it was not unusual for women to feel dissatisfied by sex, to fail to reach orgasm, and not a sin for a woman to seek satisfaction during sex through masturbation. Such information had been readily available in medical literature, but this was the first time American women saw hundreds of other females like themselves say so, and explain what they felt and experienced and desired.

The mere fact that such surveys helped people to alter their perceptions of what is possible and what is acceptable, and to talk with their sex partners about what they experience and desire, was a great step forward from the days when people repeated such public myths as masturbation leads to blindness and insanity, and sex is something women must endure and cannot enjoy. Whether or not the surveys afforded an accurate picture of American sex practices, they did offer readers an opportunity to accept themselves a little more, or to change their lives in ways that empowered them.

The Internet has become a notorious region for false identities, lies, and tall tales. Naturally, you might wonder how honest my survey participants may have been. Since I had no way of checking the veracity of what they told me, I had to judge the content on its own merits: Did it sound sincere? Did the details have a plausible ring to them? Did the men's stories as a whole seem consistent? In almost every case, such questions never even surfaced—partly because of the anonymity in which my survey participants could safely cloak themselves. If they were nervous about my knowing their true identity—and most of them were not, partly because I made no secret of my name, whereabouts, or professional writing experience, and partly because they obviously understood the importance of what I was trying to do—they didn't have to tell me and I never asked.

But the openness of my interviewees also was partly a function of the Internet itself. Many people feel more comfortable communicating intimately with someone they can neither see nor hear—someone they will not encounter on the street, in the office, or at home where the shared knowledge between them could prove an embarrassment.

Trust issues cut both ways. Some men—not many—worried about who I was and how I could guarantee their anonymity and care for their secrets. I told them about my life, sent them copies of my previously published writings. One chose to mail his answers anonymously while on trips away from his home state.

Indeed, every book involves issues of trust. How could Shere Hite have had any way of verifying what all those men and women told her? How can we be sure that Sokol and Carter faithfully quoted their respondents in *What Really Happens In Bed*, especially since few of the participants were apt to expose themselves in public to complain? How can you know that someone you care about always tells you the truth? The answer to all these questions is: ultimately, we have no certainty. But we accept many things on faith, judge people's remarks with our head and gut, try to measure the inconsistencies and false notes, and usually are justified in our judgments.

In the end, the reader will have to weigh the veracity of my subjects' remarks for themselves as I did: by how they sound.

This book will not dwell on numbers, though it employs a few to draw a rough picture of what the men had to say. It does not seek to prove or establish anything so much as to raise questions that have been too seldom asked, or not at all. Though it may not offer a statistically representative sample of American males, let alone all men, I believe it is broad enough—if not to represent every experience and sensibility one may find among carriers of the XY chromosome, at least to give a much greater sense than ever before of what men do and feel in this particular arena of sexual practice, desire, fantasy, and ethics.

If reading this book inspires you as a man to understand and accept yourself more fully, and to question yourself a little further; if it inspires you as a woman to understand the men in your life a little more, and to ask more of them in a truly inquisitive and nonthreatening manner; if it helps to make gay and bisexual men more understandable to the rest of the population as well as to one another; if it makes pornography itself seem a little less frightening or foolish, and a little more multifaceted and susceptible to positive change . . . then this project will have been worth the effort.

Unveilings:

Men's First Exposures
to Pornography

"Jack" credits Santa Claus with introducing him to pornography at about the age of 10:

> Somehow I got the greedy notion that I should write very detailed, specific Christmas lists for Santa Claus (i.e., my parents), and that I would get very upset when they would disregard what I wanted! I then got the idea of snooping in my parents' bedroom closets, to see how badly they had messed up in buying what I wanted for Christmas, to prepare myself in advance. In snooping through their room, I discovered my dad's bottom drawer, where he had a couple of "dirty books" . . . *The Bedroom Philosophers* by the Marquis de Sade, and *My Mother Taught Me* by Tor Kung.

Jack was already reading Robert Heinlein, Isaac Asimov, and Ray Bradbury at the time, so he had no trouble understanding the words in these books. Sade struck him as "a carnival circus of total weirdness, extravagant to the point of silliness." The other book was more disturbing—and intoxicating: "It was about a boy (probably my own age) who gets adopted into a rather funny new stepfamily. The stepfather keeps chasing after the French maid, the boy starts to peek through keyholes and overstuffed chairs at sexual things he never dreamed of, and then the stepmother starts to take an interest in 'teaching' him all about being a man."

Jack clearly relishes telling his Santa Claus story, but most of the men I talked to were more low-key in describing their first encounter with pornography. Many could not recall the content except in a general way, and many were hazy about how old they had been.

I purposely did not define "pornography" so each man could do it for himself. The average age for exposure to erotic materials of any sort, from mainstream cheesecake to XXX films to erotic prose, was less than 11½. This is fairly consistent with the few other studies of first exposure: The 1969 U.S. Commission of Obscenity and Pornography reported a pilot study of college students (men and women) who reported that 71 percent had seen pornography by the age of 12, while a different study showed 49 percent of males exposed to porn by the age of 12. A 1987 Canadian study indicated that the average age for first viewing of pornography among males and females was 13½, for first viewing of a pornographic film, 14½.

A few men in my survey reported that their first exposure did not occur until their early 20s, and a couple said they had seen erotic materials by the age of 5.

As for *what* they saw, about a third of the men reported that it consisted of the static, friendly female nudes of *Playboy* magazine. Before *Playboy* came along, graphic nudity was either more innocent or more raunchy. Many people assume that Hugh Hefner's magazine led the way for all the sexually explicit publications that followed, but even in 1953 it struck a middle ground—where it remains—between art photography and French postcards and blue movies. Many publications of that era took the former approach to nudity, posing tasteful nudes in half-light, carefully avoiding any hint of pubic hair and genitalia, or even nipples. A few others went all the way with pubic hair, erections, and penetration (if not genital close-ups). But before *Playboy* all forms of porn had one thing in common: They were all largely underground. Hefner put graphic flesh on the public newsstand.

Some men said they first saw the more explicit *Penthouse,* topless "Page 3 girls" in British tabloids, or "standard girlie magazines." Others saw nudist magazines first, which typically showed fully and partially nude people in nonsexual situations, such as hiking and playing volleyball, often with pubic hair and female genitals whited out.

Other "first exposures" included decks of playing cards with "cheese-cake" nudes, an adult comic book, a sex-education book with text and pictures, and paperback novels (including *Candy*, Henry Miller's books, and *Fanny Hill*). Whatever the source, a majority of the men surveyed said the first pornography they had seen showed only women.

Very few men recalled the exact content of their first pornography, however. A fourth grader was shown some *Playboy* centerfolds by a cousin—"the one I remember most was a woman named China Lee; I can still see her breasts"—and by the time he was in the fifth grade he had discovered his brother's and father's collections of the magazine. A New Zealand man recalled "*Health & Efficiency*, a naturalist magazine that, at that time, had pubic areas deleted." Two Frenchmen saw magazines at their uncles' homes showing sexual intercourse and naked men and women. A 16-year-old boy who had yet to come out as gay, joined his brother-in-law, who was a police officer, and another cop to watch a homemade sex video that had been seized: "The video was of two guys and a woman. This is what turned me on the most—the two guys, I mean. I don't mean the two guys did anything with each other. It was just hot to see two guys having sex at the same time. I remember feeling very confined in my slacks."

For most men, the first sexual materials they saw were not so much about intercourse and orgasms as they were about the female form (and sometimes her genitalia). This highlights the obvious fact that women are more interesting to the vast majority of heterosexual males, but it also suggests that whether or not they receive adequate sex education by the age of 12, many men learn to associate the sight of a solitary nude woman—more than the sight of a man and woman engaged in physical intimacy—with sex and their own arousal . . . at least until they become sexually active.

Incidentally, three men volunteered that they had used *National Geographic* magazine for sexual arousal before being exposed to material they considered to be pornography. One was a married man, one a married bisexual, and the third a gay man. Previous to seeing a photo of a topless woman another boy had brought to school (when he was about 10), the married heterosexual said he would use "medical books showing the female anatomy in both drawings and photographs, department store catalogs showing women's lingerie, and of course *National Geographic.*" The bisexual man wrote, "I think I first masturbated to images of 'ethnic' women in *National Geographic.* This magazine is more pornographic than many would like to admit."

Relatively few men said the first porn they saw consisted of XXX material. At 9 years of age, one found "Hard-core German photographs showing male/female masturbation, coitus, and insertion of objects into vagina" in his father's closet. A man who grew up in Norway was 12 or 13 when classmates showed him a magazine: "Some of it I found disgusting, like anal sex." One boy was 9 or 10 and visiting his father, who lived away from the family at the time, when he discovered magazines that reviewed X-rated movies. "I remember being surprised at some of the curved penises I saw; I had never seen an erect penis (other than my own, which is straight), and I wondered if the men had something wrong with them." A gay man who had been married to a woman for 25 years recalled:

> The first porn I saw was some stuff I found in my mother's dresser, I guess. In a brown business envelope I found straight porn—including photos of men and women fucking and sucking, interspersed with a porno narrative. My guess was my Dad got it in the service overseas.

Before photography became widespread, when obscenity laws were more severe, boys sometimes encountered drawings of explicit sex. A

67-year-old gay man recalled the popular pornographic comic books he encountered in a small Midwestern town in the mid-1940s:

> I discovered porno comics (blue books, Tijuana bibles, etc.) and written porno of similar small size. The blue books were called "8-pagers." The Tijuana bibles consisted of takeoffs on regular comic strip characters—Blondie and Dagwood, Maggie and Jiggs—both men and women. The men were usually pony-sized, the women very willing and even seductive. The pleasure derived from the fact that they were all well-known comic strip characters, from the Katzenjammer Kids to Betty Boop. I stole a couple of each from my father and Grandfather's poolroom—they had them for sale. I read them and passed them on to a 15-year-old neighbor boy with whom I was sexually active. I must have been excited about what I saw—even though it was strictly heterosexual porn, which to this day can still turn me on.

Because gay pornography was not as readily available, a lot of gay males settled for material that was not intended for them, or wasn't even pornographic. Many watched for the annual "Sex In Cinema" issue of *Playboy* because that was one of the few places one might find naked males, especially males one knew from mainstream entertainment and might already be inclined to fantasize about. One gay man related this experience:

> I entertained myself with muscle magazines and miscellaneous images of half-nude men that I encountered in daily life. I did encounter things that I used for pornographic purposes: images of partially clothed men in my father's World War II books, for instance, and even high school yearbook pictures of my favorite studs. The World War II books were commemorative albums of photos taken in the field and on Navy ships. Men were shown often half-clothed for comfort, especially on the ships. The high school yearbooks contained sports photos of various attractive boys, gymnasts, wrestlers, swimmers. Remember that "pornography" is a bit of a slippery fish!

5

Most boys were not actively seeking pornography at the time of their first exposure. Either someone else showed it to them or they discovered it in the course of searching for something else. In a sense, pornography was imposed upon these boys. Often, they didn't know enough to look specifically for porn, and some had only the vaguest notion of what they were looking at.

One boy was reading *Candy*, *Fanny Hill*, and *The Cradle of Erotica* by the age of 9 because they were available on his father's bookshelves. He said the material was "pretty good stuff, even if it was rather abstract," and began masturbating with it. Another saw his mother's copy of *Playgirl* lying around at the age of 3. It didn't leave much of an impression. A third was given a book called *The Facts of Love*. "My parents gave it to me to explain the birds and bees. There were some very attractive images of males in there."

Of course, not everyone had their grownups' blessing. One boy first saw the famous Bo Derek *Playboy* at 11 because his father had "accidentally" left it out. His Dad "showed disgust that he couldn't keep it anymore without my knowledge." A Swiss man discovered a "page 3 girl" variety of topless cheesecake when he was 8. He knew it was forbidden material, and did not let anyone know he looked at it.

Many boys were first shown pornography by male friends. "A friend of mine had some of his father's *Playboy* magazines," recalled a Canadian gay man. "We looked at them in the garage. A few years later he showed me his mother's copy of *Playgirl*." One boy was initiated by a younger friend: "I think I was 9 or 10 years old. The porn was a *Playboy* that my neighbor, who was 7 or 8, had." Another man related this story:

> I had an interest in sexually related materials since before I was able to get my hands on my first *Playboy*. At about 10, a neighbor's father had a subscription, but he kept his study locked. Around 13 another neighbor found a picture of a naked woman. We spent a lot of time looking at it. I still didn't really understand naked women, though. He had a strange theory that when they grew breasts, they also grew a penis. Needless to say, we were not very experienced.

Some boys had pornography shown to them by classmates at school. One reported that a fifth grader who lived next to the school hopped the fence from the playground and returned with copies of his father's *Playboys*. "Needless to say, all the commotion brought over the gym teacher and this kid got sent to the office."

One boy was 14 when classmates brought to school a sexually graphic comic book with pictures of "males having sex with women in all kinds of positions. Classmates also brought playing cards to class with pictures of men and women in the sex act." A friend gave a sixth grader pages from a tiny booklet about sexual positions, which he proceeded to show to every boy he saw until the principal took it away. Another man said: "I was about 11. One of my schoolmates led me into the men's room and excitedly suggested to look at some close-up pictures of male genitals, oral sex on male, and maybe genital sex, too."

Classmates also showed some outré material to a 15-year-old in 1964:

> These pictures were pretty gross, nothing like *Playboy*. (I think most of them were French and Mexican.) Large woman (almost fat) having "deep" intercourse with a donkey . . . a woman with very large vulva lips, legs spread, pissing a lot of water . . . woman with large Coke bottle almost all way into vagina . . . woman, large clit, with large penises in her vagina and anus . . . woman having bowel movement on man's stomach with his penis in vagina . . . other assorted acts of intercourse or very open vaginas. . . .

For the most part, the sharing of erotic magazines and pornographic materials was a remarkably free and egalitarian experience. Men rarely reported a boy charging others for a look, for instance. When one boy found something, he either kept it to himself or shared it freely. Youngsters were all on the same voyage of discovery into the mysterious world of women and sex (or men and sex), and everyone understood the benefits of helping one another out.

Of course when porn was brought to school, there was a dynamic of asserting power over other boys—"I'm better than you because I have this stuff"—but the material was still freely circulated as part of gaining social cachet. The everyday competitiveness and aggression of boys and young men was seemingly put on hold in the face of the mystery of girls and what they looked like under their clothes.

A number of boys ran across pornography while they were looking for something else or wandering the neighborhood. They may have been involved in a search to satisfy their curiosity, but they had not specifically expected to find pornography. It turned up in their parents' or brother's closet, dresser, or clothing, or on the street, in a field, or in the trash or a public dumpster.

In 1963, a 10-year-old saw *Playboy* "in my dad's bathroom cabinet while going on a typical kid search for mysterious, dangerous, hidden, and possibly forbidden stuff of all sorts." At age 15, he found a porn novel with hard-core photos in the same manner. A 13-year-old found *High Society, Penthouse,* and other magazines "under dad's socks." By sprinkling some dust on the top one and checking later to see if the dust was still there, the boy deduced that his father did not look at the magazines very often, so he kept them in his own room for a while.

A 28-year-old Asian-Indian man wrote:

> The summer of 1976, between third and fourth grade, I found a copy of the *Playboy* with the Jimmy Carter interview when I was borrowing socks from my father's drawer. I immediately showed it to my mother who said that he had got it for the interview. It must have been true, because I never found any other *Playboy*s when I looked a few years later, although he still had that one. One book which had a lasting effect on my life was *The Sensuous Woman.* I didn't know what masturbation was. I looked the word up in the dictionary that came with our '60s *Encyclopedia Britannica* and it said "to gratify oneself." I imagined someone staring into a mirror and saying, "I'm so great, I'm so great."

Many boys simply ran across discarded pornography while they were out playing. Recalled one man:

I must have been about 10 or 12. My friends and I were riding our bikes through an orange grove when we saw some papers and trash beneath a tree. We investigated and found a magazine with pictures of naked women. This must've been about 1964. There kneeled a beautiful naked woman on the sand on a beach. I got an instant erection. I made no use of the magazine—we left it and went on playing, throwing oranges at each other. I did not know what sexual intercourse was then.

Sometimes a boy and his friends discovered pornography where someone else had stowed it. One boy was only 6 or 7 when he stumbled upon his first, fairly graphic example:

My father was a Camp Leader in the Boy Scouts. We were at his camp one week with a bunch of kids. I wandered off by myself and found an old magazine in the hollow of a tree. It had lots of pages missing. There were some men doing men, men doing women, and women doing women with strap-on dildos.

Another man's account explained how pornography often ends up where kids can find it:

We lived in the country several miles from town. I got off the school bus one day and found some trash dumped by the side of the road. I looked through it and found a pornographic novel called *The Adam and Eve Hotel.* In later years I would find porn in trash cans and alongside the road. I understand this all too well since there were many occasions when I would buy porn and use it but then would become disgusted and angry with myself and throw it from the car. Also, on some occasions I would leave porn lying in a parking lot and then wait to see if someone would pick it up.

Forests and recycling bins also yielded porn magazines: "I and some friends always found them in the woods, or on the sides of roads," one man recalled. Said another, "When I was 11 I went to our apartment trash room and found someone's collection of old *Oui* magazines, so I grabbed a few." A married chemical engineer said, "I found some stuff out in the woods that bordered the construction area in one or two neighborhoods. I know for a fact that you can find erotica in a dumpster if you look hard enough. Kids find the strangest things when they explore."

A few boys were introduced to pornography by girls. This should not be surprising in view of the fact that there was so much of it available for discovery in parents' bedrooms and closets and on the street. Before the great divide of puberty, boys and girls can be similarly inquisitive and nonjudgmental about matters of sex and nudity. In a 1996 op-ed piece for the *New York Times*, Celia Barbour, then an associate editor for *Martha Stewart Living*, wrote: "Most women I know had a brief, intense affair with pornographic magazines when they were young. It happened around age 12 or 13 and was marked by the same avid fascination as a boy's early forays into *Playboy*."

A teenaged babysitter introduced one boy to *Playboy* when he was 8 or 9. She found one of his stepfather's issues and "we started reading and looking at it." He got the impression she had seen such magazines before. She told him, "Don't tell 'em we're lookin' at this." Several other men in the survey had the experience of encountering pornography with an older woman present who, if not enthusiastic, did not openly disapprove. One boy looked at a graphic adult comic book in his brother-in-law's home while his sister looked on with "benign indifference."

A man who first saw *Playboy* at 9 or 10 when his mother got a subscription for his father, and whose mother kept *The Joy of Sex* and *Delta of Venus* in the open, recalled looking at magazines with his younger sister:

> . . . when I was in high school and my sister was in junior high, there was a brief period when we would go through my father's closets together, looking for his porno mags. I can remember looking at *Penthouse* with her. The first couple of times, we sat side by side looking through them. I think

for her it was a novelty. The pictures didn't do anything for her, but she was very interested in the stories. After that, she started having a sexual response to the material, and wasn't comfortable looking at it beside me. Once, she took one of the magazines and knelt down on the other side of my parents' bed so that she could look at it out of my direct sight. Of course, I was still in the room, but the measure of privacy sufficed. After that, she didn't look at them with me any more.

Initial Reactions to Pornography

The boys' reactions to their first exposures to porn ranged from utter delight to sheer horror, and from puzzled arousal to complete indifference.

Nearly 4 in 10 used words like "fascinated," "interested and aroused," and "loved it" to describe their first glimpse of porn. "At the time, of course, I thought it was totally wonderful—the most outstandingly exciting thing I'd ever seen in my entire life," a British computer journalist recalled of the "tits and bums" magazine that he saw passed around at school when he was 11 or 12. "There she was, a woman, baring herself. Totally sterile, now I think about it, but I thought it was great!" A man who was 11 when he looked at *Penthouse* magazines fished from the garbage by a buddy said, "Because I had never seen a naked woman before, my first thought of all those gorgeous naked women with their legs spread open was, 'Wow!'"

"I was thrilled," echoed the American man who read *The Family's Incest Summer* at 12. "I had been masturbating for a few years by then, and it was a godsend, really; my imagination had been wearing thin." A man who discovered magazines hidden by both his father and older brother said, "I clearly remember thinking when I was that age, that I hope they still have this stuff around when I'm 18 and can enjoy it legally."

Some of the men's reactions were limited by their youthful lack of knowledge and experience. An 8-year-old shown a *Playboy* by his brother "thought it was great. I was aroused, but only as much as an

8-year-old could be. I had no idea what sexual intercourse was back then, so I just thought they were a bunch of naked people."

A few men in the "enthusiastic" group admitted to some anxieties. One who found magazines in a desk said, "I looked them over and liked what I saw," but added that he felt "some guilt—I was sure my parents wouldn't approve of my looking at the pictures." On balance the experience was largely positive for him: "I was aroused [and started] having fantasies about naked women." An 11-year-old who rubbed his erection against the bottom sheet of the bed to achieve his first orgasm "was so scared of the feelings and the wetness that I actually got my mother and told her I had wet my bed. There had been so little ejaculate she could not even feel any wetness." But by the next day he had decided the sensations were entirely pleasurable, not scary, and "something that pleasurable couldn't be abnormal."

Many men remarked that their interest was captured by the female form and its beauty. Pornography showed women's bodies and women engaged in sexual acts they had never seen and rarely had had explained to them. It sparked or confirmed a positive response toward the female (or in the case of gay men, the male) body. Not a single man reported that he felt a sense of dominance over women, or enjoyed seeing them in humiliating positions. A 22-year-old software engineer's memories of his reaction to *Playboy, Penthouse,* and *High Society* at the age of 12 were fairly typical:

> At the time, I thought it was great. It certainly was a new experience, since I never really knew what women looked like without their clothes on. Even at that age I began to appreciate the beauty of women, and I found nude women to be even more beautiful.

Most gay men in the survey would eventually arrive at a point where pornography was a familiar fixture in their lives—something that was not any cause for secrecy or anxiety because their partners and friends usually understood, were not threatened, and in fact used it as well. As youths, however, they suffered the burden of multiple levels of secrecy:

Not only did they have to hide the porn, but they had to hide the source of their arousal from their friends.

> When I was 9, a friend about 3 years older asked if I wanted to see something sexy. He pulled a tattered *Playboy* from under his bed. I remember being amused, but I don't recall being particularly aroused by it. I *was* interested in looking at the men in a "party scene," even though they were old, fat, and bald. I also somehow knew that I shouldn't let my friend know that I was looking at the men, so I made comments about the women.

A man who knew he was gay by the age of 14 had difficulty accepting the fact, so it took him some time to get used to gay porn:

> I knew what my attraction to men meant. I was still hoping it might be changeable and I'd become "normal" as soon as I saw enough female flesh to find something I liked about it. Hah! I wish someone had told me that wasn't going to do it. It would have saved me a lot of grief. The first time I saw gay male porn [at 22] I was kind of repulsed. We're programmed to think gay sex is gross, and that's how I saw it, but I imagine it was more due to the low quality of the video than anything else. Sex in bathrooms with ugly men is not something that turns me on [but] after a while I began to see aspects of it that I really liked, not to mention the individual actors as well, and got used to the idea. I was still a virgin so it was also a learning experience. I knew what sexual intercourse was (man/woman style) since I was 10 or so. I knew men had sex with each other at that time too, but I couldn't imagine it. It wasn't until I actually saw and read gay porn that I knew what was involved. "So *that*'s how . . . and *that* . . . and *that* . . . and *that*."

If, as antiporn theorists contend, the attraction of pornography lies in experiencing power over an exposed, vulnerable, degraded woman (as opposed to, say, sexual arousal, delight in the positive attitude of the models, and appreciation of feminine beauty), then one might suppose that even closeted gays would derive pleasure from heterosexual pornography. After all, gay or not, they are still men in a patriarchal society, and women are "only women." But even though some gay males wished they could be turned on by heterosexual pornography, most simply were not. As one put it, "I had 'successfully' resisted homosexual urges in my adolescence and was waiting patiently to get interested in girls. I knew homosexuals were sick and deviant and I wasn't sick or deviant so I couldn't be homosexual." When an assignment to write an essay about a magazine for an expository writing course in his junior year of college gave him an excuse to pick up an issue of *Blueboy*—his first exposure to gay pornography—he found it deeply arousing in a way that straight porn had never been for him.

> The experience of profound calm I felt at that moment when I discovered who I am made my coming-out process relatively easy. Because of the essential role it played in my development I will never condemn pornography. Gay (and, I think, lesbian) people sometimes do not have any other way to find out who they are and how they can be.

A quarter of the men surveyed said they had mixed reactions to their first glimpse of pornography. This included everything from very excited and shocked to aroused and confused; from surprised and curious to confused and not particularly aroused; from aroused and embarrassed to repulsed but tempted.

A man who first saw sexually oriented material (a sex education instructional book for children in a standard bookstore) when he was 22, had a different reason for feeling upset:

> First actual porn [was] *Show Me*, which showed kids watching their parents having intercourse. It was presented as an "enlightened" approach to sex, but I really think of it as porn. It wasn't smut but not all porn is smut. The *Show Me* book was disturbing yet seemed weirdly familiar. Much later I became aware that I had been sexually abused by my mother as a child— that is probably why. Frankly, I was entranced, but I felt it was wrong. Exciting, but wrong.

Other men recalled being confused by the material their parents were hiding and schoolmates were passing around so avidly, and not terribly aroused at all. "I didn't really understand exactly what was going on in the porn, and on some level I knew it was false, or at least a part of it was," said a man who saw *Penthouse Forum* at age 11. "But distinguishing between what was fantasy and what was reality was very confusing." A man whose younger female friend showed him *Playboy* when he was 5 recalled, "I didn't know what to think of it, because I really didn't understand it, just knew that I wasn't supposed to be looking at it, that our parents would be upset if they caught us." He would not look at anything pornographic again until the age of 20, long after realizing he was gay.

It took some of these boys a while to catch on. A man who saw porn magazines in his parents' general store at age 7 or 8 said, "As I got older, I began taking some of them into the bathroom to 'read' and looking at them more fully. Until I was about, oh, I'd say 14 or 15, I really didn't appreciate what I was seeing. Around then, I started to be really fascinated with the beautiful women appearing in them." He had masturbated in bed at night "as far back as I can remember," but connecting that activity to the readings in the bathroom took a while.

"Intercourse was one of those weird adult things which we thought bizarre and mostly snickered about," recalled a 40-year-old man. He had been masturbating since "at least age 4," but did not initially connect that activity with looking at porn—"even after encountering *Playboy*, I did so more without looking at *Playboy* than with." It was a session with some older friends and the magazine that "occasioned a comparison of masturbation technique—not by direct demonstration, but by pantomime and talking. I think that this event played some role in tying together the formerly dissociated activities of looking at *Playboys* and of masturbation—it was something that older guys who I looked up to were enthusiastic about."

By contrast, the 13-year-old who found pornography "under dad's socks" reacted in the opposite manner: "I remember being turned on at first, but then rapidly losing interest, and I stopped reading them after about 2 months." He explained:

> The people depicted were airbrushed fantasy women, not people like I saw every day, so there was no real element for fantasy, and they didn't cater to my interests, what I like in porn. I didn't really make much use of them sexually—I jerked off with them a couple of times, but they fascinated me more than aroused me after the first few times.

This man also saw "a lot of boys at school trading pictures and such, but I was never a part of that." At the time of the survey, he was working for a publisher of pornographic magazines. As part of his work, he was sent fifteen or twenty other pornographic publications for review, and he subscribed to eight himself and bought additional random issues. "I don't use them for fantasy as much as I used to—it has become business to a large degree, but there is still the occasional image I get into," he said.

About 10 percent of survey participants said they had been largely indifferent when they first saw porn. Most of them were gay:

> The first time I saw female porn I was underwhelmed. You know, I was kinda expecting *something*. After all, it was such a *big deal*. Relatives keep telling boys "oh, you'll understand when you're older" (nudge, wink) about sex and girls. Most boys in my school were chasing after girls in one way or another. Clearly it must have been a big deal for them, because they seemed to enjoy it a lot. But it really just bored the hell out of me.

A few straight men were also indifferent at first. A 35-year-old programmer, married with children, believed he was "too young to have a real sexual response" when he saw his father's *Playboy* at 9 or 10. Although he knew "that I didn't want my mother to walk in while I was looking at it, I don't think that it made much of an impact on me. For example, I had at the time a very close friend about a year older than me, and I don't think I ever mentioned it to him."

The Nature of Their Interest

Boys responded positively to pornography for numerous reasons. Men cited the pleasure of having their curiosity satisfied, the tang of novelty, the thrill of the forbidden and taboo, the tingle of doing something clandestine, the sensation of being "grown-up," and the chance to bond with other boys—perhaps even to elevate their social status to a more exclusive group.

A man who was between 6 and 8 when he saw posed stills of women said: "I saw the pictures in much the way I looked at pictures of exotic places and weird things. I was seeing things that I did not normally see in my daily life. At that time I also liked to look at *World Magazine* and the pictures of weird bugs." Said another, "It was more of an amazement/vicarious type excitement than anything." This man, a computer-business owner, first saw a *Penthouse* passed around by his hockey teammates at age 9. "The sight of a naked woman that wasn't my mother was exciting in a nonsexual way, like seeing a famous hockey player up close."

The sense of "getting away with something," of tasting forbidden fruit, can be a powerful stimulant for children that is not necessarily sexual. Sex might be the excuse, the ostensible cause, but not the real motivation, which is to do something or gain access to something you are not supposed to. "I recall it being something interesting because it was a taboo thing to have," a man recalled of the *Penthouse* he found in the trash at age 8. Of the *Penthouse Forum* guys passed around the schoolroom when he was 11, a 23-year-old bisexual in higher education agreed: "I don't think it excited me sexually in any way, other than the excitement of having something that was prohibited."

For many gay men, the manner of exposure, their response, and their interest in the material (curiosity, the thrill of the forbidden, bonding with the guys), was no different from the motivations of their straight buddies. A music student who discovered some old *Playboy*s in a neighbor's outhouse recalled: "I was turned on, perhaps more by the 'illicit' nature of it all, rather than by the women. Or perhaps I knew I was 'supposed' to be turned on by the women, so I was."

The thrill of doing something forbidden was not "just a guy thing," even in the case of pornography. Said a man who discovered Henry Miller with his female playmate:

> The overall sense of the memory is giggly kids doing something "forbidden," reading about sex, not understanding it. We were also tantalized by the four-letter words Miller liked to use. I think we would validate with each other whether the passages meant what we thought they did. I remember that neither of us was sure what an orgasm was, and we looked it up in the dictionary. I'm not sure we understood then either.

For a 35-year-old academic, the spice at 11 was secrecy rather than the forbidden:

> I found a number of issues [of *Playboy*] in the dumpster. At about the same time, some of my friends had some and we looked at them together in a fort that we had. I felt, from my friends, that there was a certain obligatory arousal that was supposed to be happening. I was not particularly aroused by the photographs, but the sense of the clandestine, the secret, was very arousing to me. I was more excited by my friends' reactions, to the small cult of secrecy that we maintained, to their arousal.

A few men described the feeling of being more grown up because of gaining access to this forbidden material. "I thought I was getting to see something very private, something very adult, and something very exciting," said a 45-year-old medical administrator whose first experience was poring over a detective novel that had a lurid cover but very little hard information inside. "It was like peeping in a window and finally getting to see something you've heard about from other kids and adults."

Some boys tied this forbidden material to fitting in with the group. The boy who regarded pornography at age 8 as similar to pictures of other "exotic places and weird things" said:

Looking at that magazine also helped my social standing among other boys in my grade, because two of the four boys were ahead of me and as a result [were] more popular. So to be able to say that I did something forbidden with older boys was a true sign of status. I made no sexual use of it. The most use I made of it was to tell other boys in my class that I had seen pictures of naked girls in a magazine. I was also careful to point out that two of the boys who let me see it were older and they chose to include me.

To be honest, the older boys' excitement puzzled him:

The two boys older than me said things like "ooh," "wow," and "look at that/those." It was definitely presented as something one should look at and express surprise, amazement, and appreciation. Their attitude was one where it was assumed that I wanted to look at the pornography and there was never discussion about why, or what one was to do with it. I cannot remember the boy my age saying anything or expressing any attitude, though he was also quick to tell the other boys in our class that we had seen pictures of naked girls.

Nudity and sex were not mysteries to this boy, whose parents had told him about vaginal intercourse when he was 5. "However, I thought that men and women only had sex when they were married, and then only to have children. I had no idea from the discussion with my parents that sex was enjoyable. I reasoned that since I was one of two children that my parents had had vaginal intercourse twice."

Just as shared consumption of pornography could foster male bonding, so traditional male bonding situations had a tendency to encourage porn consumption. Several men had their first exposure to pornography among Boy Scouts on a campout or paper recycling drive.

Men also reported considerable exposure to pornography—sometimes more than they would have liked—when they were in the military. An Army vet was delighted with the 8mm porn films that were screened in the attic of his barracks in Germany. "I liked what I saw.

Some of the acts were hard to believe, others were very arousing. The act that sticks in my mind had shown a girl on a bed with a long rubber dick; I couldn't believe it when she stuck the whole thing in her vagina. It was big. It was a lot of fun watching this stuff with all the other guys there making their comments." He did note, however, that "some of the guys just didn't want to watch the movie."

Still, the male bonding element should not be overemphasized. Antiporn feminists write about how pornography unites men *against* women, but because of the sensitive nature of sex and public discussion of it, a boy's arousal in the company of other males could just as easily be a source of isolation, even humiliation. A British student who talked of the "black market drug" as titillation in a "totally crumpled bit of paper" passed around the school added: "It did arouse me although being aroused in a class full of similarly pubescent boys was not something you wanted to broadcast."

What's essential about men's first exposures to pornography is that whatever the context, it *never* had primarily to do with objectifying or degrading women. This is not to argue the latter factors were not also present—they may well have been—but simply that other, vital elements of the male experience are routinely ignored in antiporn analyses. Not only are the responses and attitudes of grown men to pornography more complicated than antiporn feminists and fundamentalist ministers can imagine, but so are the motivations of the average 12-year-old boy.

Growing Up:

The Social Context

There is no denying that even in the absence of open discussion of the subject, men's attitudes toward pornography change as they mature. A number of men said the topic of pornography (or sex) was never mentioned by their parents; others said the subject arose only in a disparaging or joking manner. Many boys pieced together their attitudes from hints, isolated incidents, vague and general social mores, and the guesses of their equally mystified peers, rather than through direct guidance from grown-ups. They formed their opinions after braving a thicket of indirect, disapproving, and often conflicting messages from their parents and society at large.

By the time they were out of high school, most men had gotten the message that pornography was frowned upon by much of society. Some learned it from the friends who showed it to them, by observing the way their peers handled (or hid) the material. Some received clear messages from their parents, who either condemned pornography or warned their sons not to let the neighbors know about their interest. Other boys witnessed negative attitudes toward sex and nudity play out in the home, and concluded that depictions of sex and nudity must also be bad.

A boy's first signals about social attitudes often came from his male peers. "Boys my age used to leer and make snide jokes about porn, which made me believe—even though it seemed exciting and tempting—that it was a bad thing and I should not have anything to do with it," said a married musician and writer. "I was a very sensitive kid, and I homed in on other people's feelings like they were my own." An English lad reacted against pornography because of how the other boys behaved around it. "I did not see it as dangerous or corrupting at the time but as I grew older I actively dissociated myself from people when they looked at porn in a group."

"Whenever a dirty magazine was involved, it was always a big secret," reported a 24-year-old library clerk. "We always had to be secretive and make sure no one's parents saw us looking at them." A gay man in educational administration, aged 41, remembered that a friend who showed him a nudist magazine "went through this painstaking ordeal of taking it from its hiding place every time we wanted to look at it, and believe me, he really had it hidden."

Some boys incurred the wrath of their parents. A respondent who found one of his father's *Playboys* at age 6 said, "My mother caught me looking at it one day and just about gave birth to broken glass." She promptly pulled the rest of the magazines off the shelf and later argued with his father.

Although fathers as a group tended to be more accommodating and accepting than mothers, not surprisingly, some fathers were even *less* tolerant. One man who described his mother's attitude as "disinterest"—she asked him to get rid of a "smutty" booklet she found under his mattress—added: "My father had much stronger feelings about all sexual things. Although I don't remember ever discussing pornography with him (we hardly ever discussed sexual matters at all), I know that he considered it harmful and sinful."

To some extent, pornography was simply tarred with the same brush as sex. The anxiety, uncertainty, or downright disapproval with which adults addressed the subject of sexuality (if they addressed it at all) ensured that pornography would also be condemned. A 38-year-old married man said, "Sex itself was a bad thing when I was growing up. Not to be discussed or acknowledged. There was never any question in my mind that porn was dirty, if not downright sinful."

Several survey participants accused their parents of hypocrisy. Although his mother frowned on "pornography and related things," an audio engineer said she "reads Harlequin romances which have *very* steamy sex scenes in them." Another man recalled that the official parental line was "we don't want that stuff in our house," and his mother made it apparent that she considered it "filth"; but when the boy got his hands on some magazines and a video in eighth grade, they confiscated them . . . but did not dispose of them. "That irritated me— they criticize me for having it in their house and then keep it for themselves. At least I got to watch it again, though."

Obviously, some parents were conflicted about sex and pornography, so their children could hardly expect clear guidance. "My mother's attitude [about sex] was decidedly negative (even though she had her 'how to' books)," one man remembered. "My father's attitude was typical of many southern US men. A woman should be a lady in the living room and a whore in the bedroom. The attitude towards porn was secretive (he kept it hidden); however, he did use it a lot."

In some households, red flags went up before a boy even got to the forbidden subjects. A 65-year-old gay man remembered reading an article in a women's magazine that was lying around the home of his foster family, "and at dinner one evening innocently talking about some aspect of childbirth, thinking I was making a contribution to the conversation. There was a stunned sharp reaction and it was clear that we were not to talk about having babies."

To be fair, parents might find themselves in a quandary if they tried to deal openly with their children's exposure to pornography. When a parent did attempt a dialogue, the child might cut it short, as a single 32-year-old recalled:

> My mother was the type who thought she should be open about sex with her children, but growing up I was uncomfortable discussing these issues with her. My mother said that it wasn't that I was forbidden to [look at pornography], she just felt she and my dad should discuss it with me so I wouldn't get the "wrong ideas." I was not comfortable at 11-12 discussing sex with my mother, so the discussions didn't go far. After that I kept any porn I had hidden enough that the discussion never came up again.

In some cases, religious organizations labored hard to control the situation. The man whose mother had "given birth to broken glass" said: "The basic attitude of the Missouri Synod Lutheran Church (and my family) regarding *any* form of sexual relations is best summed up as follows: Sex is *dirty*. Sex is *bad*. *But* you should save it for the one you love." The problem with this regimen was that it focused intense attention on the very subject the church wanted to erase from youthful minds, which naturally encouraged the very obsessions it sought to eradicate.

Just as well-meaning churches may have stimulated undue interest in pornography, strong negative responses to childhood nakedness could also backfire on overly prudish parents. Sex might have been too mysterious a concept for small children to grasp, but keeping one's body covered was a simple one. "Little kids are taught to keep their clothes on," one man said. "So, when I found these magazines full of pictures of naked women, it was pretty obvious that someone was doing something that they weren't supposed to do."

"The nakedness taboo was weird to me when I was very young, although I quickly grew to accept it and it seems normal to me today," wrote a bisexual man. But, "As a side effect, I became very curious about what other people had on under their clothes."

In some cases, a public incident made pornography's forbidden status clear. A married bisexual man remembered that someone got caught with a magazine in junior high and "was used as an example for the rest of us." The malefactor's name was announced in all the homerooms. "I won't say that anyone called it 'evil,' but the general impression was that the administration was very much against it."

Other men cited messages in the media. "Nobody came right out and told me it would corrupt me and damn my soul," a 29-year-old virgin said, "but I heard it described as 'filth' and other pejoratives enough to absorb it—mostly from television." A 28-year-old married man said that beside the fact that his grandmother wordlessly threw away his magazines whenever she found them, "there didn't seem to be any lack of groups who liked to lecture against pornography on TV and radio."

Despite the many and varied social injunctions against pornography, few men agreed with them at the time. Some boys found it easy to dismiss their parents' warnings: "[My mother] is very antiporn, and made no effort to hide it," reported a 21-year-old gay student. "I've never agreed with her about it."

"How could pictures be bad?" a schoolteacher asked. "I was encouraged to explore other information that interested me. *And this interested me*. How come this was different?"

"I certainly couldn't see it as a bad thing, because it made me feel good!" recalled a 30-year-old gay male; "I thought it was the best thing since sliced bread!"

Societal and parental opposition served as a spur for rebellious boys. "I was extremely interested in sex, and this interest was undoubtedly stimulated by the inhibitions in my family," said a 56-year-old professor. "We had a very strict home life, sex was a forbidden topic," recalled a Christian widower. What he regarded as an innocent incident at school resulted in the strict injunction not to ask questions about sex, and "the unspoken message was that I was not to ask at home either— the topic was not welcome. This attitude probably contributed to my subsequent intense curiosity about sexuality." The man who saw the school administration make an example of a boy who was caught with porn added that the opposition of one's elders cut both ways:

> I was in junior high in the late sixties and early seventies. The pronouncements of the administration were received as something to rally against, rather than something to internalize. I don't think I ever learned that porn was bad; there is certainly bad porn, degrading porn, badly conceived porn, but generally I put it into a category of victimless crimes.

One of the dangers of vehement opposition from the church, parents, or society was that if a boy concluded they were lying or wrong about pornography, he was more likely to question *everything* they told him, which was the case for a 42-year-old electronic publishing specialist:

> I was raised Pentecostal. I suppose "porn" was considered a bad thing from the beginning, once I was aware that "porn" existed. In my childhood and adolescence, *sex* was a bad thing. I slowly began to realize that sex was a natural part of human existence, though, which shook my faith in my religion. After all, why would God build such desires within us if they were bad?

A few men in the survey said pornography only became problematic for them when they were older and became aware of feminist issues.

> Somewhere in the early seventies I bought the feminist party line that wanting sex with a woman was an evil male notion. I also started noticing that magazines were getting bad press from the feminist camp. It was not until college that I became aware of what I might feel. *Playboy* was the flag bearer for the entire porn industry. It was always "*Playboy* and all those other dirty magazines." Having read most of them at one time or another I knew that was not the case, but it was interesting to watch the media circus. [grad student, 32]

> I don't know that I ever thought of porn as a bad thing during my teen years. It was only after I learned that some women (and a few men) found it degrading. I guess I always knew the religious side of things, but my family wasn't religious and I thought most morals that didn't affect other

people (unlike murder, stealing, etc.) were pretty lame. When I learned that some women were abused to make pornography, then I grew more concerned, but I don't think I've ever thought of it as "bad." Mostly, I thought of it as embarrassing. If I admitted I used porn, then I admitted that I couldn't find a satisfying relationship with a real woman. That was the main "badness" of it. [grad student, 23, bisexual]

A few men said their impression of pornography when they were kids was that it was a grown-up thing, not necessarily a naughty or evil one. "I knew it was an 'adult' thing, maybe even a somewhat 'sleazy' thing, but not 'bad' as in, 'You should never even look at the stuff,'" recalled a 43-year-old computer scientist. Of course, the fact that it was "something that kids were not supposed to see" created "all the more reason to look," as a cancer physician observed.

A 30-year-old software consultant in Australia said:

Well, we haven't got the same lot of religious loonies that you do. I don't recall ever considering that other people thought of porn as bad, as such, when I was young. Sure, it was something, like sex, that you didn't tend to talk about or do in public, but that didn't mean it was "bad"—just private.

Even more intriguing was the blithe national self-contradiction described by a Spaniard who sometimes used pornography with his wife (who "gets very aroused, and we have great sex"):

Spain is a curious country. I mean, we are supposed to be Catholics, and Catholics used to have a narrow behavior, against sexual freedom, non-marriage experiences, and so on. But we are Latins at the same time: we are a little bit *carpe diem*. Blood is stronger than monks. Officially, pornography was a bad thing. I knew it. But I knew that I was not killing or raping anybody, and I was having a good time. I was suspecting that everybody (especially men) did it, my friends told me they did it, and I was discovering that it didn't make you blind.

I Know What
Boys Like

What do men like to see in pornography? People presume you can tell by looking at the market: Whatever is selling must be what men want. But that doesn't mean that men are satisfied with what they can get. The survey results underscored the point that different men liked different things, and while there was a lot they liked, almost no one was entirely satisfied.

When asked, "What do you especially like to see or read about in pornography?" and "What turns you on the most?", many men listed performers and sex acts, while others commented on the general tone or approach of the porn. Most of those comments had to do with credibility, realism, and overall quality. Several said pornography is most effective when it is believable. Others wanted to see the participants express genuine pleasure. A plot helped. So did good writing, characterization, decent acting, "realistic" characters and acts, and a natural progression of events instead of abrupt changes.

If everything they disliked in pornography could be summed up in a word, it would be "unreality." Many men expressed annoyance and disappointment over unbelievable settings, stories, and behavior:

> For example, a woman gets out of a swimming pool and is going to have sex with a man, but first must put her high heels on!

> I've seen amateur videos of sex and masturbation: women usually don't make much noise when they cum. They squeal a little, or sigh and tremble for a few seconds, then it's over. Knowing that, it's disgusting to see women carrying on in paroxysms of shrieking ecstasy. Also, the closeups of the "passionate faces" are sometimes hard to believe. Those contorted faces look more like they're in pain than in pleasure. Where did porn makers ever get the idea that sex has to be such unpleasant work? And the guys get so athletic, they look like they aren't enjoying themselves at all. Like it's just a big show, an athletic event. To me, that isn't sex, it's self-abuse. [musician/writer, 48, married]

Other men complained that sex and relationships as described in pornography were unrealistic and misleadingly simplistic. A 35-year-old programmer observed, "An impressionable male can easily get the impression that if you look good, women will have sex with you simply by asking them. It doesn't work that way. I'd like to see less focus on 'penetration' or 'the act' and a bit more on flirting (verbal foreplay) and facial expressions." He added it was also unrealistic to show people engaging in kinky sex acts without any negotiation up front.

A physician stated his desire to see couples seduce one another:

> Sex that looks like love-making is a turn-on; sex which is animal grunting usually isn't. In terms of particular acts, realism is best. It may include kissing, oral sex, intercourse. By the way, I once saw a didactic video about how couples can work to find the so-called "G-spot," in which this really gorgeous couple demonstrated what the narrator had described, in terms

of different sexual acts, positions, etc., which were supposed to help achieve a "Graafian [sic] orgasm" for women. The acts were accompanied by soft music. This really appeared to be intense sex between these two people, appeared realistic, and was thus incredibly exciting.

After drawing a distinction between "female" porn typified by the romance novel, and "male" porn with its focus on the sex act itself, a 25-year-old bisexual software engineer said, "I am not satisfied with either of these extremes." The ritual and symbolism of romance novels didn't speak to him—"It doesn't matter if the baron is about to inherit the kingdom but would be throwing it all away to marry a commoner"— but the voyeuristic novelty of watching people have sex on film lost its appeal quickly, too. "I tend to prefer something in between. A plot of some sort with enough characterization to allow me to identify with one or more of the characters so I can sympathetically feel the physical and emotional sensations they feel."

A number of men specifically objected to chauvinism and degradation of women in pornography. "It bothers me to sometimes see characters not treated as people, especially women—for example, when some of the male characters merely use women characters for their own sexual gratification," said a Christian widower. A bisexual Englishman who claimed to be indifferent to pornography offered a more detailed analysis:

I think a lot of porn generally presents a very negative picture of women, either as stupid, sex-obsessed, wishing to be dominated or abused by men. Of course it is not surprising it does this, given it is feeding men with a fantasy that women will be interested in them and do what they want. I would rather not see women slavering over abusive men, but I have rarely seen this anyway. It is difficult to find anything really objectionable in most porn when it is all so ridiculous and unreal.

In a similar vein, another man commented:

Basically, I want porn to give me a symbolic sexual experience, and I want to identify with the characters, but if the whole setup is unacceptable then I just can't. Usually, porn shows a man having sex with a woman he doesn't know and doesn't want to know, only because he wants sex (the man is supposed to want sex all the time), and the woman complies, even though she may have other things to do, loves somebody else, dislikes this particular person, etc. This reflects some common sexist stereotypes, and I am actively against this.

Comments were pointed with regard to blatant formulas in porn videos. "Just the same old series in porn videos of foreplay to sucking to fucking to man-pulling-out-and-cumming-on-her-buns crap," a 48-year-old musician complained; "I hate that!" The routine is so common and obvious that various men mapped it in similar terms:

What I wish were eliminated is the formula for films, which every scene follows: Kiss. Get undressed. Girl sucks guy. Guy licks girl. They screw missionary. They screw doggie-style. They screw female-superior. Back to missionary. The "come shot." Same old thing, with minor variations, over and over. . . . [computer analyst, 27, single]

I'm tired of the standard S&F [suck and fuck] routine that goes something like this: Dressed boy and girl begin to kiss and undress. She then proceeds to suck boy's penis for a good while. Next, boy goes down on girl and licks clitoris and tongues vagina for a good while. Next, girl proceeds to be mounted by boy and continue until ejaculation occurs outside vagina, usually near face or breast area. [American government technician, 46, married 25 years]

A 40-year-old programmer in Britain, married seven years, had a similar critique but argued that it was an inevitable hazard of the genre:

The problem is that by being underground, porn has evolved into a totally separate genre. Ideally one could find "red-hot sex scenes" in an ordinary drama, or Umberto Eco-quality literary pastiche in a porn novel. In practice, the market has so split that few dare try an in-between work. The literati would sneer at the porn episodes, the pornophiles would be frustrated by the breaks for plot. I'm not trying to sound holier-than-them. I normally say that I like a bit of plot with my porn, but I remember an intensely frustrating Dutch film. Every time the "action" had been going on long enough to "inspire" my partner and I, it would switch back to the plot.

A 28-year-old editor, married, complained that "too much still follows the old bachelor party mentality, while ignoring half the world's population! Until the porn industry can create high-quality movies with good plots and strong characters, they will never attract either mainstream actors or mainstream moviegoers."

A British software engineer who loved literature of all sorts, including some with highly erotic content, had this to say:

I think much of today's mass-market pornography is not about sex at all. It's about seeing how much you can get away with. As if a restaurant decided to cook, not good food, but food with as much salt in as possible. And as if they took away the chairs, tables, candles, ambiance, and expected you to stuff your face in a trough. In sum, I think a lot of porn is cheap and tasteless, and only reinforces the sick stereotype that sex is somehow improper, nasty, hole-in-the-corner or cunt-in-your-face. That sex is performed by genitalia rather than people.

"The seduction is the part I like best," said a 54-year-old manager who wrote porn novels in the early 1970s. "'Sweet reluctant amorous delay,' as Milton put it. Build up. That's what's missing most." A 32-year-old who was bored by "plumbing shots" agreed that, "The drama of seduction is very exciting and I'd like to see more of it before the jump in the sack."

A number of men in the survey cited the hyper-stylized porn videos of Andrew Blake as a welcome exception:

What mystifies me is that the other film producers don't get it—here's a guy, new on the scene, making money hand over fist, and they make much less. Doesn't it ever occur to them to try and figure out why he is so successful and duplicate it?

Another man called the prevailing style the "Fundamentals of Piston Mechanics."

Quite a few gay men also said romance was the element they most appreciated but was often missing. "Depending on the men used, some are very 'cold,'" observed a 32-year-old Mexican-American educator. "I would like to see more intimate scenes between men, more hugging and kissing before they get to the hard-core action." A 23-year-old medical student wanted "the typical romantic things, two people who love each other making love, or a lover preparing for the other lover to come home."

The interest in romance among gay men shouldn't be surprising, since there is so little of it in mainstream entertainment. Displays of affection among heterosexuals are a common sight, even in public. Advertising is saturated with it as well. By comparison, gays live on a starvation diet. If pornography is at least partly concerned with taboos—showing you what you don't see elsewhere—then gay affection could be as important as gay sex.

Several men mentioned they liked to see dominant women. Sometimes that meant simply that the female was on top during sex. For others, female dominance meant that the woman was in control. A 20-year-old political-science student characterized this as "a general being swept-off-your-feet-ness kind of thing; rather than something the man did, something that happened to the man. There's a certain appeal in having wonderful things happen to you without putting in a whole lot of effort."

In stressing that the key to good porn is fantasy, one man said he would prefer not to see condoms: "Although I am very much in favor of condoms for 'real' sex, I view porn as fantasy sex, and in my fantasies no one gets pregnant or acquires STDs."

Many men said it was important that the woman—or women—appeared to experience genuine pleasure. "In videos I like to see women enjoying themselves," said a married science teacher with two kids: "Non-faked female orgasms, whether self-induced or as a result of some form of intercourse, is a major turn-on for me."

A 28-year-old student and former business manager, married seven years, felt the same: "I enjoy when women have orgasms (or at least act convincingly like they are) onscreen." "I definitely like female orgasms, and feel cheated when all that's depicted is male orgasms," agreed a symphonic musician.

The flip side was that if a woman looked like she was not terribly excited, viewers were disappointed:

> The lack of enthusiasm is remarkable. Some women are moaning like they're having a religious experience, but when they show their faces they look like they're at an accounting seminar. The looks of boredom are amazingly blatant—so much for acting! [business owner, 30, married seven years]

A couple of men said they appreciated the rare instances when a woman looks directly at the viewer. "I'm glad to see that moviemakers are starting to pick up on the fact that it is incredibly arousing to me, when a woman stares right into the camera," said a literature professor. "Just the eye contact is crucial, and the sense that the woman is there, is involved and into it. There's this 'you are there' sense, a sense of participation." A divorced, 40-year-old software specialist agreed:

> If it's going to be still photographs, I like to see women give a look, some kind of look that says 'I want you.' Because I find that very sexy. If their eyes are closed, masturbating, that doesn't arouse me as much.

"There isn't a great deal of emotion [in a lot of porn]," a gay man observed. "It would really help to see people who either are having fun or are passionate about what they are doing, or who even look as if they are attracted to one another."

> I tend to dislike mainstream porn because the guys don't really look like they're getting into it. They act like they're acting. One of the appeals of amateur stuff is that the people in it really seem like they're enjoying it. I'd also like to see people having a little more fun. Particularly in gay porn, the scenes are these ridiculously serious things for the most part—the people don't seem genuinely aroused (even if they are hard), and they don't look like they are enjoying their partners or having fun. [research analyst, 33]

Many men had opinions on the kind of people they liked to see in pornography, although few types stood out other than attractive or beautiful women, or just naked women. A musician/writer spoke for many when he said he loved "the incredible beauty of the women." Men who said they looked for beautiful women tended to be older and had marital experience; the ones who simply said naked women generally were younger and less experienced.

Some took pains to distinguish between natural beauty, often with the underlying implication of character, and gorgeous looks. "Not everyone likes unusually large-breasted women with bleached blonde hair," said a married business owner; "I much prefer a few imperfections to the *Baywatch* Barbie look." "The most attractive women are those who look least glamorous," a 38-year-old married man added. "Porn starlets usually go for a high-fashion tarted-up look, whereas I prefer a woman with more natural beauty."

"The biggest problem with the majority of porn I see is that the women are far too similar in body type," said a 32-year-old bisexual man. "Someone once described the type as 'the body of an athletic 20-year-old with the tits of a nursing mother.' I'd like to see more women of average appearance, more ethnic backgrounds, and in less artificial settings."

Some gay men expressed similar sentiments. Said a 33-year-old research analyst:

> I think what is lacking in porn is regular-looking people, you know, the guy-next-door type. All of these buffed guys are hot, but they represent

such a tiny proportion of people, and certainly don't represent anyone who I'd be romping with.

A 32-year-old single man in public relations preferred "women who come off as self-assured and intelligent," adding that, "there is a real shortage of these in porn."

"A woman who knew what she wants and is comfortable saying it or saying that she's not getting what she wants," said a 29-year-old; "I'm very attracted to that type."

A 48-year-old musician and writer was more explicit:

> Some of the women are really stupid, like they couldn't graduate from kindergarten. They are so frivolous and dorky that even their sexy bodies can't turn me on. I'm really turned off by uneducated types in porn! I guess because I think of education as a sign of awareness, and awareness is a very sexual and sexy thing to me.

When it came to specific physical types, men's tastes went all over the map. A sizable minority liked Asian women. Redheads were popular. Smaller numbers liked dark-haired women, black women, younger women (late teens/early twenties), and multiethnic performers. A couple mentioned large or heavy women, while just as many specified petite, short, or "smallish framed."

Several men had a *very* specific type in mind. The man who disdained the "*Baywatch* Barbie look" said he liked to see "a petite, athletic redhead with freckles and small breasts who is intelligent and sexually adventurous." A 35-year-old liked to see young men or teenaged boys with women old enough to be the boys' mothers.

A *very* few men professed interest and arousal with regard to children in fantasy—*though not in their actual sex life*. A 44-year-old skilled mechanic in his second marriage said:

> I like *anything* unusual. I like heavy women, gay, animals, kids. What turns me on the most, if I had to choose, would be, and I really don't want to

freak anyone out, but I do want to be honest, would be technically considered kiddie porn. I hate that description because it conjures up all manner of low lifes, rapists and such. I would *never* do anything with a child,
but I find the sight of a young girl, say 11 or 12 thru 15 or 16, very sexually stimulating. I don't like *very* young kids, but the ages I describe. It
gives me an instant erection. I think part of the reason is that it is *very* difficult to come by, consequently, difficult to overdose on. The closest I
come in real life is my wife, who is clean shaven. That drives me wild.

A 45-year-old married man said he liked to see "she-males," or her-
maphrodites and transsexuals. But several other heterosexuals were
strongly turned off by them. "I remember seeing a picture of a female-
to-male transsexual," reported a virginal 29-year-old technical writer;
"She'd kept the female equipment and was adding on the male. She
was an ugly-looking guy, her male genitals looked pretty bad, and the
original equipment didn't look great either. I could have lived without
seeing that."

A handful of heterosexual males said they also liked attractive men
in pornography. One said attractive, "but not too muscular"; a married
physician said they should be "attractive, muscular, in good shape, but
not hulky." A 48-year-old musician said they should be "good looking,
sensitive types, not he-men and jock types." A Christian widower was
even more specific: "18-30 years old, handsome face, medium muscu-
lature, chest hair with stripe running down abdomen to pubis, spurt
semen a foot or more."

The only part of the female anatomy that attracted considerable
comment was breasts. A handful of men objected to artificial ones, and
a small group said they disliked large, heavy breasts. An Asian-Indian
man complained of "fake mutant 40++ tits." A musician decried "too
much emphasis on big tits. I *like* smaller tits." "I'd far rather see nicely
shaped breasts than large floppy or silicone-inflated ones," said a married science teacher. "It may not be entirely fair to blame porn videos,"
wrote a 28-year-old student. "From what I hear, most women make far
more money at strip clubs than they do in movies, and the women who

have had their breasts enlarged make more money for dancing. So, porn movies may not directly be the reason for messing up perfectly good breasts at all."

Some men especially liked smaller breasts. Said one, "Women with small breasts [are] perhaps [meaningful to me] because I missed out on any sex in my high school days, and the idea of being seduced by a teenage girl (16-17) excites me."

Several men specifically voiced an interest in female genitals. "I like to see vaginal shots and full frontal female nudity," allowed a Canadian government official who ordinarily did not buy or look at pornography, he said, on principle. Another fan of women's privates said: "I am fascinated by the variety of shape, color, size, etc., in women's genitals."

These few huzzahs were outweighed by a much larger chorus of men who disliked genital closeups. A 32-year-old single man in public relations called them "plumbing shots," and said he found them especially unappealing "if it's shot from the rear, looking up the performers' assholes." "The pictures are usually not very attractive," added a 23-year-old virgin, "very *un*-sexy, and I'm just bewildered that people can find this stimulating. I find it embarrassing." He felt the same way about close-ups in videos: "For as good as it feels, the actual stuff going on down there isn't particularly attractive if you're looking at it from three inches away."

A 35-year-old office worker said: "Sometimes you can just tell the area has been specially illuminated with a flashlight or directional strobe or something so it stands out from everything else. It just looks ridiculous."

No one objected to women's legs, however, and a few men praised them highly. "Legs are where it's at," said a 20-year-old engineering student. A 34-year-old British programmer agreed: "I am especially fond of long legs that are well featured."

Very few men mentioned either clothing or sex toys when asked what they most liked to see in pornography. Several liked lingerie and dildos, but almost everything else was an isolated particular that appealed to an individual taste. Two men listed stockings and garters. Another liked to see clothes and shoes on people during sex. "I find high heels exciting," said a married man with two kids.

On the other hand, three other men said they disliked the stiletto look. "I wish the actresses would take off those ridiculous high heels during sex," said a man who also hated "jesus dear god oh fuck me" monologues. "High heels are silly enough on the street, but why do the pornography producers have actresses wear them during sex?"

If the participants in this survey are any indication, clearly the sex acts men like to see in pornography are incredibly diverse. Very few acts took precedence over the others, and many different permutations were each mentioned by at least a couple of men. By far the most-cited sex act was fellatio: women performing oral sex on men. Said one man:

> I can tell the difference, when a woman "knows what she's doing" it turns me on a lot more than when she's clueless. Most lousy videos show clueless women, who suck a cock by bobbing up and down violently as fast as they can (ouch!).

Another man liked to see "women really getting into performing slow, meticulous fellatio with big red juicy lips."

Even if they liked blow-job scenes, many men voiced strong objections to the video cliché of the "cum shot" or "money shot." Said a science teacher who had been married 15 years, "I don't see the excitement of seeing a woman get semen on her face, up her nose, in her navel, on her back, etc., etc." A 24-year-old history grad student complained of "way too much emphasis on spewing penises. I don't know who likes to see that. I don't mind looking at a penis, even one that stretches the bounds of believability, but I don't want to see sperm flying around." Another man said, "Just once in a while I wish they'd cum inside the girl. I've seen a porn video in which a guy butt-fucks a woman and ejaculates just before pulling out, leaving a trail of cum and a still-squirting cock as he withdraws. Very nice."

Other men enjoyed the cum shot, especially "facial cum shots," which often occur as the climax of a fellatio sequence. "I like pictures of women with cum on their faces," said one man. "It conveys a sense of abandon that excites me." A 30-year-old gay man who had had two sex partners in his life also liked "face shots, and actual ejaculation into a partner's mouth." "My favorite stuff are gang bangs with lots of guys cumming on a girl's face or in her mouth, facials, especially face drenches," wrote a 39-year-old virgin.

Most men listed intercourse as one of many sex acts they liked to see. A few added details. A 23-year-old virgin liked "missionary-esque with him holding her legs or pushing them forward, if you know what I'm saying." "I especially like to see coitus, preferably with a good view of the penetration," said another. As one man's comments suggested, there may be a deeply emotional component to a man's interest in seeing penetration (along with the woman's evident pleasure in it):

> I like seeing penetration shots. I think this goes back to my adolescence, when I implicitly assumed that women didn't actually want to have sex. This seemed like a reasonable assumption at the time; they certainly weren't having sex with me. Even after I started having sex with my first girlfriend, I somehow imagined that she didn't really want me to fuck her; perhaps she was just in it for the orgasms. Finally, she explained to me that she derived both physical and psychological satisfaction from having my penis inside her; that she had an active and intrinsic desire to be penetrated. To this day, I see each penetration shot as evidence that one real woman wanted a man to penetrate her. This excites me. [computer programmer, 35, married six years]

Small numbers of men said they liked to see or read about cunnilingus, women in bondage, masturbation, sadomasochism, anal sex, anal penetration of males, 69, or "tit fucking." Antiporn activists who think pornography is about men exercising power over women and humiliating them should consider the fact that *the number of males in my survey who wanted to see anal penetration of men equaled those who liked to see anal penetration of women.*

41

"Seeing a straight man penetrated by a straight woman with a dildo would be exciting and different for a change," wrote a 23-year-old who considered himself bisexual, though most of his relationships had been with women. "I know that would bring up some masculinity/homophobia issues, but it would at least be different and intense and somewhat real."

Of course, many men mentioned sex between two women as something they liked to see in pornography. ("Lesbian" scenarios will be discussed in detail in the next chapter.) The next best thing was a woman masturbating alone. A literature professor said, "I love to watch women touch themselves, and my sense is that's something a lot of men feel [interested in and] I think that's a positive change."

A few people found bestiality titillating. A 35-year-old programmer, married with two children, wrote: "Pictures of people and animals having sex fascinate me. I'm not sexually attracted to animals. However, a shot of a woman putting a dog's penis in her vagina conveys a sense of depravity that excites me."

But most men who mentioned bestiality did so because they were not into it at all. "A friend has a video of a woman having sex with a pig that is repulsive to me," a 32-year-old public relations man related. Said a swingers club owner who had been a police officer, "I've seen some of the bestiality tapes. I've always thought: No wonder this stuff's illegal, or should be illegal. I've always thought that was kind of gross. Why would anybody want to have sex with a dog?"

The most unusual example was recounted by an Australian man: "I saw a porn video at work some years ago. It depicted sex with live animals and women using live eels, which disgusted me. As I recall, these women were also defecating into a container which had these live eels. They must have been drugged to do the things that they were doing. I didn't have to watch much before feeling ill."

Many men also made a specific point of saying they did *not* like depictions of violence, and some said they were repulsed by the idea of it. A 32-year-old computer consultant, divorced, described a video scene and his reaction:

> One time I had rented a film that basically featured a guy with a humongous penis just piercing a woman's anus without warning. Her screaming pretty much convinced me that [1] she wasn't acting, and [2] she wasn't crying out in pleasure. I had that video for just one day before I took it back.

A few of the other specific references to sex with violence made it clear the men had encountered it only in written stories, usually on the Internet, and not in pictorial pornography.

A couple of men said the most repulsive pornographic images they had ever seen had been circulated by feminists. One was a Canadian professor who had seen a government-funded feminist documentary. "In the National Film Board documentary, *Not A Love Story*, there were some scenes that I found repulsive and definitely not arousing. One was of a rather grisly man biting the breasts and plucking the hair from a naked woman. Another (which had 'no nudity') showed a woman performing fellatio on a cocked and presumably loaded revolver held by a fully clothed man close to his belt." A 20-year-old political science student had never seen imagery that upset him when he had looked at pornography for arousal, but he recalled images from feminist anti-pornography slide shows:

> I remember at the slide shows, seeing images that I thought were pretty disgusting. Lots of bondage-type images, where it's very clear that the woman is unhappy in the photographs. Things where it looks like there's some sort of permanent injury, physical injury. There's a sequence where a woman is ball-gagged and then tied in a rope, and then wrapped in plastic wrap, and it's very visible that this woman is in pain, and circulation is being cut off to parts of her body. And I take the word of the presenters that some people are aroused by it, and that this kind of thing is consumed, but I found it repulsive.

For most men, scatological content was the biggest turn-off of all. "I don't enjoy the sight of people playing with scat, it turns my stomach,"

43

wrote one man. "Scat is the only thing I don't get turned on by," agreed another. "One video has a guy eating it. I can't even watch it, I have to fast forward."

It should be noted that less than half the handful of men who mentioned the scat subgenre said they had actually seen any of it. As with violent porn, several said they had encountered it only in prose: "Every time I read about the use of feces in a sexual scene, I feel repulsed," a gay man remarked.

Though not a single man in the survey expressed interest in scat, several, gay and straight, said they liked to see pissing or water sports. A 35-year-old heterosexual computer programmer, married and a father, was thoughtfully circumspect:

> Just about anything else [besides torture, mutilation, murder and copro-phagy] I'll at least look at, even if I'm not really interested. I have, for example, downloaded, viewed and saved scores of pictures of men and women pissing on each other; even pissing in each others' mouths. I can't quite decide if these pictures excite me or not. (My mind is a little twisty maze of passages.)

One man wanted to see more food in pornography. "My main kink has to do with food sex," said a "very happily married" programmer of 40. "Eating fruit out of a woman's pussy, sucking pineapple rings off a man's cock, licking whipped cream and hot fudge off a woman's breasts, that sort of thing."

The Perfect Pornography

To get a better picture of what appealed to the men, I asked, "If you could design the perfect porn for yourself, what would it look like, and what would it include?" Some repeated the elements already mentioned: more romance; more buildup; more kissing; more normal people; lots of variety; and beautiful, naked women in interesting poses.

44

Several said they would like pornography that featured monogamous sex between a husband and wife.

Others said the perfect pornography would include women they knew. A Finnish man wanted to see women he knew "doing lewd things." A literature professor wanted footage of himself and past lovers. A New Zealand native imagined "making a video of my wife masturbating and then fantasize other men (strangers) watching the video while masturbating and other couples watching the video while making love." A gay male also dreamed of movies of himself and friends, "especially redheads."

Other ideas included:

> I'd pick out women with big juicy red lips and nice faces and decent bodies. I'd put them in situations with various guys, wearing weird scanty leather outfits, performing various acts very thoughtfully and intelligently although very depraved-ly. I wouldn't zoom the cameras in very much, except for an occasional exquisite closeup of a meticulous beautiful blowjob for a moment. I'd try to mostly show the whole thing, with weird far-out lighting as in *House of Dreams*. Maybe there'd be some weird games played, tying someone up, whipping, handcuffs, etc. I'd never show "cum shots." The guys could just cum inside whatever hole they happened to be in, and it wouldn't be shown. And at the end, everyone would be untied, relaxed, happy, exhausted, and fall asleep in a big pile. [Unix specialist, 36, married six years]

> For me, the "perfect" setting would be a romantic one in which the main characters would bumble through a set of dissatisfactory relationships until they happily find the right one. That's a little general, but it would suit me fine. [software consultant, 32, divorced]

> I can usually find what I like, but it's never all in one place. I think my "perfect" porn would be a video, with a good variety of men, blonds, brunettes, and redheads, some butch, some not, and different body types—not all big and beefy, not all scrawny, but a mix. There'd be a bunch

of different scenes—some "romantic" types, some athlete or locker-room type things. It wouldn't have set roles like most porn does—the bottoms *always* bottom and the tops *always* top. I like to see people surprise you by being total tops and then all of a sudden, up go their legs and they're bottoming. And really beefy, butch types who bottom. The element of surprise, the unexpected—that's what really helps make a film hot. [music student, 21, gay]

I think [current pornography] is too acted out. I would like to see more spontaneity and more lovemaking. Real relationships would do better. I would have a look at lesbians for a day, followed by newlyweds from ceremony to consummation. [telecommunications professional, 33, married]

It would be set in the Victorian era, with the proper clothes and styling. The scenery would be outdoor. Sunshine, by a beach or river. [student, 20]

I know what I'd film given the opportunities—I'd get a bunch of willing horny men into the woods, with rocks and streams and stuff, and just turn them loose and film whatever happened. [assistant professor, 42, gay]

The perfect porn for me would be to spy on someone masturbating when he thinks he is alone. I wouldn't care about the lighting or the soundtrack or the person masturbating—I guess it would be almost like a surveillance tape, which I'm sure is totally illegal, but you asked what I'd like to see in the perfect porn for me. [educational administrator, 41, gay and divorced]

My perfect porn video could not be distributed as are others. It would include insertion of tubing into urethra and anus. It would include introduction of large amounts of liquid into the bladder and rectum. It would include insertion of huge objects and/or dildos into vagina and rectum. It would include insertion of metal rods into male and female urethra at some point. And it would include sex in all sorts of strange positions. I suspect that today's S/M stuff would not even come close to what I have in mind. Yep, it would indeed be a really strange piece of video. Now, on the other end of the picture, I would love to help produce an adult movie that would help Christians understand their bodies and show how great sexual pleasures can be derived from use of the body alone. No external or artificial sexual aids would be used in this. However, it would include all present-day sexual techniques used for sexual gratification that involves the use of body parts. [government technician, 46, married for twenty-five years to only sex partner]

I have the plot for a book running through my head, working title *The Vacation.* It is the story of a couple, on a long-needed vacation, who actively decide to explore and rediscover their sexuality, sex in reality, and explore different expressions of sexuality in their relationship. It can be as graphic or as suggestive as I like. The important thing will be the exploration, not the descriptive action. [security supervisor, 48, married twenty-seven years]

A 48-year-old musician and writer probably spoke for the greatest number of men in the survey when he said:

There would be a story. It might start out with a guy and/or a girl in their apartment alone, masturbating and fantasizing about the ideal guy, then actually meeting him/her on the street or in a restaurant. It doesn't have to take forever for them to go to bed with each other, but some production value would be appreciated. You can make a decent movie with almost no money, and get some actors who want to *act.* I'd make the story completely plausible, like it happened in your home town. Take all of the grunge out, like low-lifes in the grungy part of town humping for the hell of it. That is such a lousy scenario. It really doesn't take much to put a little quality into porn. Some have done it—particularly in the lesbian cinema (women pornographers really have a sense of quality).

The Appeal of "Lesbian" Pornography

Open an issue of just about any men's magazine at a newsstand—*Chic*, *Gallery*, *High Society*, *Penthouse*, even *Playboy*—and chances are you'll find a pictorial and a story or letter that features two or more women.

Antiporn activists like Andrea Dworkin, Catharine MacKinnon, Susan Cole, and Sheila Jeffreys have regarded the fact that so many men like this so-called "lesbian" pornography as yet another sign of hatred toward women in general, and lesbians in particular. They see males' interest in watching chicks get it on as expressing a need to pry into and degrade every aspect of women's lives, and insist that pornography distorts the truth about lesbians. As Dworkin asserts, such material "does not document lesbian lovemaking; in fact, it barely resembles it."

Since "lesbian" porn does not provide an "accurate view of lesbian sexual activity," Mariana Valverde and Lorna Weir have written, "This imaginary and distorted access to lesbianism confirms men in their 'right' to have unlimited access to any and all women, even women who are explicitly uninterested in men [and] . . . undermines all women's right to say no and erodes the foundations of choice and consent."

Unfortunately for Dworkin and her cohorts, most of the men in my survey clearly understood the women were not lesbians. In making a distinction between the performers and the characters they play, a 22-year-old Canadian software engineer pointed out that plots that include "lesbian" encounters often take pains to show the characters are not lesbians. "Sometimes it is implicit that they are not, but still interested in sexual experimentation."

Some of the men addressed the question in terms of female sexuality in general rather than just women who perform for a camera:

> I think women are more likely to be more bisexual—in other words, there are more bisexual women than there are bisexual men. [programmer, 35, single]

> It seems that when women believe they are free from societal judgment or they are indifferent to it, they engage in sexual experimentation, including combinations and permutations of partners. [student, 31, single]

> A lot of women can get into that type of thing, and they really are not lesbian, or don't consider themselves lesbians. Women have a far easier way of getting along with other women, all the way across the board—sexually as well—than two men will. [construction equipment broker, 54, married three times]

Another man leaned more toward viewing the actresses as lesbians, but said the depictions in "lesbian" pornography for men are nevertheless faked:

> I'm pretty sure (from having read behind-the-scenes stuff) that most of the women are either lesbian or (usually the case) bisexual. However, I am well aware that what is depicted in most "lesbian porn" is nothing like, how shall I put it?, "real lesbian sex." [computer engineer, 36, married]

The general confusion over the issue is illustrated by the fact that "Jane Jones," a former porn model who was interviewed by Laura Lederer for *Take Back the Night*, said, "Contrary to popular belief that there are a lot of lesbians in the business, almost every woman I met there was hetero, as far as I knew." But then, "Jones" also said, "The male image of lesbian love seems to dictate that it be violent and/or include a male voyeur. . . . None of the gentle loving comes through." As we shall see, few of the men I surveyed said they wanted to see that kind of sex, so "Jones" either encountered only a small part of the industry or the situation has changed since her interview in 1979.

A 28-year-old heterosexual man who worked for a sex magazine, roomed with a lesbian, and might be presumed to have some knowledge of the subject, declared that many of the women in pornography are, in fact, lesbians:

> Well, from professional experience, I know that a large percentage of sex workers and a high percentage of glamour models (at least on a local level—we've never had a big-name star pose for us) are gay. The magazine I work on is pansexual-leaning-heavily-to-the-gay-side, so this may have some impact on it, but nearly everyone I have ever met involved with the sex industry—be it stripping, photography, massage, etc.—are at least bi.

Pro-porn author Susie Bright agrees that lesbians play a significant role in the industry. "Lesbians and die-hard bisexuals are most definitely in the front ranks of the adult movie business. In true Hollywood style, it's okay to publicly proclaim you swing both ways, but it's Closet City when it comes to revealing one's preference for women." Two questions inevitably surface in the lesbian community as soon as rumors start about a possibly gay porn actress, she writes. People ask, "Is it true she's sucking cock?—And does she like it?" Bright responds:

> Such a rude question, I think, gets to the heart of lesbian fears and alienation from straight porn. The answer is, yes, they really do suck and fuck, and in answer to the second question, what does "like" have to do with it?

51

> Porn actresses are entirely underwhelmed by male nudity, male genitals, and male studliness in general. I find their attitude refreshing. Some women are proud of their screen skills at making a blow job look good, and some have a pleasant relationship with their male co-stars, while others don't have the time of day for the cocksmen once the camera stops.... Women who prefer women, yet who are sexually active with men for money, for friendship, or for sport, are indeed kinky compared to the rest of the gay or straight world, but certainly identifiable as female sexual outlaws who walk on the gay side.

Antiporn feminists like Dworkin and Cole (who also happen to be lesbians) appear to take such pornography at face value—that is, as straightforward depictions of what men believe lesbians do together—but it is clear that many and perhaps most men do not. When men say "lesbian" in this context, it is a kind of shorthand that everyone understands, even if it is not strictly accurate.

Whatever the actual sexual orientation of the performers, the majority of heterosexual men who participated in this survey affirmed their interest in "lesbian" scenes. But when it came to details, male tastes varied wildly. Some liked it hot and dirty, others insisted on the romantic and sensual; some liked to see sex toys, many others detested them; some insisted it's better with a man on the scene, some wanted to keep all males out of it.

A fair number of men were happy just to see nude women experiencing pleasure together, and they did not care what the women did. "I guess I mostly imagine myself as a watcher—I don't have any preferences for what they do," said one. "No [I have no preference about what they do], just as long as they're naked," remarked a 31-year-old student. Then there was the wag who, when asked, "Is there anything in particular you like to see two women doing?" replied, "The dishes."

There were only three sex acts between women that more than a few men said they liked to see: kissing, cunnilingus, and 69. Kissing topped the list. "I find lesbian kisses really sexy and beautiful," wrote one. "I particularly like to see two women together when they are 'French kissing' a lot, and when they both seem as if they are truly enjoying the experience," said a 28-year-old married student. Said another: "I am a bit of a slushy romantic at heart, so I prefer to see a context for the sexual activity. My favorite lesbian fantasies involve women mutually discovering each other sexually."

Oral sex between two women had its fans, too. Nearly equal numbers of men cited cunnilingus versus mutual oral sex, or 69. Said a 21-year-old virgin: "Oral sex, if it's slow and gentle and their genitals aren't shaved, really turns me on. I definitely wonder how it would feel to receive it as a woman."

"I like to watch them doing 69, bobbing back and forth together," a 36-year-old married man said, "But I like to watch it from a zoomed-out angle where their whole bodies are visible, rather than the stupid microscopic close-ups of most lousy porn videos."

As with hetero porn, quite a few men remarked that realism or authenticity was at the heart of successful "lesbian" porn for them (although the concept of authenticity has to be rather elastic if a majority of the men admitted they were not watching actual lesbians in action).

"Sometimes it is obvious they are just acting," said a 39-year-old programmer, married thirteen years, "and all they do is lick clit or shove their hands in the other woman's pussy." A 29-year-old technical writer said: "I don't like it when you see a closeup of a woman supposedly licking the other's clit, and the tongue is a half inch away. It looks fake. I want to see real contact—kissing, sucking (nipples and clit), digital insertion, the whole thing."

How authenticity is achieved was a matter of some disagreement. Some men put it in terms of urgency or passion. Said one, "I like to see them 69ing, pumping, sweating, *really* getting involved in the action." Others thought a slow pace, a romantic approach, was more realistic and therefore more exciting. "Kissing, hugging, oral sex too, yes. But it's the tenderness that does it for me," wrote a 27-year-old computer analyst. "I do *not* like to see them ramming big dildos into each other. I'd much rather see them softly licking each other, or deeply kissing."

Plot creates the romance, a 49-year-old software engineer in England believed. "I want to see (or read) the seduction scene as well as the sex scene. In other words, I want the action to grow plausibly out of the interactions of the two characters." A 48-year-old Native American man agreed: "I would like to see them come into a place, sitting there, some kind of storyline. I mean the kissing, the touching, the lovemaking, without use of vibrators or any of that stuff. Just woman to woman on their own."

A 56-year-old professor, married 28 years, encompassed nearly all of the above considerations—"real" lovemaking (or strong acting), real orgasms, romantic tenderness—in describing what made a "lesbian" scene authentic for him:

> Naturally I like good-looking women, but even more important is that they like what they are doing. It's a real turnoff for me to see actors who are obviously bored or otherwise not enjoying themselves. One can't always be certain, but there are incidents where it's clear that someone has a real orgasm, and I like that. When I see two or more women together, I like scenes featuring kissing, soft caressing, petting, and tender, real, lovemaking.

A 36-year-old physician, married ten years, was among the few heterosexual men who disliked girl-girl scenes. "If one turns up, I'd rather fast-forward, or read a book till it's over. They do nothing for me. I'm not sure why some guys like them." A 21-year-old music student echoed him: "It does nothing for me either arousing or disgusting. I'm not sure what the big turn-on is about it for guys."

Gay men, who for the most part expressed a gracious thanks-but-no-thanks attitude, also were puzzled by straight males' fascination with "lesbian" scenarios. "I don't find any pictorials or videos featuring two women in a sexual situation as being arousing, and I find it difficult to believe any straight man would, either, although I know they are popular," one said. "In men's magazines it makes me think that as a straight guy, I could never have sex with these girls myself," suggested another. "I guess the men think they could evoke that kind of desire they are seeing before their eyes, but for *me* it hasn't done too much. It bothered me as a kid, wondering how come *straight* males wouldn't be bothered by this stuff when *everyone* is bothered by male homosexuality."

Why Are "Lesbian" Scenes So Popular?

Fewer than half the men who liked female/female sex scenes offered a reason. Though they raised explanations they thought were plausible, many frankly confessed they didn't really know.

Some suggested it was simply the greater number of female bodies to look at. "If one nude woman is arousing then two are more so," said one man. "I enjoy pictures showing two women, but the lesbian aspect isn't particularly significant to me," wrote a married programmer; "Mainly, it's just twice as much flesh to gaze at." A 48-year-old musician said, "seeing two sets of tits and cunts in a sexual encounter is double the fun. My eyes can move from one back to the other and enjoy the differences."

Men liked to see a woman enjoy sex, so the prospect of seeing two women in a state of arousal was doubly appealing. "I have a theory that most men like scenes with two women because most men like to see women enjoying sex," wrote one respondent. "It doesn't matter if the woman is alone, with a man, with a woman, with whatever. The turn-on is watching a woman so into sex, she will do it any way possible. Two women together just doubles the pleasure."

Some men suggested that not only did women's bodies present a different physical aesthetic, but there was something different about women's style of lovemaking, too. "Women are more openly sexual than men, and two women joining in their sex is extremely arousing," one man believed. "There seems to be a greater sense of self-indulgence and enjoyment in them," another remarked, "and the interaction is not so fixated on genital contact."

A 48-year-old Native American contrasted the "feel" of a "lesbian" scene with many of his own actual experiences, which ranged from military service to several years of homelessness:

> I always found it fascinating, and also a turn-on, to watch women make love. I think because of my own makeup, of the harshness of everything about my life, that in the process of looking for love, I had it equating softness and gentleness and that, and somehow I feel that women are capable of giving that to each other. And that was my idea about it.

Several responses in this vein suggested that "lesbian" pornography conveys a sense of equality, a lack of power relations between the actors, which appealed to them. "Perhaps, simply because seeing an erection is not required for the act of being 'into it,' the artifice works here more effectively," one man observed.

A different physiological response to sex was raised by a 25-year-old grad student as a factor in his fascination with women in general and "lesbian" sex scenes in particular:

> I've had some orgasms in my time which are much more deep down, in my gut, than in my penis. And I imagine that's what it feels like for a woman. I'm in some respects envious that women can have multiple orgasms. And I guess I'm just curious about the varieties of sex that women can have and I'm also turned on by the fact that I think that women are much more sensuous creatures than men.

A small group of men suggested much of the appeal in "lesbian" pornography lay in the supposition that women know best what arouses and satisfies other women. "I think it is exciting because I think women probably have a better idea how to please one another than a man does. Therefore I guess that lesbian sex is more arousing and sensual for the participants, and that makes it more arousing to watch," said a married, 24-year-old history student. "I like the way they touch each other," a mechanic stated; "They claim that one knows how and what the other likes and it shows in their acts."

This related to credibility: It becomes easier for the viewer to imagine the women in pornography actually enjoy themselves when other women stimulate them. This might have applications in the viewer's own sex life. As one man said:

> Watching a woman make love to another woman tells you about how that particular woman would want to be made love to. So when female A starts licking and sucking on female B, you can learn, to a great extent, what female A likes to have done to her. So watching two women is often more exciting because you can see what they like doing or having done to them that isn't often done by guys.

While a number of the men said they believed women were inherently more sexual than men—in the sense of greater orgasmic capacity, and a greater openness to bisexuality and experimentation—some men either believed the opposite or had personal experiences that belied this notion. Seeing two or more women enjoy each other in pornography offered these men the assurance, or the pleasing illusion, that women *could* be highly sexual. As a 27-year-old student, married, put it: "It seems that the women in such scenes are very interested in having sex, a characteristic that most women in real life don't expose publicly."

One man said, "It's often 'culturally agreed,' or was when I was growing up, that women aren't sexual, or certainly aren't as much as men. Seeing a woman practically in a trance getting off as she pushes a baseball-bat size dildo in her ass kinda blows that concept out of the water."

Some men found "lesbian" scenes appealing precisely because there are no men around. As a 40-year-old fan put it: "No hairy men. No stupid cliché cum shots."

Younger men seemed to react more strongly against the presence of males in pornography. A 20-year-old computer engineering student said, "Lesbian scenes can be arousing. I think it might be because I don't like to see men involved. The women are a lot less repulsive." A 21-year-old virgin studying math put this argument together with the idea of a "different" style of lovemaking among women: "In a way, lesbian scenes are easier to watch because I cannot stand to watch naked males. Also, a lot of the women portray a certain sensitivity that isn't there during a heterosexual scene."

Other men suggested the viewer might enjoy identifying with the players: putting himself in the position of either or both of the women he is looking at. "It doesn't require you to look at a man and sort out your feelings about that," said one:

> The appeal of lesbian sex to heterosexual males is that the fantasy of the encounter can be visualized from either partner's point of view. I find it much easier to visualize myself as a gay woman (I wouldn't have to change my preference) than a straight woman.

Of the men who said they imagined themselves as one of the women, only a few specified a role, and it was invariably the passive one. "Maybe I imagine myself in the position of the subservient woman in such scenes," one man wrote. "Sometimes I imagine myself as one of the women being seduced by the other woman," said a 33-year-old man whose wife of 8 years had been his only sex partner. This does not accord with the antiporn notion that men go to pornography to see and experience power *over* women; here, the men not only got off on pretending to *be* a woman, but expressly chose to be the subservient one.

Some of the men ruled out being one of the women because they did not wish to intrude on the scene. "I never imagined being a woman or being directly with them because I wanted to learn and see what they would do without knowing I was there," said a 23-year-old bisexual man who preferred women as sex partners. A 43-year-old accountant agreed: "I imagine I am watching them with or without their knowledge."

Not surprisingly, many men liked to think of themselves entering the scene with the two or more women and joining in. However, several said this was a sometime occurrence, only an option, rather than their sole reason for wanting to see "lesbian" porn:

> I never imagined myself "as either of the women" in the sense of *being* a woman instead of a man, but, occasionally, I would imagine that one of them would not "be there" for all or part of my fantasy. As in all of my fantasies, I imagine being "there" as myself.

Another man freely admitted the contradictions in his responses:

> I don't fantasize being either of the women, but I will often fantasize a role for me in the scene. In some of the '70s pornography, it was common to have two women having sex, then having a man drop in on them unexpectedly and join in on the action. I always wished he'd let them alone. I suppose that this sounds like it conflicts with my fantasizing a role for myself in the scene with two women, but then a lot of my fantasies don't make any sense. [math grad student, 41, single]

A 27-year-old computer analyst said his preference was highly contextual:

> Sure [I'd like to join them]. But *only* if I think they'd welcome it. I wouldn't want to be an unwelcome intruder bothering two true lesbians. But as a partner willingly welcomed into a threesome with two hot bisexual women—oh, my, yes. A "me sandwich" is a very nice idea.

Still, a fair number of men said they didn't like to picture themselves intruding on a two-woman scene at all.

> I don't imagine myself as either of the women, only as a passive onlooker. I am very excited by female orgasm. The women should do anything they like to please each other. A man is not necessary. I wouldn't like to join women making love, this perspective doesn't attract me very much. Basically I imagine myself doing the same to a woman, so in some sense I imagine myself one of the depicted women. [grad student, 22, single]

Some men observed that the presence of a man violated the spirit of a "lesbian" encounter. A 27-year-old computer analyst said, "If they look like they are really into it, like there's no one else in the world for them but each other, then I hate to see a man intruding on the scene."

One should also note that a fair number of the men who said they liked to imagine joining a "lesbian" scenario as themselves did *not* like to see another man come into the picture. While it might seem obvious that a man would find it appealing to join two women but not want to see another man do so, this undermines the antiporn notion that a primary motivation for the porn consumer is seeing women dominated by men—that any man who appears in pornography is a surrogate for the viewer.

Some men did like to see a man appear on the scene. "That's the whole point, isn't it?" wrote one. "It increases the desired reality and makes it exponentially more erotic," said another.

But the accent on kissing, and the fact that a fair number of men didn't project *any* man into a scene with two women, suggests that it is feminine beauty and the sight of women enjoying sexual pleasure— no matter whom they're with—that thrills most male viewers. That so many men said they envied women, and wished they could know what it was like to be a woman enjoying sex, flies in the face of the notion that male viewers get off on the domination, degradation, and pain of women.

60

The Image of
Men in Pornography

In his 1989 book *Men Confront Pornography*, Michael Kimmel writes that "Pornography . . . shows men what it means to be a real man having real sex." The men I surveyed would disagree. They thought men in pornography were silly, crude, unrealistic, wooden, laughable, brutal, stupid, nasty, and/or repulsively large. They usually did *not* like the men they saw in porn, and certainly did not consider them "real." The images were degrading, insulting, impossibly ideal, oppressively "perfect" or one-dimensional, and otherwise unsuitable as models for behavior, either in bed or out of it.

"They always had a kind of sleazy look about them, always needed a shave," recalled a 53-year-old who saw 8mm black-and-white films at Idaho Jaycees "smokers" in the early 1960s as well as the first mass-market porn movies of the mid-1970s.

A 34-year-old software developer in England found the men in porn "pretty ugly and repulsive. Mostly I disliked their macho appearance."

A philosophy scholar in France said, "In the late seventies, they were mostly ugly and often looked like bums."

Several men suggested the unappealing appearance of the men ruined the viewer's ability to believe in the sex: "Some men in porn are criminally unattractive and it defeats the willing suspension of disbelief: Why is this gorgeous woman having sex with this jerk???" The men struck another viewer as "always ugly, or heavy set" so "I really couldn't fathom the thought that these lovely ladies were having casual sex with the gross guys." A third called the men "butt-ugly" and concluded, "Those women must be miserable."

A few men proffered mixed reactions. "Many of them were fairly attractive, at least well-built, muscular," said a married physician, [but] "some were fairly ugly." Another man said: "Some looked good and some I thought looked ugly. Some were sexy and some repulsive—about the same as guys on the street." The praise offered by another man was guarded: "Yes, they were extremely well-built. All out of a cookie cutter it seems." By way of clarification, he wrote: "There was no variety. I wanted to see someone who looked like me in the pictures."

A 20-year-old Canadian student saw distinctions between the types of men seen in different media:

> The men are different depending on the type of pornography. A good number of men in x-rated movies are not very good looking—hairy chests (backs occasionally), beer guts, and mustaches. The guys in magazines tend to be better built and better looking. The guys in the movies tend to be horrible actors and it can distract from the experience; magazines don't have that trouble.

Not surprisingly, gay and bisexual men typically had a more positive response to the nude males in pornography. Sometimes the fact that pornographic males displayed such ease with their bodies and nudity was an inspiration to young gay men. "I admired them for being comfortable with showing off their bodies, and I wished I could be as naked and free," wrote a 37-year-old librarian. "I thought it was totally natural and it made me feel good about myself to know that these models could be so uninhibited about themselves and what others might think," added a 26-year-old Canadian grad student who found them "generally very attractive."

Gay males decried the "phoniness" of men in pornography as often as they said they loved their looks and behavior. Sometimes the same men who had positive responses also commented on the shortcomings and/or unreality of pornographic males. A 41-year-old pronounced himself not only relatively immune to the image over the years, but also pleased to see less-than-perfect specimens hit the market:

> The men in text pornography are always perfect—the handsome good looks, the body-by-god, huge equipment, and a sexual stamina that can't be beat. From early on I thought that was all phony. Don't get me wrong— I *like* to look at good-looking guys, but let's face it, there are more "normal" guys out here. When I looked at mags and films, of course, good-looking guys *had* to be in them or the films/mags would not have been profitable—and after spending years of looking at only "perfect" specimens, I find it quite refreshing now that there is a newly developing market for amateur porn. I find it incredibly exciting to see everyday people doing sexual things. I'm tired of the bleached-blonde, buffed body, California look so prevalent in the porn market. I have a circle of friends who make and exchange homemade videos from all over. That is where my interest lies now.

Many gays noticed that men in heterosexual porn were often less attractive than their counterparts in gay porn. A 42-year-old assistant professor said, "I remember finding men in the straight porn I found while younger to be mostly unattractive somehow. I'm not really sure how to describe this unattractiveness, but it was there. I still find at least some straight porn (and soft porn) features men that I just don't find interesting." "It seemed like a man's physical beauty was less important to a straight audience than was a woman's physical beauty," another gay man observed.

A married heterosexual man said the physical perfection and attitude of males in gay porn taught him a little about what was wrong with the straight porn he preferred:

> Porn that is targeted towards homosexual men displays men in the same way that porn that is targeted towards heterosexual men displays women: as sex objects. The men are young, handsome, well-muscled; they pose and strut and try to look sexy for the viewer. I must confess that my immediate reaction when I see this sort of thing is that the men are preening; that they are undignified; that they are fools. It gives me a certain amount of empathy for women who think that porn degrades them.

Many men also were turned off by the apparent attitudes of men in pornography. Several said they did not look realistically aroused by the sex. "I remember that most of them appeared bored, strained, or in some other way depicting that they were not enjoying themselves," said a casino security supervisor.

"In still shots, the men always seemed sort of phony and posed, with stupid looks on their faces," wrote another man, adding that "I find with porn specifically (and with any sort of modeling or fashion photography in general), the models usually seem to have the most unappealing expressions, sort of the 'You killed my dog; now I'm going to have to kill you' look."

An Australian programmer/analyst agreed: "They often don't seem to be enjoying it much. Also, many of the guys in videos seem to be a bit limp even when they're supposed to be hard."

This fact also struck another man as odd:

> I've seen so many videos in which the people take their clothes off, and the man still is not fully erect. The woman spends time getting him hard with her hands and mouth. This is nothing like my experience—by the time my clothes came off in most of my sexual encounters, I was hard as a rock. I wonder if having done it over and over for cameras has made sex with almost anybody less exciting for them. Bottom line: it's unrealistic and it's a distraction that takes my mind out of the fantasy.

One man pondered the emotional state of such men:

> They all seem so empty. I've found the men a real big turn-off at times. And it's not really a competition thing for me. It's not that I identify them as competition and don't want them in the picture. It's that I know there is a lot more to being sexy than just having a big dick and keeping it up for an hour. Most of the men in porn lack any kind of subtlety or expression of desire other than grabbing the nearest vagina and sticking it in.

Some men said the males in pornography were less intelligent or interesting than the females. "The guys were usually dumber than the females," one man noted. "Most of their roles are so shallow that they could easily be replaced by dildos," said another; "Roles for actresses tend to be considerably deeper than those for actors in pornography—though that really isn't saying much."

"In general their purpose seemed to be to demonstrate how good the female was," wrote a 27-year-old married chemical engineer. He added they seemed "devoid of any character or personality, almost like a person who was asleep or drugged or at work, who could do nothing except have sex."

Essayist Phillip Lopate, one of the very few men to have written personally about porn in the past, took note of the pornographic male's shortcomings: "[R]egarding the matter of sex objects, it needs to be pointed out that men no less than women have shallow, thinglike personalities in pornographic presentations," he wrote in a 1981 piece about Times Square. Lopate suggested this might be a plus, since one of the fantasies of porn was that one could engage in sex without one's personality getting in the way, but to judge by the comments of the men in my survey, they would like to see a little more personality.

These unflattering characteristics have also been criticized by women, such as pro-sex writer Lisa Palac. An antiporn feminist at the University of Minnesota when Dworkin and MacKinnon taught a course there, she confronted a boyfriend after stumbling on his pornography collection and demanded he burn it. But at his behest, she watched a video, continued her investigations on her own, and ended up editing *Future Sex* magazine and adopting a pro-pornography stance.

When she began publishing her own sex magazine as a senior in college, she and her girlfriends agreed that "Tits and ass flood our culture, but his bare body is nowhere in sight. . . . We felt that if porn was going to come of age, not only would the images of women have to change, so would the images of men." She adds, "Paunchy guys with overgrown mustaches who had little to offer except their big dicks weren't our idea of sexy. We wanted bad boys with angel faces who understood the meaning of seduction. We also wanted them to be a little, well . . . vulnerable."

In most commercial porn, however, the men are anything but. If anything, there is a tendency toward callousness. Antiporn theorist Susan Griffin wrote, "[I]n pornography, the male hero possesses an intrinsic moral rightness which, like Hitler's Aryan, allows him to behave toward women in ways outside morality. For according to this ideology, he is the more valuable member of the species." Although men agreed with Griffin that males in pornography behaved poorly, their objections suggest that Griffin is wrong when she assumes this is what men *want* to see, or that they imagine themselves as "Hitler" or "Aryans."

Some comments: "I thought some of them were fairly inconsiderate of their female partners"; "I never thought much of the way they were depicted treating women . . . some films were definitely an exception, but I generally noted a lack of respect for the women they were boning"; "A certain callousness was evident. . . . Although these scenes were explicitly sexual, they were not necessarily erotic."

A man who grew up in Norway said, "Some of the first movies I saw, the men treated the women like dirt. I don't like that very much (too much connection to rape)." A 33-year-old lit professor who recalled the "sleazy" actors of the 1970s was particularly repelled by the behavior of one man in a movie he saw:

> . . . there was much more sense of antagonism, I think, between the sexes, in the earlier stuff. I remember seeing one porn film which had Jamie Gillis,

I think, playing someone who was—you know, he raped a woman or something. And I was so upset with that, I left the theater. That I'm really against.

Such testimonies shatter the notion that men "appreciate watching men subordinate women," as Susan Cole once declared. John Stoltenberg, a gay antiporn collaborator of Dworkin's, wrote, "Male-supremacist sexuality is important to pornography, and pornography is important to male supremacy. . . . Your penis is a weapon, her body is your target. . . . Because men are masters, women are slaves; men are superior, women are subordinate; men are real, women are objects; men are sex machines, women are sluts." But not one of the men I talked to said pornography made him believe "that we are just like the men in pornography: virile, strong, tough, maybe cruel," or that "women want to be raped, enjoy being damaged by us, deserve to be punished," as Stoltenberg ridiculously asserts.

Most men did admit to having made some unfavorable comparisons between themselves and the guys on the page and screen as they grew up. After all, there was nowhere else they could see the nude bodies of other men except in the school locker room and showers, and nowhere else to learn what a male's sexual performance could and ought to be except through the exaggerated public boasts of their peers. "There was a time when I thought that my lack of success with women was due to my appearance and the fact that I don't look like Jeremy Butler, or any of the other porn kings," one man said. "I wanted to be better looking, more sure of myself, taller, stronger."

A married heterosexual male admitted he had never completely overcome negative comparisons with the men in pornography:

I've always felt inferior to other males ever since I was a kid: I was never much interested in sports; I seemed sexually behind others during puberty; and I never knew any males really closely or was involved in "male" things like all other men seemed to be. I was always more the nerdy, bookish type. But on the inside I really wanted to *be* like other men.

> And, so, in pornography, there were depicted (verbally or visually) *real* men with *real* male bodies doing *real* male activities. That appealed to my inferiority complex, in that I wished I could be like them and, I suppose, mentally I fantasized that I *was* them—a "real man."

Penis size is highlighted in pornography—in prose stories more than video, since the former have freer rein to exaggerate—and this has led commentators to speculate about the effect on consumers. But only a few men said it was a serious concern at any point in their life. A handful said they worried initially about their apparent "shortcomings" compared to men in pornography, but most got over it fairly quickly.

"I've read somewhere that every woman thinks her breasts are either too big or too small," said a 39-year-old science teacher, married fifteen years and the father of two. "I think every man thinks his penis should be bigger. Even though I knew the guys in porn were chosen for their size, I remember comparing myself unfavorably with the guys in the movies." "Yes I have been bothered with differences," another man admitted, "primarily the typical penis envy as I know I am below average in size and most males depicted in pornography are easily above average in size."

But most men said they soon left their initial concern about organ size behind.

> After a while, I thought it was funny. I have always thought it would be nice to have a few more inches, but come on! Most of these guys are way too big. I'd be afraid of scaring some poor woman to death with one of those monsters. [history grad student, 24, married two-and-a-half years]

As a 60-year-old man, married to his only sex partner for thirty-nine years, observed:

> At younger ages, differences in appearance were bothersome—difference in sizes and shapes of body components—and, yes, at times there was a

desire to be like them. But that diminished as adult years passed, and as self-confidence in sex as well as other areas increased. . . . Throughout our entire lifetime, we probably never will see another man's erect penis. That's due to a number of cultural reasons, not the least of which is homophobia. My suspicion is that where erections are concerned, we are far more a population of equals. Add to that the probability that most women don't give a damn, and it's a lot of worrying over nothing.

One man who did experience stress over penis size as a result of consuming porn was a 37-year-old bisexual who had been married fourteen years and had two children. Partly because he occasionally sought out sex with men, he continued to wish his penis were larger:

I thought they were average length [in porn] and therefore I was well below. This helped exacerbate my size complex. I would have liked to have been 7 or 8″ long, but probably my current thickness. I wish I was more of a shower, as opposed to a grower, in that I would like to have been impressively hung when flaccid. [My wife] is upset with the obsession. She says that mine is perfect for her. She once had much longer and it hurt her. She says the rest were just like me except for one guy that hooked.

One man for whom penis size and endurance had been lingering worries nevertheless refused to blame this burden on pornography. When he was 8, he claimed to have been fondled by a much older man who was joking about "how much of a man" he was. His father was in the room but did not intervene because he was passed out drunk. "I felt numb. I can still see his face, I can still smell him, and in the process it becomes very uncomfortable for even a woman to touch me. And I want a woman to touch me." Later, when he was in the Army overseas, two different prostitutes insulted his masculinity:

They compared me with the men of their race, and how big they are, telling me I wasn't that. I had to take it personally. I did take it personally. It's also a constant with me, to think that I'm not, haven't accepted or appreciated myself that I am who I am, in that department. And in the process I have three children from three different women in order to prove this to myself. And in the process also I have hurt a lot of other women by using them just for this thing, to prove that I am a man.

To read antiporn theory, you would think it was the men who feel quite comfortable with their masculinity, who align themselves with traditional social values, who would most abuse women and most use pornography. But in reality, it is the men who do *not* feel secure in their manliness, who do not feel a solid part of the larger culture, who are more likely to take pornography's lies seriously and to abuse the women in their lives.

One of the contrasts between men of different sexual orientations was that few of the heterosexuals took to heart the differences between themselves and men depicted in pornography, and most discarded their concerns after only a few years of adulthood and sexual experience. Gay and bisexual men, however, tended to express greater and more lasting envy of the looks and physique of men in porn, perhaps because they expected—rightly or wrongly—to be judged more on the basis of youth and looks, the way many women are.

When asked if he ever compared the performance and appearance of men in porn to his own once he became sexually active, one gay man said: "Always. I assumed the performances I saw in the magazines were standard/expected. I always hoped my penis and body would develop along the lines of those beautiful men."

"There was always the fear that I would be inadequate or not attractive enough," said another. "Always wanted a 'better body,'" wrote a 40-year-old musician, "Always wanted that body by god (if not the brain by Mattel)." A 44-year-old computer analyst wrote:

I often imagined (and still imagine) them as being better, braver, more courageous, and better lovers than myself. There is still an inclination to think that the world belongs to beautiful men, that they can have anything for the asking, and a longing to be one of them. It's always bothered me that I feel inferior to them, but there's not much I can do about it, except recognize the feeling as a silly one.

A 42-year-old professor, while acknowledging the physique and equipment issues as well as the premium on youth, added it was certainly not porn alone that fostered insecurity, and that time and experience softened the pressure:

> Sure, I wanted a larger cock, but I'm not sure it was just the porn that influenced it—but rather the attitudes found in many gay men (there is the well-known phenomenon of the "size queen"). The attraction for youth has also been very pronounced in the gay community so as I aged I found that I rather envied the younger men in the porn. (Oddly enough this seems to be changing—or maybe I'm just finding a lot of younger men who find older men attractive.)

On the other hand, a 38-year-old journalist disliked *too much* reality in the appearance of some men in gay pornography. "In the late 1980s I saw a couple of models with the 'sunken look' characteristic of men with AIDS. Even though the men were otherwise 'well built,' I was generally turned off by the photo spread. Porn is really supposed to create an illusion in which the 'real world' is suspended and everyone has the chance to 'make it' with an attractive, healthy man (or woman)." In general, he was quite aware that appearances were exaggerated, and currently there was such a wide range of material that no particular standard of attractiveness seemed to dominate. He said this made pornography more comforting than real life:

> Actually, "real life" can be a downer if you're surrounded by men who are adamant about only being attracted to men who are smooth (if you yourself are hairy) or who don't consider anyone sexy unless they have a larger-than-average penis. In such cases, finding porn magazines that feature men with your own characteristics (i.e., hairy bodies or average endowments) can help in maintaining self-esteem as you realize that men

of your own body type can also be considered "sexy" enough to be featured in a national porn magazine.

Despite their envy of the pornographic male's physique and equipment, success with women or men, endurance, and other amenities, men nonetheless understood at least some of the tricks of the pornographic camera and the downside to enviable traits, and they managed to belittle or outgrow their own negative feelings. A statistics professor who had been married for more than twenty years said, "I envied the life in which you can make love to many beautiful women, but on the other hand that is something I would never actually want to do":

There are both philosophical and pragmatic reasons for this. Philosophically, there is always the conflict between carnal desire and moral discipline. I am neither a hedonist nor an ascetic. Although I enjoy pleasure, I don't think that pleasure is the highest good, and I believe that excessive pleasure is bad for you. I enjoy a drink, but I would not want to spend all my leisure time drinking. I enjoy sex, but I don't want to be a pornographer. Pragmatically, there is the fact that no act exists in a vacuum. What I do now will affect my future life, my relationships, my self-respect, and the respect of others. Jeopardizing that is too high a price to pay for the opportunity to make love to many beautiful women.

How Men
Use Pornography

Opponents of pornography routinely assume men use it only to aid masturbation. In *Only Words*, MacKinnon writes, "Pornography is masturbation material," and adds this "is an empirical observation," as if she had actually studied men doing it.

For some men, that's all it is. "I never look at material except when masturbating," a British software developer, 34 and bisexual, declared. "The idea that anyone would be interested for any other reason baffles me."

But quite a few other men indicated that MacKinnon's "empirical observation" doesn't always hold. A 28-year-old editor/publisher, married seven years, who said "most of the time when I look at porn I do not masturbate at all," explained: "I have on occasion used it with friends as an element of foreplay, and I have also used magazines such as *Playboy* to demonstrate poses when taking my own pictures." The latter consisted of "personal pictures we [his wife and he] have taken for our own pleasure, or perhaps something to give to a close girlfriend of my wife."

A 42-year-old electronic publishing specialist in his second marriage said, "I sometimes look at erotic materials without any intent of arousing myself to orgasm, but this is because I have developed an intellectual interest in the subject."

A 60-year-old man said that at least 20 percent of the time, "it is observed without much arousal, and I go on to other things in the day's events. The material is consumed as a turn-on which does not lead to orgasm, and is not the prelude to extending the fantasy." A 26-year-old married man who preferred written porn had this to say about the photographic content of *Playboy*:

> I guess I could say that when I look at the pictures in *Playboy*, I actually look at them without a desire to masturbate. It's like looking at artistic pictures. It's aesthetically pleasing. I may find it to be a sensual picture; I may think about it at a later time. But just looking at the picture rarely ever gets me turned on. I may look at a woman in a picture and say, "Woah, she's really attractive," but I rarely ever get an erection because of it.

A few gay men made similar comments. "Sometimes I use porn without masturbating at all," reported a Canadian math student, aged 23. "Some people are just attractive nude, but in a non-sexual way. I would probably have some of these decorating my room, but that would be a bit much for my parents."

In a couple of cases, men said they might start looking at pornography and stimulating themselves, but discover they were not in the mood and did not finish.

A 21-year-old virgin engaged in a little autoerotic foreplay when he turned to a pile of magazines, videos, or lingerie ads and stared at them to "set up" a long masturbation session. He did *not* masturbate *while* looking at the material, however. "I like to concentrate on the feeling [when masturbating], and pornography is a distraction," he explained. What he fantasized about when masturbating was having a friend as a sex partner, or being a woman. A 48-year-old librarian and software developer had a different motivation: "As a widower, I need to masturbate periodically to relieve sexual tensions. At my age it gets a bit more difficult to get and maintain a solid erection, so I will often use written porn to help things along. I masturbate (usually with porn) probably one to three times a week."

More gay men than heterosexuals indicated that they "almost always" use pornography to aid masturbation. Rather than yield to the temptation to conclude from such findings that gay men are "oversexed" or "dependent on pornography," one might consider the notion that using pornography is simply less of the loaded and secretive act for gays that it often is for heterosexual men. Gay males often discover and establish their sexual identity with the help of pornography. It is a haven in a hostile world rather than just another adult or illicit substance. Their partners usually understand this because they have had the same experience, and sometimes share its use. There isn't a need for total privacy, to hide the material, to wait for opportunities to be alone. Gays don't feel the weight of feminist theory, or the likely disapproval of current and potential sex partners. As for disapproval of pornography from the community at large, gays are used to disapproval of their mere existence, which makes the "sin" of pornography minor by comparison. This crucial difference between straight and gay men's experiences may account for much of the difference in the frequency of their porn use.

A 23-year-old virgin reported that he occasionally went on a pornography "binge" with no orgasms to supercharge his arousal:

> Eeeevery once in a while, maybe once every few months, I'll go "off" porn, or more specifically, off masturbation for a week or so. I'll enjoy a tape or a magazine or whatever for a couple hours, and then stop (or continue for a few more hours, but the point is, I just won't finish). And then on successive occasions (which become exponentially more, uh, desirable), the sensations are heightened even more, to the point where it can feel almost like a continuous orgasm. After a few days of this, your (well, my) mind can be so screwed up by hormonal imbalance (or somesuch), that it's basically all ya feel like doing, all day long, and often it would take up most

of the time from when I got home to when I went to sleep. Eventually it becomes so overpowering that you absolutely cannot stand to hold it in any longer, and then you must release. This is a weird feeling, unlike your "standard" orgasm. There's a tremendous amount of semen, however. This is how the binges occur.

As for the general frequency of their porn use, the men's responses varied considerably, from a few times a year to once a day or more. A separate group said it varied a lot. Most of those men said sometimes they used it one or more times a day, and then not for a week, or even months. "Sometimes I do it as often as ten or more times a day; sometimes I do it as little as once or twice a week," said a 26-year-old single man whose ten times a day was the highest reported by anyone.

For many men it depended on the whereabouts of their partner. One reported that he normally looked at porn only once every few weeks at home, though if his wife were away for a day or weekend, he "might drag out the videos and magazines two or four times in a day, in between doing other stuff. But that's pretty rare these days." On the other hand, a 47-year-old New Zealand native in his second marriage reported his range as "sometimes four or five times a day, sometimes not for a week," and the activity sometimes involved foreplay with his wife "or maybe I'll watch her watching and masturbating while I also masturbate."

A solid majority of men affirmed that they used pornography more often when they were not in a relationship or were temporarily apart from their partners. "During the ten years I lived alone, it was essential," wrote one. Said a 42-year-old gay male, "Usually when I am alone and unattached, porn can fill (or attempt to fill) a void, but it is at best a feeble means and an inadequate one. A relationship is far preferable to a vacant look in a photo or film." Others said their porn use stopped when they were in a relationship: "When the preferred alternative (a partner) is available, I don't use porn."

But several men wanted to make it clear that use of pornography did *not* cease when they were involved with someone. Said one, "I think that I watch about the same amount now that I am with someone as I did when I was single."

A "very happily married" 43-year-old man said three to five times a week he masturbated with an oil lubricant in front of the VCR "after putting the kids to bed while the wife is downstairs with the dishes."

A 36-year-old computer systems specialist, married six years, believed his use was fairly constant, if a little high at times, and the source of some shame:

> I can get quite excessive and compulsive about it, renting four adult videos and spending a whole weekend just getting high, masturbating, napping, eating, when I'm alone. But I don't feel good about this. A more reasonable balance is when I am making love with my wife a few times a week, but still sneaking out to masturbate to videos or magazines once a week too. It doesn't interfere with my relationship with her; in fact it helps balance my needs with hers, because when I'm most randy and horny, she doesn't always want it as much as I do, so I blow off the excessive steam on my own, and I can focus and concentrate on squeezing out every drop of intense pleasure that I know how to do, prolonging and ecstasizing it as much as possible.

A 38-year-old married man said he usually made an "almost-medicinal" use of video porn two or three times a week, "when I'm not interested in having 'real' sex with my wife but want to relieve sexual tension." These sessions lasted no more than ten to fifteen minutes. Once or twice a year, however, he managed to find a hallucinogenic drug like LSD or psilocybin and saved it for an occasion when "the stars align so that my wife goes out of town and I have no pressing obligations; when that situation arises, I'll drop a hit of acid and watch porn videos for hours, remaining aroused pretty much the whole time. The images on the screen take on an amazing depth, and become very involving, at such times."

"My use increases as stress increases in my marriage," reported a 33-year-old who was eight years into marriage with his only sex partner. "If

I am feeling distant from my partner, I don't want to share myself with her, including my sexuality." Another 33-year-old, married five years, had the sobering response: "I will use porn more often when at odds with my spouse. That is most always though."

A 35-year-old programmer noticed that although he typically did not use porn as an escape from marital difficulties, it helped reduce the pressure of occasional anger toward his spouse:

> My wife and I basically have a pretty good marriage. One aspect of that is that when I'm unhappy about something in our marriage, I usually discuss it directly with her, rather than channeling my feelings into something else, like porn. In the past, I kept porn and my marriage completely separate in my mind. However, as I've gotten older, I've gotten more comfortable with my own feelings, to the point where there can be some spillover. Recently, sometime in the last few months, I've been angry at my wife about something, and furthermore, I didn't feel that talking to her about it was going to help. What I do remember is preferentially reading stories about women getting spanked, and using those stories as an outlet for my anger.

Quite a few men also said that difficulties with a partner made them *less* able to enjoy pornography. "If I'm having problems with my SO, I'm not likely to be feeling very amorous," a 32-year-old divorced man said, "thus, I'm not likely to seek out sexual excitement." A 20-year-old Canadian said problems took all precedence over pleasure or escape: "When I've had trouble with my SOs I usually had other things on my mind, such as why we broke up (most of the relationships didn't last long enough to have fights). With my present GF I am too occupied with the problems between us to even think about using pornography, let alone feel like it."

Implicit in many responses to questions about use of porn was the notion that sexual energy consisted of a certain level of need or immediate tension that could only be relieved by sex with another person or masturbation with pornography. A 26-year-old student in theater and photography described the utility of pornography:

I tend to get sexually aroused easily, especially when I am not having sex with another person regularly; it is often distracting, because I will find it difficult to concentrate on what I am supposed to be doing when I have an erection. It is easier to regain my concentration (and much more enjoyable) to masturbate, and have an orgasm, thereby blunting my sexual appetite for the time being, rather than to ignore my urges.

Of the men who said they had noticed a pattern in relation to their overall mood, two thirds said they tended to use porn more when they were unhappy or in a negative mood. This included a wide range of perspectives, though. A man who believed he had been molested by men as a child and gave up pornography in high school, said "I used it more when I was unhappy, but it didn't make me happy. It only increased my sense of guilt and worthlessness." "When I am out of control then I need the porn to escape from the pain," said another man who was separated from his wife; "When I am emotionally well I don't feel the need to use porn or act out in other ways." A third man agreed that while "porn has tended to be an idle or back-burner hobby," his use of it "increased during a depressive time in my marriage."

Though increased porn use coincided with depressed moods for a 46-year-old man who had been married twenty-five years to his only sex partner, he stressed its therapeutic value for him:

. . . depression does bring on more active use of pornography. In several cases, I couldn't sleep at all and after viewing some of my material and then masturbation to completion in a hot tub of water I fell right to sleep.

A gay journalist's experience was similar: "I definitely use porn more when unhappy or during periods of unwelcome stress. In periods of career setbacks or work difficulties, I spend a lot of free time looking at porn, in essence to overcome depression and regain a motive for life."

The remaining third of men who linked porn use to mood said they used it when they were in a happy or positive mood. "I would say I use

79

porn slightly more when happy than unhappy," said a 28-year-old student, married seven years.

A 32-year-old in public relations reported, "I use it more when I am unhappy, but it has a place when I am happy (but unattached) as well." Said another man, "It is like medication when I am unhappy, like recreation when I am happy. It seems like a 'need' when I am down, as contrasted with an 'option' when I am happier." A 38-year-old man, married fifteen years, said it was even more complicated for him:

> It does make a difference, but not a consistent one. Sometimes when I'm depressed, I lose interest in having sex with my wife. She is, after all, nearly 40 years old, and overweight. At such times I might hit the videos harder than usual. Other times, depression leads to a total loss of libido. Conversely, happiness improves my marital sex, which reduces interest in porn; however, good moods (such as come with spring) raise my libido to the point where even frequent sex only whets my appetite for more, in which case I might turn to porn.

Still, the majority of men in the survey downplayed any connection between how often or when they used pornography and their mood. "It's more of a neutral release valve for me, so I don't think it correlates well with periods of stress or happiness," said one. "For the most part, Happy or Sad, I have and will use Porn," was how an African-American man put it.

Some of the men who said there wasn't a connection between their mood and their use of porn nevertheless said they *avoided* porn if they were down. "I sometimes get more depressed watching it," a 35-year-old programmer wrote, "particularly if that depression stems from relationship problems." A gay man, 38, felt the same: "I have noticed that pornography is not a panacea—at least not for me—for unhappiness. In fact, when I am feeling blue or particularly lonely, pornography quite often will compound those bad feelings. I've learned to stay away from it during those times."

Other men pointed to the simple fact of extra time on one's hands (so to speak) as the most salient influence over how often they turned to porn. "When I am very busy, I use porn less often"; "Obviously, if one's free time is spent with another, there are fewer opportunities."

Some men described the use of pornography within a sexual relationship. Said one who rented a video on Saturday nights with his wife, "We hardly ever finish watching a film. We will have sex in the living room, where we watch the porn, or sometimes in the kitchen on the table [and] just let the porn run in the background." A 23-year-old chemical engineer said he usually used pornography alone but he had shared it with a girlfriend: "We tend to watch the whole film first and then have sex" because "it's that 'aching wait' that we go for." (Men who share pornography with their partners are discussed in greater detail in the next chapter.)

As a possible method of gauging how men felt about their use of pornography, I asked what they did after using it and how they felt about themselves at that point. Their answers to these open-ended questions were particularly impressionistic but the overall picture was one of contentment, relaxation, even reflection, often followed by a return to an earlier activity. For most men, pornography was little more than a break in the routine. Some had mild feelings of shame, mixed emotions, or violent ambivalence about their use of porn, but relatively few.

The mere act of looking at porn and masturbating to orgasm tended to act as a relaxant, so that many men went on to rest, nap, or turn in for the night. Others felt refreshed before returning to their daily tasks. A corporate manager said after using porn, he felt "ready to go on to something else, like playing the piano. Music and sex, what else is there?"

A 26-year-old data processor said he thought about "Whatever problems or pleasures surfaced in that day with a fresher perspective. It's like exercise for the psyche." A gay professor in Canada called it pretty accurately for all orientations: "After I use porn/jerk off I usually feel really mellow. I think that goes for gay and straight, doesn't it? I don't feel guilty, if that's what you want to know. I just have a warm glow through my body."

A few men whose post-porn emotions were mostly positive admitted to occasional negative feelings. But these tended to relate to the content of the porn or circumstances in the man's life, not the use of pornography *per se*. "I feel fine unless I've also sexually fantasized about a female friend, in which case I feel guilty or regretful," reported a young math student. "If the [Internet] story was particularly raunchy (pedophilia, rape, whatever) I sometimes get a nudge of disgust of the 'how could you have been turned on by *that*' variety," a 25-year-old bisexual wrote.

Several gay men admitted to tensions between their use of porn and sexual relations with their partner, even though they had little problem with using pornography themselves. "I generally feel a bit tired afterwards, perhaps relaxed, and sometimes a bit guilty about having played with porn rather than with my partner of 14 years," a 44-year-old man said.

Some men expressed feelings of shame and reported a total loss of interest in porn once they had orgasmed. "I'm a red-blooded male with a 'quarter in the vending machine' sexual response," said a 35-year-old in library and information management. "As soon as I recover from orgasm I pick up the porn and put it away. My interest and arousal evaporate quickly and often I don't want to see it or think about it after I've come." Said a 35-year-old, married office worker, "Sometimes I feel a little silly, like: What was all that excitement about? I don't feel like looking at any more nudes, and wonder a little about why I felt such a need to ten minutes before." Another 35-year-old, a married programmer, described his response thus:

> When I use magazines, particularly bondage magazines, I often find that I feel a little bit stupid about the whole thing after I cum. I think what happens is that the magazine starts to deconstruct itself in my hands. Before I cum, I'm wrapped up in my sexual response to the women I'm looking at. After I cum, my sexual response fades, and I'm left with just the women. And then they're not women, they're just pictures of women. And then it's not pictures, it's just little dots of color on the pages of a maga-

zine. And finally it's not even a magazine, it's just an object in my hands. And I paid $8 for it. How stupid. I'm happy to report that this doesn't happen after I've been looking at porn on my computer. I suspect this is because there is no persisting object to deconstruct itself after I cum. Close the window, exit the program, and there's nothing left.

Highly mixed responses were described by a 22-year-old physics grad student who whose feelings about pornography were mostly positive:

[I] relax and return to whatever else I have to do or was doing. I feel sometimes completely free of any sexual desires, even on occasion feel strange that I could be sufficiently motivated to spend time on it. Most of the time I feel like I wasted my time. Also, I am thinking about the ideas that were implicit in what I read, and I usually find them quite primitive and often wrong. In this way I hope I am not getting too brainwashed by all the garbage that is present in the porn.

Stronger negative feelings were reported by the 36-year-old who discovered porn because of Santa Claus:

Sometimes I feel sort of yucky afterwards, but still relieved that I "got my rocks off." I never would want to force this private world on anyone else publicly. Just like you would never want to force others to observe your bathroom toilet habits, would you? At times when I'm more alone, I sometimes go through severely depressed periods where I shut myself up alone in a hole, and masturbate frequently, multiple times per day. When I was without a girlfriend, when my wife is away, I got into the bad habit of doing it often. I say "bad" because it made me feel rather degraded and animal-like unclean afterwards, yet still I was compulsive about it, about the moment of ecstasy and the whole sort of private, personal ritual surrounding it.

A 35-year-old man whose wife filed for divorce during the time he was taking the survey said: "I usually feel pretty sick or depressed for a while. I don't like it and to this day I still don't understand how a few seconds of ecstasy can be so addictive."

Several men said they had gotten over their shame. "Currently I know that I enjoy it and like the feelings it gives me," reported a 39-year-old married man. "I've wondered if I spend too much time thinking about sex and viewing porn, but what the hell, it is fun."

Sharing Porn
with Others

Although pornography use is typically a solitary pursuit for men, it can be a shared experience. In chapter one, we saw how young boys show it to one another. If the story of pornography is men exercising control over women, then it would make sense if, as adults, men gathered to enjoy the experience and direct one another toward the choicest bits of female humiliation and degradation.

However, half of the heterosexual men in the survey said they never even discussed pornography with other men, let alone perused it in their company. "I am a fairly solitary, introspective individual," a corporate manager wrote, "Too embarrassing [to share or discuss], I would imagine. A private vice." Though he had swapped computer image files with friends, a 38-year-old married man said, "'Consuming porn' remains a private matter, being, as it usually is, part of masturbating."

Heterosexuals were likely to have looked at porn with other males only in their youth. Three recalled seeing a porn video with friends in high school. At the college level, eight men had seen videos with other men, eight had seen movies either at a theater or in a public screening on campus, and five wrote of shared magazines. "Many of the frats would hold Saturday night showings of porn flicks as a way to raise money for the house," a married science teacher said.

A Duke graduate said his fraternity brothers would host smokers, during which they would "drink heavily, smoke cigars, and watch porn movies together. The whole thing made me very uncomfortable. I brought up the fact that I didn't like smokers a couple times at meetings, but they ignored my comments and refused to think about it." The others called him repressed or politically correct. "I think deep down, they all felt that I really wanted to be like them but that I was too scared." He acknowledged that the films aroused him, but he also had objections. "I think all they heard was that the films excited me and that was enough info for them to believe that my critique wasn't strong enough."

Other men said they had enjoyed such situations: "In college it was good, wholesome Saturday night entertainment for the guys to go to the on-campus porn flick," said one. "It was a lot of fun watching this stuff with all the other guys there making their comments," said another who had watched 8mm hardcore films in a U.S. Army barracks.

Still, many men who recalled viewing pornography with other males (and sometimes females) said it had not been a pleasant experience:

> When I was about 18 or 19, a bunch of my college friends would gather in a girl's apartment (she was there too) and we'd all drink beer and watch pornos. It wasn't our reason for going to her apartment, though; we just went to parties at her house frequently, and she often had porn videos there to watch. I think she was comfortable with the idea of watching porn, because she was always the one who rented the videos. It was rather uncomfortable to be watching it in the presence of all those people. The only men I've ever watched pornography with were the ones at the party. However, my wife and I often watch X-rated movies together. [computer student, 28]

Shared experiences declined considerably after adolescence and college. Only eight men said they had viewed porn videos with other men as adults. One mentioned businessmen's smokers in the early 1960s and attending the cinema with male and female friends in the early 1970s, and three mentioned swapping videos with friends. Several men who were out of college and in the workplace described what sounded more like a routine matter: "Most of my friends look over my shoulder when I get in new .gifs/.jpegs at work," one said. And a 45-year-old Canadian professor recounted an interesting story:

> I saw my first stag movie only about seven years ago. Some of my colleagues had a poker party, and after the poker game we watched videos. Some of them were definitely hard-core, but nothing illegal like kids, or animals, or violence. It was fascinating to watch them. Although I am too old to be shocked by anything, I did find it a little bothersome to know that respectable people I worked with, including folks who counseled students, actually watched such things. Somehow, I expected higher standards from mature, respectable university professors. One was assistant dean for student affairs, another was soon to take that role. Another was a senior, churchgoing fellow, and part-time church organist. What surprised me most was that this seemed to be a regular form of entertainment for some of these fellows. The conflict between personal inclination and moral imperative is still strong with me. Generally, I am not comfortable viewing porn in the company of others.

Greater access to regular and fulfilling sex with a partner may be a factor in men keeping their adult use private. Less curiosity about naked women and sex, as well as less casual contact with other men—in the locker room, up the dorm hall, in shared living arrangements from fraternities to bachelor pads—play a role as well. Simply being among enthusiastic people versus those who might be hostile (in the grown-up world of work and disapproving partners) undoubtedly made a difference.

Men were also usually hesitant to talk about porn with other men. A 21-year-old music major said he had discussed pornography only with his closest friend, "usually about a particular article or model." A 23-year-old virgin said "the latest female stars" were the topic of choice with a friend of his. "Once I got into describing the pictures in *Lips* magazine [a publication devoted to closeups of labia] to an old friend, who seemed amused and delighted by it," a 48-year-old musician recounted.

Quite a few men said the topic had come up only in a joking, indirect, or shameful manner, according to a British college student:

> It's mostly comments that deride or make fun of it. Never have I heard anyone say something along the lines of "There's a brilliant porn mag out this month—go buy!" or someone recommending pornography to me in a serious sense. It's all "nudge, nudge, wink, wink, say no more!" It's all got that humour(less) edge to it which makes all sex issues become base and points of derision, which they're not really. *Yes*, sex is fun and sex should be laughed at but not *all* the time and in ways that make everyone feel it to be something to be hidden.

A 23-year-old bisexual added:

> Sometimes my friends and I would joke about using it to masturbate to, but nothing serious was ever discussed. In some ways, it was cool, but in others it was a symbol that you couldn't find a real girl to have sex with if you needed porn. There was definitely some shame attached to it, but then again, that went along with masturbating without porn as well.

In only a few cases did men report having a serious exchange with another man in connection with pornography.

Most men generally didn't share their porn with the women in their lives, either. They hid the porn away, sometimes to maintain their partner's ignorance, but more often with her silent, grudging tolerance, or rarer still, consent.

Most men said their partners knew about their use of pornography. A few were certain the woman did not know, others said they believed she didn't know but might suspect. A few more were not sure because it had never been discussed.

"None of them have known I wrote or used anything like this," said a 54-year-old manager. "They were almost always of a jealous nature, and a woman can be jealous of a magazine photo as easily as a real woman." "We never talk about erotica and its uses," said a 60-year-old man who had been married thirty-nine years to his only sex partner. "I am sure she would disapprove. And it's something I am not eager to have linked with me in her eyes—or in anyone's eyes."

"I have a stash now and my wife might suspect but would rather not know," a Black telecommunications professional said. "I try to have a permanent collection. My wife throws them away if she finds them. She openly detests it."

Other men operated under an uneasy truce with a disapproving partner. "My wife knows about my pornography and is very displeased with it," a 46-year-old government technician reported. "She would throw most all of it away in a minute, if I gave her permission to do so." Religious scruples had inspired this man to purge their home of pornography several times over the course of a 25-year marriage, but "later, during depressing periods or fights with my wife, I would restock my supplies."

A few men said their partner's attitude was not entirely rejecting, but reluctantly acquiescent. "She sees it as demeaning to women," a musician said of his wife. "She is tolerant of my use. I don't think she likes it, and wonders how my life, which is so gentle and caring, can have room for pornography. But she knows it's important to me." "My wife tended to have the same attitude as the other women who were disgusted or disappointed," a 35-year-old office worker reported, "but over the years she has come to accept that I treat her and other women with respect, and my use of pornography doesn't seem to affect that, so she accepts it. She doesn't really want to know about it or share it, though."

A fair number of men reported encountering mostly negative attitudes in past relationships as well. "Most companions felt that porno was disgusting," recalled a 24-year-old physical education student. "My ex-wife knew I used porn occasionally," said a Canadian public administrator, 48. "She refused to watch it with me, or read erotic letters. This bothered me, and I think I felt there was something wrong with me. Now I believe there was something wrong with her, and that I was the more 'normal'; meaning, I was responding openly to my needs, and was by no means a member of some small minority of perverts."

Others said they had encountered a variety of attitudes in their partners. A 35-year-old bisexual grad student, married for two years, said that of his roughly fifty sex partners, attitudes ranged from "disgust to complete acceptance and use." The employee of a sex magazine naturally tended to have girlfriends who used it with him and owned pornographic materials of their own. Their initial attitude when they learned he used it was "usually, 'oh, let me see,'" although even he sometimes encountered ambivalence.

"You deal with feelings of an individual," said a 44-year-old. "Most often the reaction is that porn somehow implies a failure on the part of a partner to be adequately sexual in the 'right' way, and that requires considerable reassurance. Discussion is always helpful, but not necessarily enough; sometimes you have to hide the porn." In some cases, if he suggested early in the relationship that they read some of the porn he liked, they ended up watching movies together.

A 35-year-old computer programmer said he had also encountered the full gamut of attitudes. "One woman who was Southern Baptist was highly offended by it." He called her a prude, "possibly more so than a typical Southern Baptist," with what he saw as a variety of psychological hangups. "Basically, she had the typical attitude of 'you'll burn in Hell for looking at that stuff,' and my reply was, 'I'll take my chances.' On the other hand, she read and liked steamy romance novels and the Anne Rice novels."

Some men sensed a woman's negative attitude toward porn without ever discussing the matter. They kept a discreet silence regarding their own use of porn and feelings about it. When the issue came out in the open, the violence of a woman's reaction could shut down any further communication. From then on, the man avoided anything that might lead to a similar explosion.

A 36-year-old Unix administrator recalled a vivid incident with a past lover:

> I had a box filled with magazines in a closet and I had tried to show my ex-girlfriend but she had gotten upset. Sometime later she was angry over something else, I forget, and she stormed in and started shredding magazines in the box, one by one, tossing the bits up in the air, not stopping until the whole box was gone and the bits were scattered all about the room. I was right there, standing and watching. No, we didn't really discuss it. I knew after that, that this whole magazine thing must have hurt her more deeply than I realized. It's kind of sad and scary because I really need to trust and open and share, even the bad parts along with the good parts, but [the women I loved] generally haven't "gotten" it.

In cases like these, a violent emotional reaction led the man to resort to secrets and hiding, and the woman to willful ignorance. Because she did not wish to face up to or discuss her emotions and fears, he was forced to bottle up his, too; his curiosities, desires, and interests often took a back seat to her strong negative response.

Some men said their partners intimated or specifically said they viewed porn use as a direct criticism of themselves. "My fiancée is bothered, mainly in wondering if, after seeing it, how I can stand to look at her (she's overweight)," said a mechanical engineering grad student. "I try and show her how she affects me (getting hard just looking at her, etc.), to try and dissuade her of her feelings of inadequacy."

"I've never explained [my porn use] to any of my partners, partly because of fear of ridicule and partly because of fear of insulting the partner ('Aren't I good enough?' or 'I don't provide enough?')," wrote a New Zealander.

Among the men whose partners did not like porn, the notion of their wife suddenly taking an interest in pornography gave them pause. One said, "I [would] wonder what I was doing wrong; I would want to know what I could do differently or better to eliminate her need for the porn."

A 48-year-old Canadian public administrator did not see anything wrong with his porn use but found himself stopped short by the thought of a partner's use. "I couldn't deal with it. I would think there was something lacking in me. I am fully cognizant of the double standard here, and just don't understand it."

Some women did share in their partners' use of pornography on occasion, but mostly for the man's sake rather than out of their own interest. "My wife will sometimes watch a video with me or will read to me or have me read stories to her," said a 30-year-old, married seven years. "It's rare, but when it happens, it's generally her idea. She's not very interested in it, but I think she sometimes likes to use it because she knows I like it and that it can excite me."

Other men used porn as a sex aid with a willing partner. Wrote a 28-year-old, married seven years:

> Our typical experience when watching porn together is just what happened this evening: We watch the movie(s) while "petting" each other, then afterward we have sex. Sometimes we will try new sexual ideas that we have seen in a movie. I have discussed pornography openly with my wife, and she is a willing participant in watching it with me. I don't really think she gets as sexually excited by it as I do, but I may be wrong.

Said a New Zealand man of his second wife, to whom he has been married twenty years, "On occasions (maybe 15%) my wife and I use porn together as a prelude and/or accompaniment to sex. We've used video, magazines, and literature. If she's alone she sometimes uses porn in masturbating." He added, "My wife understands my use but probably doesn't realize the extent."

In a few other cases, the woman's tolerance and even encouragement was part of an agreement between the couple: If I allow *this*, I can expect *that* of you. A self-described "Kinsey 5" (bisexual close to the homosexual end of the spectrum) who was married for fourteen years and had two children, said he masturbated with pornography nearly every night, even some nights after he and his wife had already made love. Curiously, he often began by looking at straight pornography, then climaxed with gay porn. Though he had had more female sex partners than male in his life, of late his interest had turned primarily to men. He negotiated with his wife as to how often and when he might have sex with a man. Thus, her attitude toward pornography was "initially highly against, now tolerating and sometimes encouraging or suggesting the idea," perhaps to quell his appetite for seeking out real men for sex. "She looked over my shoulders when I got the first gay magazines in years."

Another man who identified himself as gay had been married even longer, and had a child with his wife. She tolerated his porn use partly because they no longer shared a sex life:

> My wife knows I am gay and since we no longer have sex, she knows and allows me to indulge myself, even being so kind as to wait until I am finished when it's time to go to bed. But I try not to abuse the situation, and can usually cum within a half hour. Once you get to that plateau, you usually want to cum anyway and enjoy the wave. I am so glad my wife allows this outlet for me, even at age 52. I am open with my wife about this and always have been. My wife never had any porno stuff and never will. My gayness has turned her off.

The most surprising finding about the shared use of porn with a spouse or lover was that *just as many men said their wife or girlfriend was totally supportive of their use of pornography as those who said their significant other absolutely hated it.* "My wife and previous long-term girlfriend aren't ashamed to admit that they too like porn," wrote a 40-year-old British programmer who had traveled to Europe with his wife in order to see live sex shows and to purchase hard-core pornography unavailable back home. He admitted that "wife/girlfriend would prefer it if I never wanked and was always gasping for them, but they're realistic." A Black desktop publisher who was also a minister said, "My wife is almost as into it now as I am." He added that he also traded pornography with his best friend, who was a woman.

A 44-year-old bisexual man's response was brief and pointed: "My wife is the only person that has ever known about my sexual taste in real life and in pornography. She is also turned on by it which is *really fuckin' convenient*!!!" "She does like to look at it, almost as much as I do," a 32-year-old specialist in computer graphics said of his second wife. "I've often caught her masturbating while watching a porno that she rented."

Some men knew women who not only enjoyed looking at pornography but had some of their own. A 35-year-old bisexual grad student, married for two years, said he once had a bisexual girlfriend who "really enjoyed it—we shared watching videos, and sex after, and she turned me on to a few bi-magazines, more narrative and political, that I had not heard of."

Several men had seen *Playgirl* magazines among a lover's possessions. "My last girlfriend and I actively enjoyed reading erotic materials together and watching videos together," recalled a 24-year-old audio engineer. "A few actually surprised me," a Bangladeshi man said. "They didn't seem the type. You could imagine the expression on my face when this quiet, shy woman pulls out a 12″ dildo and a bunch of *Playgirl* magazines."

"I think *Playgirl* is today's porn for women," a Canadian professor thought; "They seem to like their sex less aggressive than most men. They also like to play games about sex more than men, who like to get right down to it and get it all out in the open." He thought this explained why "all the photos in *Playgirl* are so laid back, trying to look like you just happened to come by when they were undressed, instead of being undressed for the purpose of having sex." A 35-year-old librarian who had looked through *Playgirl* a few times and found it "interesting," commented, "the stories contained descriptions of what the characters were wearing, how the room was decorated, etc.—all that context stuff that females insist on and men eschew." (Gays hotly disagreed about whether the true consumers of *Playgirl* were men or women, incidentally; urban, experienced gay men tended to find the magazine laughable, while boys who grew up far from the cities found it one of the few affirming sources of gay identity and pride available to them.)

Many men felt romance novels constituted female pornography. "The largest consumers of porn are women, and the best-selling porn genre is written for them," a 49-year-old British man declared. He asserted further that force is used in this women's genre more often than in male pornography. "It's called 'romance,' but usually referred to as 'bodice rippers.' The prevalence of rape fantasies in this literature has often been remarked upon. That doesn't worry me; in fact, it's a useful thing to cite when hypocritical feminists attack men's pornography."

Another Englishman ventured the opinion that "many women are interested in porn and much of what I have recently read in 'women's magazines' is very sexually explicit. I know that recently a U.K. women's magazine got rid of naked centerfolds because women were not interested in them without erections!"

Some men had either heard of or seen videos directed at women and couples, most notably by Femme Productions—videos directed by former porn actress Candida Royalle and other female veterans of the industry. "Candida Royalle's stuff was intended that way, and there are a number of 'romantic' videos available from *Playboy* and others," noted a 48-year-old widower.

Men disagreed about how appealing these productions really were to women and their partners. "I enjoyed [them], as well as the girlfriend that I watched them with [did]," said a 24-year-old library clerk of the movies he had seen that were "more artistic or romantic as opposed to just raw sex." But several other men told a different story. "Yes [there's porn for women], but it's boring," said the 27-year-old Black man whose wife was "almost as into" pornography as he was. "Despite all the faults in the mainstream stuff, the 'feminine porn' lacks a lot. Even my wife didn't like it." A 28-year-old White male backed him up: "I've seen some of it, from Candida Royalle's Femme series. I didn't like it—too soft, not raw enough or explicit enough. I know this sounds like a traditional male chauvinist attitude, but I don't think it is; my wife watched it with me, and she disliked it for exactly the same reasons."

In several cases, the pornographic or erotic material owned by a woman consisted of photographs or a video of the woman herself. A 28-year-old with a bisexual wife had made photos "for our own pleasure, or perhaps something to give to a close girlfriend of my wife." A 43-year-old man said, "A couple of lovers had pictures and videos taken of themselves either posing in an erotic manner or during sex. I guess that could be considered pornographic although I prefer the concept of erotica as a name."

Among the men whose wives did not fully share porn use or possess erotic materials of their own, a few said their partner's attitude appeared to be in flux; it varied over time and depended on the situation. "My wife also started out thinking it's totally disgusting and still basically thinks so," said one, "and fights with me on occasion about porno-related subjects, but I have gradually introduced some bits of this world to her. We have watched a few 'adult' videos together and even had sex while watching them, which is an incredible accomplishment for me in coming out of this dark private hole into sharing the world with another human being."

Most of the men I interviewed wished their female partners were more interested in pornography. Many believed this would lead to more and better sex, and greater intimacy in general.

The experiences of a number of men and their partners suggested that openness and communication could alter the woman's attitude and the course of the relationship—especially when it led to sharing rather than isolation and private consumption. This happened with some of the men whose partners accepted their porn use.

"At first she was kind of stunned," a chemical engineer said of his wife. "I've gotten her interested in erotica, but she still has problems with actually going into a store and renting a video. (She sends me in.) Now I get the feeling that it excites her when I say I've rented a movie because she wants to be with me to watch."

A widowed librarian, teacher, and church organist said his wife had known of his porn collection and "viewed it as a sinful flaw in my character but understood that it was not used as a substitute for her." Late in their marriage, as he found himself opening up to her more, they watched several of the "Better Sex" instructional videos together and "watching made both of us quite sexually hot." Another man said:

> I'd never admitted using pornography to any other girlfriend until my present one. Originally she was rather perturbed by the thought that I needed a magazine to get satisfaction. She felt inadequate and jealous that I would be giving my thoughts to a picture. She finds mental images much more satisfying and hence has trouble understanding why I would need a picture. After some very long and open conversations, I finally got her to realize that I have no kind of mental attraction towards these women. I merely use it as a visual stimulus for masturbation; I have sexual urges and pornography helps satisfy them. While she thinks of the magazines as being very pathetic, she no longer feels jealous or inadequate—it's just a pathetic guy thing she has to put up with.

A high school chemistry and physics teacher, married fifteen years, said his wife also initially regarded his collection of magazines as a threat. He spent much of the first year of their marriage "explaining to her that 'they were just pictures' and that it was physically impossible (paper cuts on the penis—*oww!*) to have an affair with a photograph." No single incident turned the tide. "I think what happened was that over the years we've been together she's learned that I'm not going to leave her for 'Miss May' or whomever, and that my liking these things doesn't mean I don't find her attractive." They went to an X-rated drive-in once—"which she enjoyed, once she got over the initial shock of 'They're actually *fucking* . . .'" It took about five years for his wife to become fully comfortable with his magazine collection. Eventually, they bought a VCR and started renting videos. "She finds at least some of them as erotic as I do. To this day, I have to fight for first dibs on *Playboy* to see who gets to show the cartoons to the other."

One man whose wife's initial resistance and disgust changed over the years to acceptance and even delight was a 48-year-old who worked as a security supervisor, and had been married twenty-eight years. When they first married, she did not know of his porn use, but she learned soon enough. "At first she felt threatened by it; the old 'why masturbate when you have me' syndrome." But this changed as they got to know each other and she had her first pregnancy. Intercourse became painful for her and she saw the value of an alternative outlet for him. In addition, he worked graveyard shift for much of their life together. "This put a crimp in our sexual relations [because] when I was coming to bed, she had to be up to care for the kids and get them off to school." With some regret, she recognized his need for regular orgasms and permitted him the continued use of porn. "Since I had promised her never to expose her to STDs, she had to allow me a safe alternative."

Eventually, the wife accompanied her husband to X-rated theaters out of curiosity and discovered that she enjoyed the films, although "being of a strong religious background, she has had problems adjusting mentally to porn and the question of harm or victimlessness."

> Today she is not upset by it and even enjoys it, doesn't feel threatened. She has walked in on me in the middle of masturbating and, when there wasn't time, has enjoyed the sight; when there was time, she has joined me and completed the sexual act (a wild time). There are things I enjoy that she has not been able to adequately perform, primarily oral sex. Porn enables me to mentally experience these. In return, I have learned new techniques that I have shared with her to our mutual satisfaction. All in all, we have arrived at a very workable accommodation of porn in our lives. While my wife has never bought recognizable porn, she does read romance books (and is beginning to break into writing them) that have strong erotic elements; some have called the genre soft porn for the housewife. My wife does read my porn and masturbates to it. I have found books and mags under her side of the bed. She has tacitly admitted to doing this but has never come out and said so openly. Perhaps someday I will walk in on her!

Although a woman's attitude was more likely to shift from negative to tolerant, or even positive, a few men in the survey said their wives' attitudes had gone the opposite direction, from initially tolerant to negative. Married ten years but separated from his wife at the time of the survey, a 34-year-old reported: "Specifically, my wife thinks porn reflects the evil side of humanity, and that my contact with it makes me less desirable and respectable. In the past she had accepted my porn consumption and tolerated it."

A 35-year-old man regarded his own problems with pornography and sexually arousing materials and activities as an addiction. He had spent a lot of money on phone sex services, indulged in "cybersex" with several women on the Internet, and had filmed his wife in the shower without her knowledge. (The couple had also taken nude photos of each other with knowledge and consent.) A number of times he had thrown away his porn collection and assured his wife it was gone, only to begin collecting again and hiding it from her. "She claimed that it was OK but one occasion when I was in bed masturbating to a story I was reading she specifically asked me not to do that when she was around." For a short time she read porn stories herself, and they viewed some video porn together. He characterized her attitude over the course of their seventeen-year marriage as toleration, then collaboration, then back to toleration "with the caveat that I did not use it around her." Eventually, she filed for divorce, citing his "sexual acting out—including use of pornography" as a significant factor in her decision.

It may be that these particular men had a problem with pornography, or it may be that pornography was only a symptom of larger problems in the relationship. In any case, the fact that the women's attitudes could change over time suggests that pornography does not have to play an inherently positive or negative role in *any* relationship.

Of all these examples—men whose partners enjoyed sharing pornography, men whose partners were not as interested but sometimes shared porn use for the man's sake, and men whose partners tried it once or twice and indicated they did not want to anymore—none conforms to the scenario depicted by opponents of pornography, in which men routinely cajole women into unhappy viewings of porn and force sex acts upon their partners after seeing them portrayed. In nearly all the relationships described by men in this survey, both partners sought to be considerate and discreet. Either the man sensed the woman's distaste without any discussion and kept his activities private; or he broached the subject and respected her responses; or he waited for her to raise the topic herself if she was so inclined or curious about his interests.

In only one case did a man relate a story anything like the one described as the norm by foes of pornography. This was a man who liked to see fists and bottles in vaginas and anuses, enemas and the like, and whose wife was "very displeased" with his pornography and would throw it all out if he said the word. He admitted, "As a Christian I know deep in my heart that pornography is *wrong*," and "If I could get a handle on my problem I would probably give it and some other unnatural things I do completely up." Over the years he negotiated with his wife to perform sex acts he desired, such as giving him an enema. "For years she would not even hear of it! Now today, she will reluctantly help give me an enema when she is in the mood." He noted that the first time she gave him a high enema and fisted him, she got seriously sick to her stomach and threw up. She tried to leave him several times over the years and "every one of them was due to me trying to force a sexual fantasy upon her in some way or other."

As unnerving as this sounds, the couple was still together after decades of marriage. There had been no infidelities, and all unusual sexual activities were heavily negotiated beforehand. "I have learned my lesson and take things a good bit slower now." Unlike the classic anti-porn scenario in which a man sees something happen in pornography and wants to inflict it on a woman's body, most of the sex acts this man sought involved manipulation and penetration of himself: fisting, enemas, and the use of "diddle sticks" (technically known as urethral sounds, used medically for opening the urethral tract during infection and swelling) on his penis. His wife had also benefited from his arousal by pornography: After being turned on by a rented video in which a microprobe went up a vagina, he had sex with his wife three times in one night. "She was very curious why I was on such a sexual high; I told her about the video but did not go into any great detail. I also laid some real serious 'loving' on her and she really liked that."

Unlike the many heterosexuals who had kept their thoughts and activities largely to themselves, nearly all the homosexual men in the survey had both used pornography with other men and discussed it often. This was one of the areas where the experience of gays differed markedly from that of heterosexual men. It's no surprise, since all the players were males, and had had both comparable exposure to pornography growing up and similar interest in it. Not only did nearly all gay males say their partners knew about their porn use, but their partners used it too, sometimes with them. And where there were disagreements over taste, frequency, or even the use of porn at all, gays were much more likely to discuss the matter openly and/or arrive at compromises that satisfied both parties.

"I think many gay men tend to be pretty open about their sexuality with their gay friends," said a 42-year-old professor, "and I've sometimes watched porn with men to laugh at it—though a couple times I know that both I and the other men who were laughing on one level were pretty seriously aroused on another."

Quite a few gay men said that while partners tended to be understanding and tolerant of porn use, sometimes they didn't care to share its consumption. A 35-year-old in library science and information retrieval said he could share pornography with some sex partners, less with others, but in the final analysis pornography was rarely the center of interest:

> Some [lovers] just aren't interested in it. Some are but if we try to include it in our own sexual encounter we soon get so involved with each other that the porn is forgotten. Porn is distracting when I'm with another man. The physical medium (television screen or magazine) is inconvenient to turn and look at when one is interacting with a flesh-and-blood partner. Thus, it makes me a little uncomfortable in the context of a relationship. A porn user, to me, is withdrawing into himself and gratifying his own needs on his own terms. I have sat on a couch or bed and viewed tapes with a sex partner occasionally, usually as a prelude to sex with each other.

> Also, once in a while I have the pleasure of meeting somebody with sim-
> ilar tastes, and we can compare materials, share ordering or store infor-
> mation, or giggle and dish about our preferences. Some but not all of the
> men I share porn with are sex partners of mine.

"My ex-lover also enjoyed pornographic movies on occasion," a 38-year-old library director recalled. "The funny thing was he would never watch these movies with me, but he didn't mind if I watched by myself. And I was aware that he often watched these movies when I wasn't around. He said he felt that I should be more interested in satisfying him than watching total strangers on a video."

A 36-year-old publicist whose taste differed from that of his partner (his partner's porn "generally has more spanking—he went to Catholic school"), said, "I like finding the tapes he bought and 'hid' and watching them." Gay men also subscribed to the idea that porn use enhances a sexual relationship more often than it detracts from it—even if the use is not shared. "My ex-lover *did* like to look at pornography, but he wouldn't watch it with me," a 38-year-old librarian recalled. "It really didn't bother me. When I was at my least appealing (because of weight), it put him in the mood for sex."

A bisexual male who preferred men and had been in an on/off, nonexclusive relationship with one, said pornography played a stabilizing role in his relationship because it helped to keep his partner satisfied. "[His use] does not bother me, because I know that I am unable to fulfill his sexual desire. He wants more than I am able to give to him. If it helps our relationship, then I am all for it."

Others were more prickly. Said a 23-year-old medical student: "I take great offense at being asked to share [pornography] with someone that I have only been dating for a short time. Contrary to someone I just want to have a sexual encounter with, I feel that someone I am dating should find me enough at the time to be a fulfillment of their sexual needs. If they look at pornography while they are home alone, I don't care, but when we are together I want us to spend the time wrapped up in one another, not watching someone else have sex. I guess in short if I don't turn him on and he has to go to pornography then I have no business dating him."

A 26-year-old in school for a human resources degree suggested that not being entirely out of the closet could inhibit sharing of pornographic tastes and activities among gays:

> My current lover gets really bothered by my use of pornography while I am away at college. I tend to internalize that apprehension. He thinks it is a substitute for real contact with another person. I don't really view it as that but it bothers me that he gets upset by it. I'd rather be using pornography than having casual sexual encounters. I guess it's a form of denial or escapism, the feeling of being able to put it away at my own discretion and not deal with the issue of being gay. I guess that's what happens when you are primarily in the closet. Pornography kind of reassures me that it's okay to have these feelings when you see these gorgeous guys who seem to be enjoying themselves immensely, with no apparent reservations. It gives me a sense of connecting with other people who are inclined like me. My lover also has a small collection of porn that he acquired before our relationship two years ago.

In at least one man's relationship, the issue had become a highly sensitive one. "I think my lover resents it [pornography] now that we have sex so seldom," wrote a 40-year-old musician who did clerical work. "Before, I don't think it bothered him as much." The situation was complicated by the fact that this man was HIV-positive and his lover was not. "I have been much less physically active with my lover since I found out I have AIDS. I turn to porn because I can do it during the day, it takes less energy, and my lover doesn't initiate sex."

There are even gay men who accept antiporn ideology, though none that I talked to. A 32-year-old graduate student in the social sciences reported:

> Once in a while, I will take home a guy who believes the Dworkinite crap (not to insult coprophiles with the comparison) about how porn is degrad-

ing, un-PC, etc. I try to explain the importance of porn in gay male culture, and how homophobic the antiporn "feminists" really are. I talk about how antiporn laws have the effect of facilitating government repression of gays—and specifically those who are marginalized and most defenseless: rural gays. I cite the ways the Dworkin/MacKinnon legislation in Canada has resulted in confiscations of gay and lesbian political literature by customs. And that I *like* porn.

A fair number of gays said pornography proved a useful tool for "breaking the ice" with a prospective sex partner. "A sort of stereotypical gay male thing is using porn to try to arouse someone so you can have sex with them," a 42-year-old professor explained. "This even figures in some porn I've seen. I've been to parties where porn was used as background—either as wallpaper or as a sexual inhibition breaker." "I have also a few times used porno as a seduction ploy," reported a 67-year-old retired programmer. "I have been the perpetrator of this as well as the 'victim,'" a 23-year-old ex-Mormon wrote.

A surprising number of gays said they had seduced heterosexual and married acquaintances—even strangers—with the help of pornography.

Because I was so pathologically shy, pornography provided a means to male/male intimacy. My college roommate and best friend was very attractive to me, in fact I was very much in love with him, but could never have verbalized these feelings to him. One night, he came over and brought a couple of *Penthouse* magazines. He was aware, at this time, that I was gay and I think he intended something to happen this night. Anyway, we looked at the magazines and, as he became aroused, I started to touch him—here and there. He didn't ask me to stop, so I continued until I got to his mid-section. I started to rub, then I unzipped him and pulled his cock out and the rest, as they say, is history. He kept looking at the magazine while I was fellating him. He came over to see me three or four times after that expressly for the purpose of getting off. By exposing him to pornography (heterosexual) and waiting for the inevitable arousal to occur, I seduced him. Perhaps you will think this was a dishonest way of expressing my feelings for him. At the time, I believed he was denying his true "bisexual" orientation. I won't pretend, though, that there was anything altruistic in my actions. We haven't maintained contact with each other. He's married and has 2 or 3 children, I hear. [library director, 38]

I did get together with a guy at work who liked to look at porno with me. We would stay late, drink beer, and look at porno. He showed me his collection at work because his wife wouldn't let him have them at home. After the beers he let me know he felt comfortable with me and asked if we could check them out together. Well, first you're rearranging yourself, then rubbing yourself, pulling it out, beating off, hell, let's get naked and relax. Before I knew it I was in front of him and had his dick in my mouth. He was a buddy in need. We would both cum at least three times each. Once just wasn't enough. He would let me suck him maybe once or twice. One of the three would be solo. No, he didn't blow me, but a little touching. The plus was he was HIV negative and had been with his lady for years, so I could swallow his cum without worries. And he had a great cock. He was straight, married, and had 2 children. [video/film industry employee, 41]

Consent was clearly a factor in all these cases, whether curiosity, opportunism, or sheer lust lay behind the heterosexuals' participation. (Notice that although the library director says "I seduced him," it was his straight friend who brought over the porn.) One gay man who said he would "test the waters" by broaching the subject verbally ("I realize that not everyone is turned on by pornography, and I fully respect that choice") concluded: "I've run into all types of men over the years—the petrified straight guys who made up all types of excuses to leave; the boy-was-I-drunk-last-night types; the liberated ones who just wanted to enjoy some porn and get their rocks off; and regular queers who just enjoyed what was happening. And I usually had a good time too."

Off the
Beaten Track

By now it should be clear that there are as many different kinds of pornography as there are ways to respond to it. But despite fear-inducing warnings by antiporn activists and the media about "what's out there," the worst, most kinky and violent materials are rare, and most men who look at porn on a regular basis do not spend their time and money on them. Men are largely content with garden-variety magazines of posed nudes, and videos of pleasant-looking people engaged in consensual sex.

There are men whose tastes run toward material not commonly available at the local video store. But even they express a wide spectrum of points of view and motivations. They are not all "sexual pioneers" who push the envelope to find the most extreme content. Nor are they hermits drawn to deviations from the norm because they simply don't know what "real" lovemaking is. Some are highly experienced sexually, and have seen a lot of porn. Others are young and uncertain where they may end up, in terms of what they look at or do. But they know what they like, and it isn't *Playboy*.

Mark: It's a Skin Thing

"Mark," 54, was a manager in a Fortune 50 company and reported income of about $75,000. His current marriage was seven years old at the time of the survey. He had had no homosexual experiences.

As he grew up in the 1950s, arousing material consisted of the novels of Frank Yerby, with their romantic sexual component, and an occasional softcore paperback. "All this was very soft stuff, but I guess it spoiled me for the cruder varieties of porn, which I've always found sort of distasteful." It was a "schizoid environment" that he thought was quite normal for the time. He loved girls from afar, but never associated them with the "real women" in books.

Until the late 1960s, the only pornography he knew were soft-core paperbacks and *Playboy* and its imitators. Mark didn't see a man in a magazine or movie until about 1970. "Never to this day have I seen a male homosexual video, though once I thought about viewing one in one of those peep-show video stores, but I was too shy and embarrassed."

His first exposure to serious pornography was in 1969 or 1970 when his marriage was collapsing:

> In a magazine store I accidentally came upon a publication with about 15 pictures—including the cover picture—of this absolutely exquisite Black girl. Really gorgeous, with a stunning, perfect body. The girl was, it seems to me, only about 16 or 17 years old, certainly an illegal age for this kind of posing. But at that age her body was pristine and pure and perfect.

Asked to describe her perfection, Mark wrote:

> She was beautifully proportioned, not fat or thin, her breasts perfectly suited to the rest of her body, not too large or too small. She had a beau-

tiful face, if you like that kind of face (I love it), with large but not Ubangi lips, a largish but not unattractive nose, bangs (I love bangs), straight white teeth. She also had a perfect bottom. There is a condition called steatopygia which predominates among African races and gives them large, protruding buttocks. You can see these women (especially) on the buses of any major metropolis. But when this condition is not exaggerated but normal, it gives a woman a beautifully sculptured round bottom that can be breathtaking (for me) to behold. Finally, what she had most of all was that special, dangerous look in her eyes. Examples: Lauren Hutton and Stephanie Seymour have it, but Christie Brinkley and Claudia Schiffer don't have a clue; movie stars: Lena Olin, Nastassja Kinski, Julie Christie yes; the young Lana Turner, yes (see *The Postman Always Rings Twice*), but Marilyn Monroe, Ingrid Bergman, Ann-Margaret, Jessica Lange, no; Faye Dunaway sometimes, Susan Sarandon never. These women have a sort of "fuck me if you dare" look in their eyes. This is something that knows no racial boundaries, of course, but when you find a woman who fits all the other criteria, and she has this extra something, you are bound to be much more affected. This quality of danger is infinitely attractive, and this girl in the magazine had it. I still have those pictures. They are as stunning as ever.

There was an ad in the magazine for a Super 8mm film of this girl, and Mark sent for it.

She started out lying on a bed wearing a yellow nightie. She took it off, very tantalizingly. She caressed and stroked her body, then picked up two long feathers and stroked it with them. She ended up with a pillow between her thighs, simulating an orgasm. It was heaven. The movie was grainy and dim and fuzzy, but she was young and radiant and shockingly sexy. I would give anything to have it again. I bought a small projector from Sears and watched this picture for years, until it deteriorated. I can still recall every frame.

This girl, or the image of her, became a significant part of Mark's inner life. He wrote a novel in which she appeared. "It almost got published, and had a few favorable notices from editors, but I'm now glad to say didn't make it." Under a pseudonym, Mark published a number of pornographic novels in the 1970s that included this woman, whom he named Rina. He spent his 30s and early 40s looking for a woman like her. At the time of the survey, his wife was black, as an ex-wife and another former girlfriend had been.

Aside from twelve sex partners, Mark had had three encounters with prostitutes: one in Tijuana when he was a teen, one when he was about 30, and a third five years later when a buddy purchased her for him. It was the second who most closely resembled his image of feminine perfection:

> I picked up a prostitute on a corner in the Black area of town. She had a body just like the magazine girl, though not a beautiful face, just average plain, I would say. But she had definitely the most beautiful body of any woman I have ever been alone with. She was seventeen. I know because I asked her. I felt a little guilty about her being so young, at the time, and about using her that way. The prostitution business is a very brutal one, and I don't think anyone but the pimp really profits from it. I certainly never got any memorable pleasure from such an encounter, except for the memory of this girl's splendid body.

Mark's interests were totally focused on black women. He did not buy pornography if it did not have particularly alluring black females in it. "That's really all I'm interested in." He preferred especially dark-skinned women to "high yellow" or tan ones, and was very attracted to African features. Angela Bassett or N'Bushe Wright were more appealing to him than, say, Halle Berry.

> I know some would consider that a racist orientation, something like Boswell's inability to enjoy coitus with a woman of his own social class, which made him seek out servant girls and whores. But I think otherwise. I think of it as an esthetic preference, which is very strong. I went for dark girls even when I was a teenager: Mexican girls, olive-skinned girls, Fil-

ipino girls, etc. At an earlier age, I was vaguely troubled by why I might prefer black women, but I have outgrown it. It can't be because I think they are hotter in the sack, or anything like that, since I have had many of them and know that isn't true. Some I've known have been absolutely frigid, or sexually awkward, or inhibited. Just like everyone else. I don't have any unrealistic expectations of them. I just find their looks more appealing.

Feminist writers have made much of racism in pornography. In a fiery essay, Alice Walker wrote of the legacy of the old slave societies of the South, wherein white "gentlemen" used their slaves as "breeders, raped for the pleasure and profit of their owners." Such treatment resulted in what they called "beautiful young quadroons and octoroons," who became increasingly "indistinguishable from white women, and were the more highly prized as slave mistresses because of this." But Mark explicitly was not interested in fair-skinned black women.

Patricia Hill Collins writes of the exploitation of black women in pornography as "animals that can be bred against their will." Violence and subjugation, she asserts, mark the relationship between a white male and a black female. Reviewing a porn novel entitled *Black Fashion Model*, Andrea Dworkin writes, "She is punished in sex by sex and she is punished as a consequence of sex: She loses her status." But this does not describe Mark's tastes or life choices. He married two black women he desired, and had a child by one of them, whom they raised together. The beauty of these women drew him, not a need to subjugate.

This is not to deny the racist slant of such pornography as *Animal Sex Among Black Women* or *Seductive Black Bitch*. But to apply a template of historical significance to an individual man's life, to each and every exchange between the sexes and the races—even in pornography—pushes the argument too far.

In most other respects, Mark was fairly conservative. "A woman's face is absolutely the most important thing about her. Eyes, expression, mouth, etc." The idea of group sex appalled him: "The only 'sharing' I have ever done is to enjoy a few casual, passing jokes or *bon mots* with friends about certain recurring themes or images in porn."

Mark's ideal woman lived on as a character in an ongoing pornographic novel he wrote for himself. The market for porn novels largely collapsed after the advent of video, so Mark did not expect to publish the work, which had grown to more than eighty chapters. The protagonist was a beautiful white woman named Laura, who resembled Stephanie Seymour. "I see her chiefly as a surrogate for me, since she gets to screw all these darlings I would like to screw myself." Including, of course, Rina.

Mark's wife didn't know about his pornography, purchased or composed, which he kept hidden and locked, and neither did most of his past lovers. "They were almost always of a jealous nature, and a woman can be jealous of a magazine as easily as a real woman." To some extent, Mark felt his wife was entitled to view pornography as competition, which may be one reason he didn't use it much anymore. Although he would look at pictures three or four times a week, and a video once or twice a month when possible, masturbation with them occurred once a month at most.

> I have to save some steam for my wife, who is younger than I and expects a certain amount of attention. And who is very attractive, by the way. I must say she has first ownership rights to my orgasms. The ones I don't need to devote to her, I devote to myself. I think our sex life is fine, but I also like my secret life.

Jay: Fit to Be Tied

"Jay" did not recall seeing any pornography before the age of 14. He may well have, but nothing made an impression until he encountered John Norman's novel, *Kajira of Gor*, "which I found *enormously* erotic." It was not the story's slave women per se that startled his libido into gear, but the fact that they were tied up.

Jay remembered playing cowboys and Indians about age six, and getting tied to a tree. "I found it profoundly exciting to be tied up this way—it felt much more fun than most other games." He recalled playing Houdini games in fifth grade with his younger sister and two boys his own age. "I have a very distinct memory of being strapped to a wicker chair in my parents' family room, with two dinky leather straps around my wrists. I was thrilled and panicked to discover I couldn't undo the straps." A similar opportunity presented itself during a trip to the ocean when he was 12:

> There was an old boat pulled up on the sand a quarter mile from our beach house. I remember one day I played pirates with a couple of other vacationing girls, one my age and one around seven. The older girl wouldn't hold still, but I did manage to tie the younger one's hands quite securely behind her. And of course who came walking up but her parents; she jumped onto the deck of the ship and yelled hello, with me freaking out at the thought that her parents would find out what we'd been doing. I untied her *really* quickly and no more was ever said about it.

The girl showed no resistance to the game. "She enjoyed it."

By the time Jay encountered the Norman book, the pump was primed. "I'd always enjoyed tying people up and being tied up, and finding a whole *book* about slave women was very sexy indeed. I kept it hidden from my parents, as I knew they wouldn't approve—even though, back then, I understood the differences between fantasy and reality, and knew my fantasies were OK."

Jay was introverted as an adolescent. "I had a very graphic and extreme fantasy life, and I think the porn I read contributed to that." The gap between what happened in his fantasies and teenage dating was so huge that he remained intimidated by the real world. "I was desperately curious to find women who enjoyed the same fantasies I enjoyed—I knew they existed—but I was nowhere near ready to act on that desire." From ages 14 to 16 he subsisted on John Norman books and *Variations* magazine from the newsstand. Between ages 17 and 19 he was able to find bondage magazines at an adult bookstore near his home.

Jay called bondage his "fundamental turn-on." He liked to see "well-done bondage on attractive women—men in bondage don't arouse me so much unless there is a woman being explicitly sexual with them. I like images of struggle and surrender and explosive helpless orgasms." Asked to define "well-done" bondage, Jay said "if it's easy to escape, it's not well-done." That can vary with the scenario: "latex fetish goes well with elaborate harnesses and suchlike, while a woman tied outside in the woods may look best with hastily looped (yet securely knotted) ropes." Jay found a wide variety of women attractive in such images. They didn't have to be any particular body style. Nudity or sexual activity did not even have to occur: "Even if neither is involved, I fantasize about how easy it would be—given the subject woman's helplessness—to remove her clothes or have sex (perhaps forcibly) with her."

The crucial element was that the activity—no matter how forceful, "violent," and vivid—be consensual:

> It is necessary for me to believe that the woman in the picture is consenting to being in her situation. She may be role-playing an unwilling participant, but at bottom she is there by choice. If I do not believe this, I do not enjoy the image. Enormous amounts of trust, lust, and sexual confidence are implicit in that decision of hers.

Jay had seen images of women who didn't appear to be enjoying themselves at all, on any level: "One that comes to mind is a German S/M flick in which a woman got pins inserted into her breasts. It was very disturbing for me to watch this video, though there were erotic overtones present."

It must be stressed that Jay had no investment simply in exercising power over women, because it mattered little to him whether he did the tying or was tied: "I have found that in my personal bondage play, my arousal at making my partner helpless reinforces her arousal at being so, resulting in a ravishing coupling that takes us both by storm. This works as well if it's me being bound and her binding."

He took equal pleasure in "the hunger to be taken" and in "the power of taking." He got just as much enjoyment from "the human response to constriction and pleasure, both of which can produce deeply calming and stimulating responses on the physiological level," as from acting as if he had utter power and enjoying the fact that someone had placed complete trust in him.

"The pleasure in being bound is being able to thrash and struggle, of experiencing overwhelming waves of sensation and penetration while chained securely in place." When his lover ties him up and gets him off, "I feel on cloud nine afterward—it is an extremely mind-blowing experience to be so focused on what she is doing to me. It's wonderful to lie back and receive so much from her, and to squirm so shamelessly that she finds me irresistible."

When the tables are turned, "I relish controlling her experience, leading her right up to the edge of orgasm, then sending her over." It was also pleasurable to use his lover to gratify himself, because his pleasure sent her into "further paroxysms of ecstasy." Being top and being bottom are pleasurable for both parties, "but the energy flow is different. I associate topping with voyeurism, mastery, lecherousness, and power. I associate bottoming with exhibitionism, submissiveness, shamelessness, and helplessness." In the end, regardless of which position Jay and his lover took, "we wind up naked, breathless, sweaty, and happy. So although the energy in the scene is different, both roads lead to the same destination."

Jay knew what it was like to have the trust misused. Once he attended a workshop in S/M shamanism and was so attracted to a workshop assistant that he allowed himself to be led to a basement dungeon. They proceeded to perform many of the acts Jay had long fantasized about. "He was the person who first dressed me in corset, stockings, and heels, and all three have been mainstays of my erotic life ever since." Unfortunately, about four months into their twice-a-month liaison, the man attempted something to which Jay had not consented: anal sex without a condom. "He didn't get anywhere, as I didn't want it and wasn't receptive," and Jay stopped seeing the man. All of his other bondage relationships had been with women.

Jay acknowledged that his tastes were not the norm. Though he had bought bondage porn in print form for many years and downloaded stories and images from the Internet, photographs of restraint and of explicit sex—common by themselves—almost never appear together. "What I wish for is explicit bondage with explicit penetration, but that's very, very rare in the U.S." It is as if the two together are too potent.

Jay did not agree with the "slippery slope" theory, wherein a man seeks ever more vivid and violent pornography after an initial taste. "Lovemaps tend to be more fixed than that, in my experience. Consensual violence, rough sex play, is enormously exciting to me. I have had worries about being addicted to it and about the 'slippery slope,' but again these worries have over time proved unfounded."

Twenty-five years old at the time of the survey and reporting an income around $70,000, Jay was getting better at "bringing my real sex life closer to my fantasy sex life, for which I feel very blessed." When asked if he had ever committed a violent act, he wrote: "If strapping down my lover, gagging and blindfolding her, putting clothespins on her pussy lips and tying them apart with strings, shoving a butt plug up her ass, then fucking her pussy while simultaneously stroking her clit and dripping hot wax on her counts as a violent act, then I plead guilty."

The average person might respond to such a scenario with horror. Sensing that Jay knew this, I asked him to deconstruct the scene by describing the context. He had met his girlfriend at work, was struck by her beauty, and they developed a friendship, then a relationship, over several months. A year and a half passed before they performed the act described above. (By the time of the survey, they had been together four years.) Before it happened, they discussed their sexual fantasies, and had several erotic conversations about BD/SM. It took about five weeks before they tried the above scenario:

> The clothespins were her idea—she finds it incredibly erotic to feel the intense pinches on her labia, while also finding her pussy so very exposed and open. The fucking-while-stroking clit technique was one I'd learned after lots of experience making love to her—it demands a certain flexibility but often results in devastating near-simultaneous orgasm for us both. She

enjoyed being strapped down because it enabled her to struggle and exert all of her muscles as I was having sex with her, without throwing me halfway across the room. She also liked feeling like I had the power to decide what she was going to feel and how she was going to get fucked. The butt plug felt good to her because I inserted it in a way that was both hygienic and painless, and because having something up your ass can greatly enhance orgasm. Gagging her both gave her something to chew on and increased her perceived sense of my power. Blindfolding her made it easier for me to surprise her with sensation and made it easier for her to trance out and focus on what she was feeling. As I'm fucking her, I hold the burning candle at a height of probably 18 inches above her naked breasts, and dripping drops of hot wax from it onto them. It feels like burning needles gently touching the skin, before (almost immediately) cooling. When in the throes of hot sex, many intense sensations are perceived as pleasure when ordinarily they might seem just painful. This was a perfect example.

I asked Jay if his girlfriend ever told him what an experience like this meant to her—why she pursued it. He said, "She finds it very cathartic to be hurt like that. She was struggling and screaming while it went on, until she finally reached a point of acceptance, where each stroke felt not like agonizing pain but like a blinding biting kiss."

The context of a solid relationship, a shared desire, and total consent enabled Jay and his lover in the end to feel "Very very happy, relaxed, tired, gratified, and slightly sore. She was very happy for days afterwards, feeling the lingering pain in her ass and remembering how intense the experience was."

Frank: Realizing the Inner Woman

"Frank" was never turned on by *Playboy*, *Penthouse*, or any other men's magazine when he was young. He described what he called "classic porn" as something "designed to be stimulating by describing more-or-less ordinary sex." This never interested him.

I frequently wondered in what way I was different, that *Playboy* et al. did not do for me what it was reputed to do for others. However, as no one of my acquaintance ever displayed any particular reaction to *Playboy* or other porn, I eventually concluded that the issue of porn exciting men was yet a Big Lie—that only crude and uncivilized morons were excited by it, but that the Myth was created that such was the state of all True Men.

It wasn't until he was in his early 20s that Frank saw something that caught his interest: letters in the *Penthouse* Forum by transvestites describing their fantasies. "I found even more stimulating stories clearly designed to appeal to my interests—stories of the feminization of men." He described a typical story line:

Young man or boy is coerced/tricked/bribed by female authority figure (girlfriend, wife, stepmother, kidnapper) into wearing female clothing (perhaps extremely frou-frou, perhaps with elements of bondage, perhaps just ordinary); usually he is brought to appear socially as a woman/girl. In nearly all the stories I've read, the man/boy is predisposed to like this (he'd confessed as much to his wife once; the kidnapper has sensed this in him; he's answered an ad, thinking it would be just for a lark); the feminization is sometimes viewed as punishment, which the man/boy grows to accept as natural. Sartorial elements are lovingly described, with much attention to undergarments; one common subtheme is that of Victorian-style clothing, complete with corsets.

Frank explained that the appeal lay in empathy with the male subject: "placing myself in his shoes, imagining how I'd feel in such a circumstance, imagining how it would be to be 'forced' by a woman to become feminine." If he thought about the story in retrospect, "I typically will alter the storyline to better fit with my own particular inclinations. I may imagine interacting with the woman involved, in much the same way as in the story."

Domination, in this case, meant physical control by means of bondage or threats. Mere exertion of a strong personality was not usually sufficient, "although that could, conceivably, be the means by which to assume control of the man." Although Frank at times imagined himself magically transformed into a woman, he never saw himself as a dominating one, and both situations were fairly peripheral to the main source of his arousal.

Frank kept encountering homosexual elements in the stories, which did not accord with his tastes at all:

> Many of the TV porn stories end up with the man engaging in oral sex with a man—I have always found that portion exceedingly unappealing. For some folk, complete feminization means becoming capable of sex with a man (or, at least, having sex with a man). Hence the usage of fellatio in many TV porn stories ("I'll make a good little cocksucker out of you!"—typical line). Possibly, these stories also appeal to men who have a repressed interest in engaging in sex with men—though I've not met any such TV's. I have no such interest.

It's a common assumption, especially among antiporn activists of the religious stripe, that transvestites are homosexuals, and transsexuals are bisexuals, and everyone who is "different" goes in for bondage and excretory activities. Once you're off the beaten track, the theory goes, you could not only end up anywhere, you *will* end up *everywhere*. This is not true for most people. Frank skipped the male-to-male incidents in TV porn. He was repulsed by anything that involved excrement. Other things left him unmoved, "such as pain or sex-change operations or anything degrading to women."

Frank said he identified himself strictly as a man, with no particular fantasy of actually becoming a woman. "I have had a few fantasies about appearing in public as a woman, but these are not very strong. I lost interest in stories in which the subject eventually underwent sex-reassignment surgery. My feeling of connection to things feminine, achieved by putting on a bra and panties daily, is a feeling of connection to a layer within me, not to a 'model' woman."

Though having sex with women appealed to Frank in his actual sex life, it was not all that interesting to him in pornography. "Sometimes

there is described sex with a woman, but that has always left me cold—
not that I find that idea unappealing; rather, that its description does
nothing for me. My libido is not engaged much by descriptions of sex.
I don't usually fantasize sexual acts at all—rather, relationships that I
find exciting (being dominated by a woman, generally)."

Although he said he currently did this much less often than in the
past, Frank described what he did with TV porn when he used it
frequently:

> Typically, I would sit down and pore over a story, perhaps going through
> several stories or episodes serially, while maintaining a high level of
> excitement, and perhaps (especially with something new) coming soon to
> a climax (with no or minimal masturbation) and then stopping. Sometimes
> I would first dress in feminine attire, but that actually made little differ-
> ence, and I frequently did not do so. This would happen several times a
> week, for the period in question—now I may do it once in several months.

Asked about the importance of wearing feminine clothing, Frank said
it "is always pleasing to me, it's just not necessary to enjoy the stories.
The mental idea is what is paramount for excitement (the idea of being
feminine or being made to be feminine)." Other pleasures associated
with wearing women's clothing were not, however, strictly related to
sexual arousal: "A pleasure at thinking myself connected with things
feminine, and also a sheer sensual delight in the satiny textures; these
pleasures are not what I would call sexual excitement, except on a very
low level (erection may come, but not much and not for long; the low-
level pleasure, the 'glow' is there in any event)." Frank habitually wore
bra and panties and nightgowns for years. Less often he donned skirts,
blouses, and dresses. "I obtain these in the most prosaic of ways, by
purchasing them at department stores or specialty lingerie shops."

Frank said he didn't masturbate with TV porn very often, preferring
"to maintain a steady state of excitement." In the past, he frequently
read porn without reaching orgasm, because he did not intend to:
"Occasionally I did orgasm, even without much masturbation, and

sometimes orgasm was my intent, though that was not the majority of the time." He estimated that he currently used TV porn as a masturbation aid less than five percent of the time.

Looking back, Frank remembered some incidents that hinted at things to come: "The earliest fantasies I can recall were from about age six; they involved my being chased by girls, being caught and then tied up and kissed. This was clearly exciting to me, even at that age."

When he was 23 and a senior in college, Frank had to put on a skirt for a concert performance. Several girls teased him about it, and this incident inspired many subsequent fantasies. "In my fantasies, I would go over to the girls' dorm, they would have me take off my pants and put on a slip 'in order to get the measurements right'; my pants would then mysteriously disappear. Eventually, dinnertime would roll around, and I'd just have to wear the finished skirt to go to dinner with the girls— maybe with suitable blouse and heels."

Some years before taking my survey, Frank found a large and inexpensive mail-order source of TV porn. Most of the material did not include sex; instead, the focus was more directly upon "the feminization of men by women." However, since the primary intent was to arouse the viewer sexually, Frank was content to label it pornography. "I grew tired of it," he said, "though it can still catch my eye on rare occasions."

Part of what caused him to "drop it cold" two or three years before he took the survey was discovering "the joys of the net: alt.sex.bondage, IRC #crossdress, Transgen listserver . . . . Suddenly, I was no longer alone!! I cannot overemphasize what a difference this has made. I no longer felt compelled to engage in solitary pleasures, when there was so much to be gained in communing with others. It's been an incredible experience, as the level of discourse on Transgen is often (though not universally) exceedingly high."

There were at least two facets to Frank's use of the net: discussion and learning about himself through the experiences and ideas of others, and direct pleasuring. He had had sex on the net with about half a dozen "near-strangers, and, so long as it involved items of erotic interest to one or the other of us, it was somewhat exciting." The best encounters developed from electronic conversations "in which one can no longer call these people strangers."

The idea of becoming "close" to someone you've never met, whom you know only through words, may seem delusional to anyone who has never experienced the Internet (or conducted a romance by old-fashioned postal letters), but Frank insisted otherwise:

> [By "someone who cares"] I meant people one has known on the net, exchanged many hours of converse with. For instance, I was most affected when one Domme I had been having a few scenes with berated me for engaging in a net.scene with someone else—not because she was jealous of the other, but because I had allowed myself to become involved with a scene which made me uncomfortable (involving sex with another guy, at the other woman's direction); she was disturbed that I had allowed myself to be taken advantage of in such a manner (feeding the other woman's penchant for control in a manner destructive of my own sense of self). That such concern for me was in her heart made future sessions with her much more heartfelt on my part—I was more "into" the scene, wanting to make her feel into it.

Some of Frank's most interesting encounters took place on systems that use a "tinyMUSH" code. MUSH stands for Multi-User Shared Hallucination, in which many people occupy the same electronic space at one time, as if they were all in the same room but could only hear, not see, one another. A coding language allows all players the ability to "create objects" and give them descriptions, as well as allow the objects to interact in complicated manners with other players.

Frank achieved a kind of apotheosis in a MUSH environment that was a simulation of Milton's Hell. He played the role of a woman, and eventually a man asked to have sex with her:

> I had, for some months, been playing the part of a woman on Pandemo-niumMUSH (the lost soul of Boudicca, to be precise). No one knew

Boudicca's player was a man (and I exhibited none of the telltale traits so many guys show when playing female characters; they're often easy to spot, ridiculously female-stereotyped). One fellow, a notorious rake in the game, fell in love with Boudicca, wanted to marry her (marriage in hell! it was a first for the game). After a courtship, I consented. He then wanted to get some intimate play in. He told me his real name as we started—and so I told him mine! I could hear his jaw drop over the net. He was still so taken with the image of Boudicca that I had created that, some days later, he wanted to go ahead with an intimate scene, anyway, just relying on me, as a consummate role player, to create the appropriate responses. For me it was interesting, an acting challenge—but not exciting. I'm not sure how it was for him, but I know he was much more identified with his character than I was with Boudicca. Still, I made Boudicca into my idealized woman—the kind I'd have fallen in love with, had I seen her. Bou was one of the most successful players in the MUSH—towards the end (a year ago the MUSH went down) she had virtually no enemies among the hundred or so players (and a score of good friends)—and this in a simulation of Milton's Hell, with endless rivalry between lost souls and fallen angels.

Of course, being a grown-up human being involves more than the ability to play computer word games and pleasure oneself. As with all the experiences and perceptions described in this book, this portrait of Frank unfairly highlights a few aspects of his life, which does not all take place through mail-order and MUSH. Frank was a 43-year-old professor. He had been physically intimate with about ten women in his life. And he was in transition.

At the time he began the survey, he said: "I have never told anyone of my extensive collection of TV porn, save for a few people similarly inclined. I have not discussed it with my SO." By the time he had finished the survey a month later, however, she knew. When I asked why he had chosen to participate in the survey and whether there had been any benefits, he said, "Basically, I am interested in increasing the general scientific knowledge of people like myself. Also, all such surveys help me in seeing myself, as I probe inwards for answers. Now that I have an SO whom I share everything with, it also helps that I can show her my answers, telling her more of who I am." I asked if it had been a safe and productive exercise to share this information with her.

> It has, indeed, been productive to share this information with my SO—I have yet ever to regret sharing any piece of me with her. I think I was just a bit nervous in sharing some of this with M., but not very—and there has been nothing but good that came as a result. I really do want M. to know all about me, and she seems pleased to know as much as she can.

Having come so far in understanding and acknowledging his desires and fantasies to himself, and now to the most important person in his life, Frank was still constrained to keep it between them . . . and perhaps a few distant, faceless friends on the Internet. I asked if he found this unfair:

> Is it unfair that I cannot, without risking social opprobrium, express my feminine leanings in public? "Fairness" is not something which properly applies to the way in which society is constructed in such fundamental matters. I don't like the fact that this is the way things are, I wish they were different, I rejoice in the movements I see leading to a liberalization of such attitudes. I do a few small things to encourage them.

Harold: Like an Animal

"Harold" was a 24-year-old Canadian college student. Like many men in this study, his first exposure to pictures of nude women involved his father's copy of *Playboy*. He was 11, the year was 1981, and the subject Bo Derek.

> At first, I thought it rather strange. I never saw a fully nude woman (and frankly the most beautiful woman I ever really saw at that time) in sexual poses before. When I first saw it, I thought she was wearing a swimsuit,

> then realized she didn't have any. Then I tried to rationalize as thinking of an Adam and Eve mentality in order to excuse the stimulation that I couldn't explain that I got from it. I was Christian for a while, I guess I sort of got the idea that sexual feelings were somehow wrong. So in order to excuse that to myself, I tried putting it in a Biblical context to fool myself into thinking that I was contemplating the Bible instead of thinking "sin." Chalk it up to a typical Christian attitude that if you enjoy yourself, you must be sinful and damned. It was only later that I used [the images in *Playboy*] to found my sexual fantasies.

At 11, Harold had no idea what intercourse was or what caused pregnancy. A sex-ed book helped clear that up. His father caught him with the *Playboy*s and "showed disgust that he couldn't keep it anymore without my knowledge." His father and brother later "graduated to cruder stuff which I find repellent."

Harold did not associate the people he saw in the magazine with anyone he knew. "I regarded the models in a rather detached manner as having nothing to do with my life or reality." Although he naturally was interested in the female form and, "to a lesser degree," the male form, he did not explore until later.

> Later I was interested in porn letters and digests that depicted explicit sexual activity. I would say the exposure to pornography was occasional. I only bought a porn magazine once, but with[in] four hours of buying it, I threw it out in disgust. I prefer erotic stories, considering it forces the sex characters to display something of character.

About four years before he took the survey, Harold found some material that appealed to him much more than what he had seen in *Playboy*. It was "furry erotic literature and comics," which depict human-like creatures in erotic tales. "I find these vastly superior in artistry and the stories are largely extremely well written. I know it sounds strange but I regard it as healthier than regular porn." Some examples were *Omaha the Cat Dancer*, *Genus*, *Katmandu* and *Wild Kingdom*.

> *Wild Kingdom* is an anthology series of furry erotica stories which has funny animals for characters. [Issue] #1 had three stories. The first one was about a young vampire bat who went to a finishing school to attack a young virgin mouse girl. She woke up and greeted him like a romantic hero come to deliver her from that prison. This left the bat totally bewildered as the mouse girl offers herself to him. He tries to attack her, but when he moves, she interprets this as heavy petting and opens her shirt to get him to nuzzle her chest, where her cross necklace is. When he is burned twice on the nose for it, she removes it and this confuses the bat even more to see a would-be victim trust him. Thus the story shows the bat is as much an innocent as the mouse-girl as they make love. At the end of story, he decides to stay with her, using tomatoes as sustenance.

Asked to explain the appeal, Harold suggested there was a distancing factor with imaginary creatures which made sex acts and intimacy less threatening than they often are for young and inexperienced readers. "I feel more comfortable with furries engaging in sexual activity than humans." The "cuteness" was appealing in general, and Harold could allow himself to be aroused even by "handsome male furries." Perhaps, he theorized, the human sexuality depicted in pornography "is too close to reality for me, or the human stuff is what I associate with the artistic schlock of regular porn." He added that the limited market for what he called "furotica" tended to encourage more personal visions among the artists.

Harold also said "my furry stuff allows me to see women without getting caught in the beauty myth. Thus, I can see women without imposing impossible standards of beauty."

> Furry stuff allows me to see sexually arousing imagery while being continually reminded that this does not exist. The chance of meeting a real furry is about the same as meeting a woman of the beauty of Christie Brinkley. Thus, if I get my rocks off with furry imagery, I can relate to women without my sexual perception of them interfering. Thus, I will not denigrate a woman for looking less beautiful than the artificial imagery of

the cover girls. With furries, I can avoid the blinds of race and (sometimes) culture. It distances sexual activity to expose me to things that I wouldn't accept seeing in humans.

Harold added that "furries" appear in mainstream entertainment:

Art Spiegelman used furry imagery to illustrate the social dynamics of the Holocaust in the Pulitzer Prize-winning comic, *Maus*, though it doesn't work all the time. For example, the Jews are represented as mice, Germans cats, Poles pigs, and Americans as dogs. To illustrate how Jews had to hide their culture, he showed the lead character, a Jew, with a pig mask, thus showing he tried to pass himself as Polish. *The Lion King* has a powerful story and themes. The fact that the characters are represented as animals in an animal society gives advantages to the format that any human can identify with.

Harold stressed that the material he enjoyed was "strictly nonviolent and nondegrading" and "I have no patience with stories that are violent, as in rape, or deal in humiliation."

When he used these materials, Harold was usually in bed with the computer on or he looked at a comic on the bed. As he read, he masturbated, trying to time his orgasm to the climax of the story. He did this twice a day, morning and bedtime. Harold estimated that he looked at the stories without masturbating perhaps a quarter of the time.

His personal fantasies tended to involve sex between humanoid animals with mild domination, jungle or island settings, and "often ridiculously elaborate" scenarios of persons, animals, and sexual tools. Very occasionally Harold fantasized about rape, bondage, or S/M, and "then I find myself beating myself up for it." He wanted to see the "basic sexism of pornography" eliminated, because "a basic sense of humanity, love and considerate fun towards one another" was missing from most of it.

Harold cited one other guilty pleasure, one that he rarely had the chance to indulge because it was hard to find: mud and jello wrestling videos.

> Maybe it's a latent sexism that gets a strange thrill out of seeing beautiful women wrestle and getting covered in the stuff while tearing their clothing off. It could be a latent egotism I have buried that gets off imagining that those women are fighting for the right to fuck me. I don't know, but I often feel shame for getting off like that.

Although Harold was quite satisfied with his chosen form of erotica, friends had given him grief about it. He once showed a copy of *Wild Kingdom* to them and the reaction was very negative. "My friends reacted thinking that I was weird and considered getting me some regular porn to 'cure' me. After all, funny animals are associated with children, and the furriness suggests bestiality to others."

Fortunately, one of his closest woman friends expressed interest in the vampire story because she was a fan of vampires in general. He told her he thought "Taste of Blood [the *Wild Kingdom* story]" was the best erotic vampire story he had ever seen. "After all, when was the last time you saw a vampire with puppy-dog bewildered eyes? I asked her for her honest opinion and she said that it was a neat tale and very funny and charming. Almost no one outside a few confidants understands my attraction to this and the reactions I usually get range from uninterest to suspicions that I am some sort of pervert. Hence, the conventions I plan to go to with other fans are gratifying in the extreme."

Since Harold hadn't had a sex partner in life, I suggested perhaps he might lose interest in furry erotica once he became sexually experienced. "I don't expect to, but things do change," he replied. "Maybe, if I get real sex, the need for the vicarious kind could decrease, but it is so beautiful on its own that it could survive."

As a hypothetical, I asked Harold what he would do if he were to fall in love with someone who objected to pornography, especially his furry erotica. "I would hold my ground and show her that the vast majority of my stuff has a great deal of artistic validity. I think I would win her over, but otherwise it is a minor quirk in my personality and not a great flaw to [have to] tolerate."

The "Slippery Slope" and the Question of Addiction

When discussing the effect pornography has on men, its foes often apply a "slippery slope" model. After a while, the theory goes, the friendly nudes of *Playboy* no longer suit; the viewer *must* move on to more kinky and violent material. I asked the men several questions to investigate whether this were true—whether there had been times in their lives when they used significantly more (or less) pornography than at other times, and whether the style or content they preferred had changed over time.

If the antiporn theory is correct, the men would have used more pornography over time, and its content would have become more vivid and violent. Although most men said there had been times in their lives when they had used pornography more than at other times, high use tended to correlate—as we have seen in previous chapters—with external circumstances: not being in a relationship, being in college, amount of privacy, extra time on one's hands, or when depressed, under stress, or experiencing relationship troubles.

In reality, only a few men reported that they had gone for the more vivid and kinky over time. "Sam," whose experiences are described in detail in the "Pornography as Hell, Pornography as Therapy" chapter, was one: "Once any flick off the shelf was fine for me, but as the addiction escalated I needed stronger and stronger material," he wrote, especially anal penetration.

"Normal stuff is somewhat boring," a 46-year-old married government employee said. "Just pure, clean naked girls was once a total turn-on. They still are exciting, but now I want to see some really heavy and nasty stuff. I want to see underage stuff, animal stuff, kinky stuff and waterworks stuff. Most of this I cannot purchase due to present laws." This man was a Christian, had sworn off pornography a number of times, and was married to the only sex partner he had ever known—to whom he had been faithful.

A bisexual male who watched video porn with his bisexual wife said: "I used to be satisfied with naked women. The pornography I view now tends to be of young girls (or boys), gay men, animals, and fisting. I've been on an 'Asian' woman kick lately. Don't want to sound racist or anything, [but] something about them is a little exotic."

A third of the men in the survey said the porn they had liked in their youth was the same porn they liked today. "Still the same," affirmed a Canadian government employee who almost never bought magazines or rented videos, for feminist reasons: "Mainly photos of nekkid wimmen."

"I've generally just read your basic convenience-store-type porn (*Swank*, *Velvet*) as opposed to anything very explicit and fetish oriented," said a 20-year-old Canadian student. "Never been interested, never will be." Two men whose taste ran to bondage had keyed into it since puberty or before, so they also could truthfully say their preference had not changed.

Some men had lost interest in pictorial porn over the years. A Spaniard who once liked girl-girl pictorials later turned to that scenario in story form. Another man who watched porn videos with his wife said he was pretty non-discriminating: "When I want a video, I just go to the store and pick one. In my mind, they are all pretty much alike. What I have been watching over the years didn't change much. Probably only the faces."

The only change many men cited was toward higher quality. "I look harder for well-produced, more interesting stuff, like Andrew Blake's films," said a 29-year-old married man who thought his tastes "haven't changed radically." Said a 29-year-old married custodian, "I feel that I've become more judicial about what I view now. When I was younger, anything with naked people in it was good enough; now I'm more picky about the performers, directors, and video companies. I tend to go with the ones I know by experience or reputation. With our having a child and my wife getting bored of the 'same old porn movie junk,' we rent fewer in a year than we used to in a month."

Some men said their taste had narrowed to very particular types and little else. "I used to be into the pornographic videos with amusing plots, situations, pick-up lines, spoofs on TV shows, etc.," a 21-year-old music major reported, but "these days, I'm into the sex marathon tapes with as much sex as possible and no dialogue whatsoever, just grunting and moaning."

Is Addiction Possible?

Porn users who commit heinous crimes, such as serial killer Ted Bundy and Canadian Paul Bernardo (who had his girlfriend videotape him in the act of raping teenage girls he later killed), have provided an easy weapon for antipornography activists to claim that pornography is not only addictive, but inherently and dangerously so. While a majority of the men in my survey thought it was possible to become addicted to porn, almost all were sure *they* were not addicted and had never been.

Many said a variety of substances and activities could be addictive. "Anyone can become addicted to anything: sex, drugs, tobacco, alcohol, sugar, caffeine, driving, television, the Internet," wrote one. Others listed food, the Blazers, the Beatles, fast cars, video games, Pepsi, running, dancing, soap operas, gambling, shopping, and chocolate. A few qualified the condition as "psychologically addicted," or "dependent."

A 24-year-old married student drew a clear line between the few who are susceptible and the many who are not:

> I use the analogy of role-playing games and heavy metal music. Some kids have killed people after playing role-playing games, and others have killed themselves after playing heavy metal music. Are these things inherently harmful? No. Many role players develop problem-solving skills through the playing of these games. Most kids listen to such music with no adverse effects.

A 40-year-old Englishman suggested that notions of addiction lay in the eye of the beholder: "If someone enjoys something, and *in your opinion* he indulges too often, he's an addict." Although he saw addiction to pornography as a symptom of a more generalized addiction to sex, a 22-year-old American suggested something of the same when he said the word "addiction" presumed the existence of a problem. Many people "would generally not really say the same if one spent hours a day talking on the telephone, watching television, playing video games, or using a computer. All are forms of entertainment."

Other men could imagine situations where addiction to porn was possible. A 20-year-old Canadian believed addiction "probably more likely would occur in someone who has severe social difficulties," adding, "I don't think it happens very often." A 45-year-old in manufacturing was of the same opinion: "I believe there are some who become addicted but they are generally those who do not or cannot lead a normal life; it is something in their personality."

Another man took a double view of the matter—unconcerned about his dependence, but uneasy about others':

> I am addicted to it. I don't see anything much wrong with that. I'm addicted to coffee too, and whiskey, but I only drink 3 or 4 shots of whiskey on the

weekends. I used to be addicted to cigarettes (22 years) but stopped that addiction because I thought it had control of me. I have control of the others. I do, however, think that some men who have trouble relating successfully to women may become addicted to pornography. In many cases it may be a pale but useful substitute for them, and in some few cases a terrible vice, leading to rape or some other awful mayhem.

A smaller group of men spoke with certainty of the dangers of porn addiction. "Dan," a Christian who avoided pornography himself but sometimes obtained erotica for his wife, said, "It doesn't matter what I think on this—this is a proven fact." Several men thought they had witnessed it in others. "One or two people I know seem to live porn," commented a mechanic. "They know all the actors and movies. It's unreal how much time they spend with porn." A Frenchman who hated pornography was certain some people he knew were addicted because "they cannot bear waiting more than a week between two porn videos."

A couple of men voiced worries about becoming addicted:

At times I've felt it's become too compulsive; this particularly applied when I frequented peep [shows]. Perhaps I was concerned more about the cost and the chance of being seen rather than any negative effect the porn was having on me. I could at that time perhaps be regarded as a porn binger—I'd spend entire nights at the peeps, perhaps weekly but rarely more often. These concerns have passed since video emerged. This has had the effect of lessening the financial price and porn has become more of a part of my day-to-day life.

Only three men in the survey declared flat-out that they were addicted to pornography. Two were married men who had attended meetings of the twelve-step program Sexaholics Anonymous. "I am addicted to the feelings and actions and lifestyle that is characterized by lust," said one. "It is a progressive illness. The level of porn consumption that was more than enough 10 years ago doesn't even begin to satiate me today. In fact, it may hardly arouse me. I need more quantity, more erotic, more fanciful, more different porn as time goes on in order to 'benefit' from it." The other, Sam, declared that "porn is destructive to many, it has done great damage to me," but he added: "Porn is not the root cause of my sexual addiction. I would blame porn for exacerbating it, however I would blame growing up in a family in which physical affection was rarely seen for causing it." The third man was a 39-year-old virgin. "I regard myself as addicted to pornography. I recognize the need to stop it, but don't feel there's a snowball's chance in hell of doing so."

Although not one of the gay men in the survey said he was addicted, and only a few said the possibility had ever crossed their minds, several believed they had seen it in others. "It is certainly possible and I have known people who I would say have been addicted," a 36-year-old systems analyst remarked. A 42-year-old professor said, "I do know people who spend a huge amount of money on porn—sometimes more than they could afford. Is that addiction? I'd say so."

Quite a few men wondered about the definition of "addiction" and questioned whether it was applicable in the case of pornography. "Sex is a powerful drive, and the use of pornography as a sex surrogate can create a psychological dependence," a law student wrote; "[But] I don't know if it should be called an 'addiction' in clinical terms."

"In true 'addiction' terms, I don't think it is possible to become addicted to porn, just as I don't believe in the notion of 'sex addiction,'" said a 33-year-old gay researcher. "But that is just my background in psychology speaking. I think it is possible to become a bit obsessed with it—and one can certainly allow it to upset other areas of one's life. But as a true addiction—no."

"Pornography is not cocaine or crack!" a 24-year-old engineer exclaimed. "Having lived with a drug addict, I know how consuming true addiction is," added a 38-year-old homosexual. "I don't believe a compulsion for pornography—if, in fact, there is such a thing—can in any way be likened to an addiction." "I don't get physically ill when I stop using pornography," a 41-year-old math student dryly observed.

Another man spelled out the differences between truly addictive substances and porn:

In recent years, it has become fashionable to tag various behaviors as addictive. People will claim that they are addicted to sex, or relationships, or anger, or overeating, or whatever it is in their life that troubles them. The people who exhibit these behaviors may have real problems. In particular, there is often a compulsive component to their behavior. However, these behaviors do not fit the model of real addiction. Someone wrote a book on this subject a few years ago. She suggested that what these people are suffering with is not any true addiction but simply existential anxiety: "the terror of knowing what the world is about." She felt that it debased the word to call these problems "addictions." Some people define addiction so broadly that it loses all content and becomes little more than a synonym for "want." Real addiction generally involves use of psychoactive chemicals. Characteristics of addictive substances include craving, euphoria, tolerance, and withdrawal. Also, use of addictive substances is self-reinforcing: the more you use, the more you want. A few behaviors, such as compulsive gambling, possess some of these characteristics as well. I drank heavily for three years in college. I managed to stop before my life was an utter shambles, but it was a serious problem. I consider myself to have been close enough to real addiction to have some authority on the subject. Pornography is not addictive.

Reality
versus Fantasy:

Do Porn Fans Associate Figures
in Porn with Real People?

Contrary to the assertions routinely made by antiporn activists, most of the men I talked to were quite clear about the distinctions between pornography and real life. Perhaps those distinctions are what make porn so attractive to men. If so, their taste for porn does not mean they wish real life were more like it, any more than most people would want to live in a D.H. Lawrence novel. The average person is drawn to most entertainment precisely *because* it is different from life. It provides a temporary respite, a brief thrill, whether it's a Disney movie or *Debbie Does Dallas*.

I asked the men whether, when they were first exposed to pornography, they associated the characters in it with people they knew. Almost everyone said no. "Real people were different from the ones in the magazines, that was clear to me," said a Dutch man who first saw porn at 12 or 13. "I've never associated people I saw in pornography with people I knew," a 41-year-old grad student declared; "I knew the naked women in the photographs were simply models who were paid to pose nude or topless. The photos were simply fodder for fantasies." "I made no associations between the figures in porn and real people—it was merely a bridge to active fantasy imagery," declared a 43-year-old professor. "I think even at an early age I could distinguish between the magazines and real life," recalled an African-American who first viewed porn at 10 or 11. An Australian man said, "These people were merely images and seemed too unreal. It wasn't until years later that I realized that they were real people and were simply doing a job."

"The first stuff I saw was from *Playboy*—not a cheap sleazy rag," recalled a 35-year-old gay man in information management. "But even such high quality porn seemed contrived and lurid to me. I knew real people didn't look or pose like that. I could see that real life was one thing and porn was another."

For one thing, the women in pornography just didn't look like any of the girls the men knew, though each was fascinating in her own way. "Since I was in high school, the girls I knew were teenagers," Mark recalled. "I loved several of them from afar, but I didn't at all associate them or compare them with the 'real women' in these books." "I lusted for adult women like the ones in the pictures and on TV," another man said, and "I had crushes on girls my own age, but could not think of them sexually." A 21-year-old student in England said, "Girls then weren't overtly sexual and I didn't make the connection." More coarsely, a 21-year-old American student said he never associated the women in porn with girls he knew because "I'm from Illinois, so all we have is corn and fat chicks." (He added, however, that he was more comfortable around large women and that "women that look like goddesses really intimidate me.")

Some men said the people in pornography were so different that it was impossible to associate them with real folks. "None of the women I was acquainted with were as pretty as those in the magazines; I did then, and still do, associate the women portrayed with a high level of beauty and attraction," said a 48-year-old married man.

For others, it was behavior that set figures in porn apart. "The people I read about were completely different in their approach to sex.

They were uninhibited, and I didn't know anyone who *wasn't* inhibited," said a 45-year-old gay man. "Pornography was a sexual fantasy that had no connection with reality. I absolutely did not associate any of the characters in the novels and magazines I read with any real people."

One man came to view porn as entirely separate from life as he knew it because of the general disrepute with which people around him regarded it:

> Because I had absorbed the idea that porn was dirty, I attached that association to people involved in porn—assuming that the photographers, models, publishers, etc., were part of some truly seedy underground thing. I don't recall making connections between the people in the pictures and the people in my day-to-day life, but I think I could say the same about people I saw in non-porn magazines or on television.

"It actually took a long time for me to picture people I knew in the same (literal) positions as models/actresses," related a 26-year-old in desktop publishing. "The people I grew up with were either excessively private about their sexuality or very unsexual." Like the figures in other entertainment media—rock music, films, books, TV—folks in pornography were "strong people with character and personality," he went on. "People trapped in the 'everyday' always seemed a bit lost. Porn merely emphasized that feeling." A 43-year-old gay man echoed this sentiment: "They were real, but not people I knew. They were just like any celebrities to me."

An Englishman wrote that not only was he wary of the pretense he saw in pornography, but that other sources of information offered him a better perspective:

> I fairly quickly came to the conclusion that the images and stories in porn magazines were fantasy. My theoretical knowledge of sex was greatly improved by listening to a radio phone-in program which dealt with sexual problems. By about age 14 I knew very well that porn images and stories were completely unreal. [software developer, 34, bisexual with female preference]

Sometimes a boy's particular milieu was too different from the world of porn to equate the two. "I went to an all-male school and knew very few girls," a 40-year-old Englishman reported. "The only girls I knew went to Catholic school and the only women were nuns," said another man, "and none of them looked like the girls that were in that magazine."

Some men traced their assumption that porn was completely separate from life to their childhood. "I was a very introverted person for most of my adolescence," said one; pornography contributed to the enormous gap between his bondage fantasies and "the realities of teenage dating games." This was likely if the material a boy saw was especially graphic, like the novels Jack found when searching for Santa Claus:

> There was an incredibly huge separation between the outside world of "reality" and this new sick, twisted, mysterious dark world of the pornography, etc., at least to me as a 10-year-old boy stumbling deeper and deeper into it. Other kids were holding hands and going on dates with girls and "trying to get to 1st/2nd/3rd base," while I was reading graphic descriptions of bondage/S&M, etc. Somehow I probably grew to view real live girls as being more sacred or something, that there was a "bubble" of reality around them which had to be protected, lest they fall into the fantasy porno world and become one of the weird fictional totally fake creatures who inhabited it. I went for years, until age 23, before actually having intercourse, because I always waited for them to OK it and none ever did—I was so paranoid, so afraid of the "underworld" I had been sucked into in visual fantasy, that I was extremely careful in all real world contacts. The last thing on earth I wanted was to be accused of forcing anyone to do anything!

Despite Jack's inner conflict, the crucial point of his story is that he never confused fantasy with reality, never felt impelled to force his attentions on a woman, and never thought women should be any different from the way they were with him because of porn.

A man who said he was addicted to pornography explained that when he was young, he had a positive stake in believing that porn fantasy and reality were two separate things:

> The people in the movies were held apart in my mind. For one thing, the experience of pornography and masturbation was so overwhelming that I was satisfied with it for a long time and did not worry about whether real girls I might meet would be like the girls in porn. I was and am so shy that pornography worked for me in a way that nothing else would. Real sex with a real person was too scary for me. I preferred the fantasy, which admittedly is pretty pathetic.

Some men said they began to place real people they knew into fantasy situations later on, but still they stressed the distinction between reality and fantasy:

> I would sometimes fantasize about real women I knew the way I would fantasize about porn images, but I knew that was fantasy and fantasy was different from real life. I still react that way. [symphonic musician, 52, married twenty-six years]

> As time progressed I began to associate erotic images with women I knew and actively used the images in fantasy. I believe that erotic imagery or pornography has led me to the belief that women are inherently beautiful, and not the opposite view—that women are to be used and degraded. [audio engineer, 24, single]

A few other men recalled making connections between porn imagery and people and events in their lives. "It made me aware that others, including women, could be just as interested in sex as I was," recalled a New Zealand native.

"At times I would project the faces of females I knew onto the models," said a 29-year-old engineering student. Another man reported that if he was particularly taken with a girl at school, "I would consciously seek out erotic or pornographic material that featured a woman who closely resembled the girl of my affections. A couple of times I recall being uncannily fortunate enough to find magazines that featured girls who could have passed for the local girl's twin."

What these men did was the exact opposite of what antipornography activists fear: They brought a desired piece of reality into the fantasy, rather than trying to impose the fantasy on reality.

A 12-year-old who found a novel called *The Family's Incest Summer*, about a couple in their 30s and a 17-year-old boy and 18-year-old girl experimenting with sex, began fantasizing about "this family that lived across the street. The mother was in her thirties and she had a son in high school. I substituted them for the characters in the book." Again, this boy did not try to remake reality to conform to porn, but merely to animate the fantasy of porn with real people. Significantly, "Her daughters were younger than me, so I didn't factor them in."

Only two men reported an inability as boys to distinguish between pornographic images and real life, and both claimed to have been sexually abused by adults.

Another method of testing the line between the fantasy of porn and the reality of their actual sex lives was to ask the men whether they had ever tried to import something they had seen or read about in pornography to their own sexual practices. Antiporn theorists regularly assert that porn teaches men to use, dominate, and humiliate women. What a man learns to want, they say, are sex acts the woman presumably *isn't* going to desire or enjoy—such as fellatio, anal sex, or ejaculation on her face and breasts—and the man has to cajole, negotiate, or just plain impose the practice by surprise or physical force. The underlying assumptions are: Women are never equal parties in what happens in sex; women never want to do the things men become interested in because of pornography; and men don't really care about women's sexual pleasure or that they might not wish to do certain things. These assumptions were not supported in any way by the experiences and attitudes of the men in my survey.

"It added a few positions to my love life," said a 39-year-old married man. A 65-year-old gay man remarked, "Sometimes it is interesting to try a position, or act out a fantasy suggested by the video or reading." "I think watching porn has given me ideas as to positions, etc., but I'm pretty sure I would have thought of those on my own had I not ever viewed porn," said a "very happily married" 40-year-old, "but maybe not as soon."

Moreover, a number of practices men took from pornography into life were intended to increase their partner's sexual pleasure more than their own. "I have learned to be much better at cunnilingus by watching it in porn," a 35-year-old married man said. A 48-year-old widower said porn had given him useful information about "how to sensuously lick nipples and how to perform cunnilingus, both of which I think my wife appreciated." An unmarried 23-year-old British man said, "My technique for masturbating her by stroking her clitoris has improved since watching 'educational' films (barely distinct from mild porn except by the fact that they are introduced by a doctor)."

A 52-year-old married man recalled mixed results whenever he tried to import sex practices into his real life from pornography, which he did "only two or three times, over the years." One that worked was "a way of manipulating my wife's breast, a combination of oral and manual. There was one other position I wanted to try but never got anywhere, and suddenly one day she started doing it without my mention. That was 1) to lift her legs up over my back, and 2) from that position to roll onto our side. At the time [I suggested it] she was not interested. Years later, when I assumed she had forgotten about it, she started doing it."

Of other staples in video porn, most men said they tried only one or two. A 24-year-old man who said he became interested in "facial cumshots" after seeing them in porn admitted that "not all girlfriends find this as interesting as me."

In a number of cases, men reported that the imported practice was not successful or the man himself was dissatisfied with it. "I have tried many of the positions I've seen in videos to see if they were comfortable, let alone pleasurable," a 30-year-old business owner said. "I've found most are uncomfortable and are [done] for the benefit of the cameras." Another man said, "I remember one time, pushing the woman's leg on my shoulder here, and I did not realize that was highly uncomfortable for her. But that was what I saw in a movie, and it looked neat [laughs]." The man stopped when it became clear these moves were not working for the woman.

Two other men made unsuccessful attempts to perform auto-fellatio. One, a 41-year-old heterosexual grad student, said, "I wasn't successful, since my body wouldn't bend that far." The other was a 45-year-old gay man who liked to experiment when he had a long-term partner. "I'd always thought auto-fellatio would be great, but since I'm not that greatly endowed, nor am I very flexible, the act couldn't be performed. We came as close as possible to it, though, with me standing on my head and cumming in my mouth while my partner held me up and watched. The first couple of times were exciting; after that it became more ridiculous and funny to me until I couldn't do it at all."

Whenever men referred to sex acts that antiporn crusaders claim all men are driven to by pornography, it was always in the context of consensual play. "I have tried to encourage my women partners to perform fellatio in manners like what I've seen, but more importantly to understand it in terms of how I like to work on my own penis with my own hand," said a 36-year-old married man. Porn "helped me explain to my wife how I like my cock sucked," a 39-year-old man said. And a video enabled him to "show her a way that felt better than the ways she was doing it. My wife has never been able to deep throat me. So the technique is to use her hands to slide up and down the shaft of my cock as she is sliding the head of my cock in and out of her mouth." Evidently, he did not insist that she keep attempting to deep-throat him.

Another oft-cited "forced pornographic sex practice" is anal sex. First off, this requires the assumption that no woman ever freely chooses to do it. Said one 30-year-old, "Viewing videos with anal sex in it led one partner to reverse her views that it was not something that people really did for pleasure, and she decided to try it."

A few men said they had imported nothing from pornography, because their real-life sexual tastes were conventional, and they were content to leave fantasy where it was. "It has perhaps made me more desirous of trying a position or activity, but nothing I haven't done before," said a 47-year-old New Zealander in his second marriage. "My sex life is fairly conventional for the times, and I have plenty of fun with 'normal' sex," said a 27-year-old single American who masturbated to pornography at least once a day. More gay men explicitly said they kept pornographic sex and real-life sex entirely separate. Although "I have tried to do some of the things I have seen" in pornography, said a 30-year-old in higher education who had been in a committed relationship for three years, "My partner and I are pretty conventional in the bedroom. We aren't too wild and crazy. I think I live out that part of my life through porn."

Only two men in the survey said ideas they had gotten from pornography had been a source of conflict and tension with their spouses. One who had improved at cunnilingus by watching porn also said, "I have attempted other things, but my wife has always rejected them. Those things would include planned fantasies of sex with strangers, multiple partners, sex in public places, etc." There was no indication that he had ever tried to force any of these proposals on his wife. One who might have was a 46-year-old government employee and Christian who said he had tried to import "new sexual enlightenment from viewing some forms of pornography" into his marriage, "sometimes with great success." After initial resistance, his wife enjoyed inserting marbles and then a vibrating Ben Wa ball in her vagina at his behest—but fisting, enemas, and sticking metal rods into his urethra and bladder made her sick. At times he traded days of housework for some of the activities she disliked. Although such activities may not be to many people's taste, it should be noted that most of them involved penetration and manipulation *of the man's body*, not his wife's, so even this doesn't support the antiporn argument that men force acts on women's bodies to dominate and humiliate them.

At the far end of the spectrum, two men said they owed nearly everything good about their sex life to pornography. One was a 32-year-old married man in computer graphics whose wife watched porn with him and who recalled, "I watched porn long before I ever was with a woman. The first woman I was with, I did everything I had learned from porn. It drove her crazy and she told me that I was one of the best lovers she had ever had! Boy, my ego shot up then." Since most analyses dwell on how *poorly* pornography instructs men in pleasing a woman, I asked what he had done. "I ate her pussy like I learned from the porn videos," he replied, "and I knew all the positions."

The other man was a 27-year-old bisexual with a preference for males, who wrote, "I have imported a lot of what I see in pornography. It was the only way I knew what to do in a sexual situation. My family never talked about sex (hetero or homo) so I never knew what would be expected of me by my partners. If it had not been for pornography, I would still be a virgin."

A 42-year-old professor implied that, instead of porn imposing its reality on his life, he was drawn to porn that reflected what he had already done and desired: "I don't know that I've ever seen anything in porn that I didn't either imagine or try myself previously. I find porn the more interesting as it more closely reflects my own fantasies. In fact, I think I'd say that pornography is, for me, a way to solidify and give a touch of reality to my fantasies."

Most men, if they took anything from pornography, did it either quietly to see if it worked (and if it did they continued, and if it didn't they stopped), or negotiated with their partner as an equal. Far from assuming they knew everything, men were willing to learn from every source of information, whether pornography or their lovers, and not give greater credence to the former, despite the claims of antiporn activists. As a 41-year-old math student put it:

> The first time I had sex, I asked my partner lots of questions, both of the "Would you like?" and "How does this feel?" sort, because of my seeing

things in pornography. I also had no hesitation about cunnilingus—other than asking my partner if she liked the sensation, of course.

If men sensed that their partner might not be amenable, most were content to leave it as a daydream and not push the issue.

Thus, many men's answers reinforced the sense that experience, if not simply their own judgment, taught them that pornography and real life occur in different and mostly separate arenas. As the gay man who had only short-term and incomplete success with auto-fellatio put it, "Most of the things which are erotic on the videos or in the magazines are not in real life when I do them." Some understood that difference and valued pornography for just that reason. Others, like a 22-year-old physics grad student, found the gap irritating: "A lot of what porn is picturing reminds me that, in my sexual experience, the particular sexual technique didn't work as described. This, of course, degrades the value of the porn."

But whether delighted or annoyed, most men clearly know the difference between fantasy and reality.

Pornography as Hell, Pornography as Therapy

Men's responses to pornography are as varied as pornography itself. One may suffer porn as a scourge that blights his life while another finds in it a savior—from ignorance, religious intolerance, or fear of sex and women. Since this is one of the few areas where the experiences of gay men truly diverged from those of heterosexuals—pornography appeared to be almost universally a positive force, or at worst a matter of indifference, for nearly every gay man I talked to—this chapter exclusively relates the experiences of straight men.

HENRY'S STORY

"Henry" said he never looked at pornography anymore. He had mostly avoided it since his teens. He did not believe it qualified for protection by the First Amendment. "I think the use of pornography is inherently detrimental," he said. "It encourages fantasy that denies life as it really is." A government employee in security systems management, Henry had been married for more than twenty-five years. Although he was honest about being aroused by various forms of porn (as well as mainstream references to women's bodies and sex), he felt a moral objection, even physical disgust, along with the excitement. All his experiences with porn had been negative.

> I was about 9 or 10 when I first found some of my dad's stuff (sometime during 1958). I was playing around wearing his Air Force Reserve uniform when I found a story book in the pocket. The booklet had scenes of sex with young girls, sex with young adult women, sex with black slave or servant women, women masturbating the man, oral sex, anal sex, masturbation in public areas (on an airliner, for example), sex with multiple partners, voyeurism, homosexual practices, and defecation during sex. It focused on the size of the man's penis, the size of the breasts of the women, the amazing sexual equipment of the black women and men, and the insatiable sexual appetite of the women.

The material did not consist of photographs. "It was like a comic book, drawings with thoughts, dreams and dialog in word balloons." The material Henry saw was so graphic and different from anything he had seen before, that he experienced a negative reaction.

> It was quite plain that the experience of having someone defecate on you was neither normal or pleasurable. To this day, certain words from that book are very repulsive to me. My understanding of some terms that are not particularly vulgar was corrupted as well. For example, I cannot bring myself to use the word "grunt." The term was used in the defecation scenes. I puzzled for years at why people ("nice people," even) would use such a dirty word. It wasn't until a couple of years ago that I finally realized that the word did not mean excrement. I tried after that to bring the word into my vocabulary, but it just felt too ugly and I quit trying.

Although Henry was repulsed by the book, he went back to look at it repeatedly. "I had already formed a desire to have sex with women and the booklet was the subject of repeated visits for the visual pictures of what that would be like, masturbating with those images in mind." His response was strong partly because the activities he saw were not new to him.

> I had already experienced repeated oral and anal sex with an adult male. External behavioral evidence indicates I was first abused before age six. I don't know [by whom] or how often. My clear memories of sexual abuse are with a neighbor man about 35-40 years old. Masturbation was already an ingrained daily practice. When I told my abuser that I did not want to do that stuff any more, I found that I was now an outcast. He made it quite clear that I was now unwanted and somehow tainted. So since some of the material in the pornography reflected my "perverted" experience, I knew it was bad.

The "external evidence" Henry cited was that he taught another boy to perform oral sex when they were both just 6. "I can remember thinking about how to have that pleasure again and deciding to ask him to do it." Instead of asking, Henry performed it first. Later, people who work with children told him kids normally have no concept of oral sex at that age. They understand the act of urinating, so usually the idea of placing a penis in a mouth appears "yucky." So Henry believed someone older, with more experience, must have taught him how.

The images in his father's pornography were repulsive, yet compelling, and they made Henry afraid of what he might do himself. "I thought of carrying out my ideas, but never actually did anything since I was always afraid of being found out." He watched diapers being changed at the church nursery in order to get a glimpse of "a real, 'naked' woman." He had opportunities to abuse children 3 to 5 years old several times before high school, but he never did anything. "I'm not sure whether it was my fear or my better judgment or both." Once, an 11-year-old male friend invited him to participate in using a girl who was their age:

He was getting ready to meet her when I knocked on his door. He told me he had paid her to undress for him. It seemed obvious to me at the time that he intended to touch her sexually but I don't know what actually happened. He met me at the door of his home in his underwear, fully erect and apparently had already masturbated in conjunction with this episode. He even feigned masturbating when I noticed his erection. That was the end of my friendship with him.

Four or five years after Henry discovered his dad's porn, his parents divorced. Although at the time his mother cited money problems as the reason, more recently she told Henry his father's pornography was a greater factor.

It is hardly possible to overstate my mother's hatred for pornography. It was an embarrassment and humiliation to her throughout 20 years of marriage. She has never remarried. The primary mode of her "abuse" was that he forced her to duplicate the activities portrayed in the pornography.

Henry said he initially assumed the images he saw were real. Until some time after high school, "I used those kinds of images when thinking about what I would do with—or, more accurately, to—a girl or woman I liked." He described a "split view" that divided girls of "pure fantasy" from others, generally ones he actually got to know. At that age, it was difficult, however, to separate fantasy from reality altogether. If the content of porn did not make sense, yet was powerfully arousing, what was "real"? One thing was clear: Henry did not like the behavior of men he saw in porn.

I didn't like the way they treated anybody—the women, other men, or themselves. Somehow, I couldn't believe that women would really like men treating them like that. In the original piece [the book in his father's jacket], the woman/girl went to work in her daddy's office dressed in a very short skirt with no underwear. For a top, she wore a piece of string draped across her nipples. I knew that wasn't real. The customer who came in almost immediately started sucking on her breasts and fingering her under her skirt. All this in a business environment where someone could walk in at any moment. To make it worse, when her father arrived he approved of the man using his daughter. Maybe that's where I first tripped off-line. I had been used without my permission, too.

At the same time, he admitted, "I was attracted by the sexual activity even in the midst of all that I didn't like."

Though he fantasized about women, "My fantasies never included sex with men even though I was molested by a man/men." Pornography's image of men was too ugly:

I never compared myself to the men in any of the pornography I saw. I already felt dirty and disgusting and didn't need to add to the image. I think I also had some fear that I was actually like some of those men and hated that intensely.

This image of men was confirmed by the males around him:

I generally thought most men were sexual boors with no thinking processes other than what their penises would provide. The junior high and senior high locker room conversations pretty well confirmed that for me. The pornography displayed the same sort of manly "thinking." My own secret thoughts about women were enough to make me dislike myself in the same way. I was separated from the world of women by being a man and from the world of men by the disgust born of the abuse. I don't know how to describe the feelings I had when I kept hearing the various vulgar references to oral sex or anal sex or homosexual activity. Nobody knew it, but that was *me* they were talking about.

All of this led to Henry's decision in high school to give up pornography completely. "I came to realize that it had a hold on me I didn't like. It reminded me too much of the abuse in some ways. It made the battle with masturbation more difficult." Asked why he associated photographs of men and women having consensual sex with his own experience of being abused against his will by someone older, Henry said, "I recognized the possibility that I could take advantage of someone else like I had been taken advantage of, that I could use somebody else, and recognized that process at work in my use of pornography."

Married at age 20, Henry and his wife bought *Playboy* a few times early in their marriage so she could read the interviews. He read them too but "probably focused on the pictures." His wife had been his only romantic and sexual companion his entire adult life. But he was not free of the effects of the sexual abuse, nor had he been able to avoid pornography entirely. It became even more difficult when he was in the military in Southeast Asia:

> It was almost impossible to not see it and I had to devise some real solid strategies to keep it out of my mind. I was fortunate to have a bunk room to myself in Vietnam and could keep it out of my living space. The worst areas were the break room and the entrance to the base I was assigned to. While I had learned not to look at pictures on the wall, the loud discussions in the break room all seemed to center on the prostitutes in town and lots of specifics. It was not possible to close my ears and they wouldn't let us take our breaks anywhere else.

One time, Henry told the other men that he intended to remain faithful to his wife, and that he would not go to prostitutes. After a stunned silence, another man praised him for his convictions—but the talk resumed the next day, and Henry learned that a transfer order to Thailand had barely saved him from a scheme some men had cooked up to get him forcibly drunk and raped by a prostitute.

If anything, Thailand was worse:

> They all loved the stuff, if the amount of it lying around was any indicator. One evening, I returned from the servicemen's center to my usually darkened cube. I lay down on my bunk and raised my eyes to see my first porno movie in progress on the wall right in front of me. I was really

dumbfounded and left as soon as I could figure out what was going on. Even during that short span of time, I was subjected to a sequence of a man ejaculating on a woman's face.

Prostitutes lined the road to the base entrance and flashed their breasts and genitals any time a GI passed by. This presented a gauntlet for men like Henry who merely wished to go about their duties. One of Henry's coworkers had an 11x14 photograph looking directly into his girlfriend's privates with her legs spread wide. He displayed it on his desk under Plexiglas, facing whoever came to see him. Henry learned that his comrades not only consumed local pornography but also manufactured it:

One of my roommates was berating a friend of mine for his "two-faced" conversion to Christianity. He called J. a hypocrite for professing to be a Christian and still cursing, using pornography, and so on. I intervened, physically stepping in between them, and told my roommate that we are all hypocrites in one way or another and that J. was a new Christian and was trying and told my roommate to leave J. alone. Shortly after that, J. left. Almost immediately, my roommate came over to me and began explaining his rationale for using pornography and [for having] a live-in "girlfriend" downtown. (He was married back in the States.) He produced pornographic films using local people and exported it back to the States in [soldiers'] personal belongings. He was not at all interested in the welfare of his actresses, only in the money they provided him. He lived with a couple of them through the year, promising to marry each in turn and then leaving both of them to go back to his wife in the states. He lied about their future (acting careers in Hollywood) and about who he was. He informed me that his wife didn't know anything about it and it wouldn't have any effect on her when he returned to the States and, and, and. . . . He went on for 45 minutes. I was amazed by the obvious burden of guilt he was carrying over these issues. He was consumed by his year of betraying his wife.

Back in the U.S., keeping away from pornography did not mean that Henry managed to clear his life—let alone his head—of all unwanted

sexual images. Porn-style objectification of women in mainstream publications was everywhere. Auto magazines he read had photos of
"beauty contest winners" posed around the vehicles:

> I find I am embarrassed when I purchase one of these. If the clerk is a man,
> I don't say anything but wish he knew I wasn't interested in the magazine
> because of the women. If the clerk is a woman, I usually mention some-
> thing about being unhappy with the stuff on the cover. So far, every time
> the response from the woman is something about her being unhappy with
> similar magazines her husband buys. I tend to fold the magazine so as to
> conceal the cover until I take it to the check stand.

Henry was raised in a house without television (as were his own children), which minimized exposure to mainstream culture. He and his
wife had a policy of skipping R-rated films. Henry avoided novels with
sexual content—he preferred nonfiction anyway—which left such writers as C.S. Lewis, George McDonald, Tolstoy, Shakespeare, Bunyon,
Dante, and lesser-known Christian writers. Antipornography literature
by feminist theorists interested him, but could pose a dilemma:

> I have read a number of works in the area of pornography, *Take Back the
> Night: Women On Pornography* and [Dworkin's] *Pornography: Men Pos-
> sessing Women* among them. I have read portions of the [Meese] Commis-
> sion report on pornography. Some material in *Pornography: Men Possessing
> Women* was arousing as the author went into great detail to illustrate some
> of her points. It was very close to reading some of the hard stuff itself, even
> worse in some ways since she concentrated the plot to illustrate her points.

Henry also struggled with the unaccountable behavior of some of the
women he knew. On occasion, female coworkers seemed to delight in
exposing their bodies to their male colleagues. "They would lean very
far over while wearing a very low-cut blouse or sit across from me with
their legs uncrossed while wearing a very short skirt." A coworker would
come up behind him and make bodily contact with her breasts, either

pressing them into his back or brushing them across it. "While the touch was 'electric' in a sense, it was the same 'electric' I felt when a 35-year-old man first touched my penis when I was 8. It was all wrong and arousing." In Henry's view, such behavior was sexual harassment and should be strictly discouraged in the workplace.

Most disturbing, perhaps, was that even a woman who had been victimized by pornography—Henry's own mother—might employ a similar type of intimidation, though probably unconsciously:

> I was talking with my wife about the issue of my mother and her 'personal space' being so small that she often touches me with her clothed breasts when there is no particular need for the contact (i.e., other than giving me a hug). My wife reminded me of some other things I forgot. She remembers witnessing an instance where my mother was exercising in her bedroom, jogging on a mini trampoline. Her door was open and she was bare from the waist up. My mother, while so jogging, called my brother to come and get something or do something. While she continued to exercise (holding her arms over her bare breasts), she told him what she wanted. The way she covered her breasts was minimal, she used her wrist and forearm to cover the "important" part. She seemed oblivious to the impact of her actions on us. The fact of the matter (from my current perspective) is that there was no need at all to have her door open, to exercise half-dressed, or to have conversations with her sons while she was undressed like that.

Henry said the act of coming up behind and pressing her breasts into his back was a fairly recent thing with his mother. "I don't remember her doing that four or five years ago."

Recovering from the effects of his childhood abuse had been a long and arduous process. Occasional flashbacks—such as the sensation of an adult penis in his mouth—haunted him. "I have had a number of nightmarish flashbacks to the sexual abuse when actually making love with my wife. That was disturbing." He also had a longtime problem with compulsive daily masturbation, even after sessions of lovemaking with his wife:

> Over the years, I grew to have a mixture of feelings about it. I hated me; I hated my wife for not being more willing to meet my needs (never mind that I never told her about my "needs"). All this was an internal reality that I managed not to notice. It was part of my defense mechanism I created following the abuse as a child. I think even the "not noticing" was part of the same mechanism. I didn't think I was an angry person until after I faced the issues of abuse three years ago. Even then, it wasn't until about six months later that I realized how enraged I was inside. In the three months before my initial healing experience, I had begun to lose control of my anger and the rage-filled words would spill out when nobody was around. There were two instances when I struck a door post or wall and nearly broke my hand. But I didn't think I was an angry person. I just ignored the danger signs.

Henry believed the compulsive masturbating was a way of punishing his wife for "rejecting me"—even though the rejection was all in his mind. "I was giving myself what I felt I had been denied. On the other hand, I renewed my feeling of being dirty or perverted every time I did it." His theory was that the compulsiveness was driven by a feeling of rejection that he perhaps needed to prove was justified: "The rejection I refer to was by the pedophile. Even the lowest of the low didn't want me anymore." Because of that emotional legacy, Henry took any sign of anger on the part of his wife as hate and rejection, and assumed she did not love him.

When he masturbated, however, it was to mental images of love-making with his wife, "most often when we've been outdoors and made love." The compulsiveness had come to an abrupt end several years before he took the survey, when he began to deal with having been sexually abused.

His experiences led Henry to conclude that "pornography should be outlawed and its production and distribution vigorously pursued and prosecuted with large penalties and jail time."

Because of the abuse, scenes that featured fellatio elicited the strongest response in Henry: "I am aroused most intently by (and hate my being aroused by) scenes of oral sex. It doesn't make any difference who is doing who. The primary mode of the abuse I experienced was oral sex." Not all pornographic imagery struck him, however, with the same repellent force. Scenes with two or more women, especially performing oral sex on each other, did not repulse him as much as others because they reminded him of positive experiences with his wife. "I really enjoy giving my wife that pleasure as much as she enjoys receiving it," he said; these scenes "recall good and wholesome experiences for me with my wife." And because it was his wife and the emotional context was their marriage, Henry could experience fellatio as a warm, not an overwhelming or threatening act:

> My wife suggested the practice to me very early in our relationship, a few months into it, and we have both enjoyed giving and receiving oral sex. She was unaware of the abuse at the time she suggested it.

Through the years, the abuse flashbacks and images that lingered from his own encounters with pornography gradually left Henry's mind—and his life:

> The images I have been exposed to have, once in a while, gotten in the way of loving my wife and enjoying her for who she really is rather than some "ideal" body. Thankfully, that period of my life is behind me. I can now really enjoy her body for the fact that it is hers and not another's. She finds this quite a compliment, even though both of us are aware of the fact that neither of us are 20 any longer. This also frees her to offer herself to me without fear of comparison. We have a varied, imaginative, and intense sexual relationship that would be the envy of many men I've known.

SAM'S STORY

Like Henry, "Sam" was happily married to the only woman he had ever known sexually. Unlike Henry, he had not managed to control his compulsion to use pornography. While he believed porn "has done great damage to me," he didn't think it should be banned. Sam described the damage thus:

> The most apparent effect has been to totally separate the concepts of love and sex in my mind. When I think of the ideal wife and the ideal sex partner, I am thinking about two completely different women. The sex partner wears revealing clothing, lots of makeup, she smokes and swears, and is willing to participate in any type of sex act. Outside of the bedroom the only use I have for her is to show off what I scored. The wife is an ordinary looking woman, introverted, whom I rescued from some bad situation, maybe even from the ledge of a building, and whose self-esteem I am building up by constantly telling her how beautiful and wonderful she is. It is your basic hero-to-the-rescue fantasy: After years of not having anyone of the opposite sex show any particular need for me, it only stands to reason that I would conjure up an image of a wife with the strongest need for me I can imagine. Bottom line: strong mutual dependency. Thoughts of sexual relations with this woman don't really come into the picture.

Sam's actual wife was like neither of these fantasy women. He saw no relation between the fantasy images and his relationship with her.

Sam's father had subscribed to *Playboy* and picked up *Penthouse* occasionally—"for the articles, of course." Sam believed he first saw this material about the age of 11. "The pictures didn't have much effect on me; simple nudity has never provided me much arousal. Instead, I was drawn to the section of *Penthouse* where readers send in letters bragging about experiences."

Though Sam was raised with no formal religion and regarded his upbringing as "basically amoral," he knew porn was "bad." "Dad claimed that he only read the mags for the articles, implying that there was something wrong with using magazines for arousal."

At the age of 17, Sam discovered a local XXX theater. "The first time I went I was asked for ID. I showed it. 'You're not 18.' 'Yes I am, just turned 18 on my last birthday.' 'Yeah, you're right.' He never asked again." Sam went to the theater every Friday for several years. "That's when I feel I got hooked."

Sam believed the pornography at the theater stunted his understanding of sex and intimacy. "I got my ideas of what sex is from porn flicks, and in these sex is mostly portrayed without love or relationship." It did not help that he felt confused about gender identity and unsupported by his environment:

> At that time I hated my male identity, wished I had been born female, and cross-dressed (privately) for excitement. Girls just seemed to have it so much easier. In the suburban SF Bay area schools I attended, a boy could not show weakness, and school officials did absolutely nothing to keep bullying in check. On the playground, if a bully picks on a girl, those around him will tell him to leave her alone. If a bully picks on a boy, those around him will watch to see if the boy will fight back. When they become old enough to date, girls are not obligated to make the first move. A boy must take the risk of being rejected (a girl who seems very nice can turn out to be very cruel), or he will never go on a date. I felt then, and I continue to feel today, that girls/women have it a lot easier in life.

The self-hate did modulate itself. By the time he was 20, Sam had lost interest in cross-dressing and was "completely comfortable" with his male identity.

He was deep into a struggle with pornography, however. Sam joined a church at the age of 19. He would swear off porn for several months, even a year at a time, only to be drawn back. "After a prolonged avoidance I would feel terrible about giving in, and I would struggle to keep my hand from shaking as I paid the clerk." After he got married, Sam rented and sometimes bought pornographic videos, "looking for more and more bizarre material. It got to the point where I would fast-forward through most of the thing, hoping the next scene would be even better."

The first time Sam had intercourse was with his wife, at the age of 25. That was when he learned how deeply his past experiences might have affected him:

I discovered, to my horror, my inability to achieve climax on our wedding night. This made those first few days of the honeymoon very stressful for me. I tried fantasizing, and afterwards, to this day, it is absolutely needed if I am to complete the act. It is rare that I can achieve climax during intercourse without fantasizing. The fantasies I use are the same ones I use during masturbation. There have been times when I have gotten so aroused [during sex] that the fantasy is not needed, but if it happens twice in a year I count myself lucky.

Sam traced the evolution of this dynamic:

During many years as a celibate young adult I came to regard "real sex" as something I will have in the future, but don't have now. This premise, though now no longer correct, remains with me. Thus, try as I might, I cannot accept anything I have as "real sex," and simply through self-conditioning I long for that which is "real." This has led to some really warped thinking. In order to define "real sex," my mind has contrasted what I have and what I fantasize about. The result is that "real sex" is the most kinky and unnatural acts my mind and the pornographer's lens can produce. My partner [in these scenarios] is not someone I care about, but rather a promiscuous slut and there is no act she is unwilling to participate in. Outside of bed I really want nothing to do with her, and I would be extremely embarrassed if anyone I know found out that I have anything to do with her.

Sam's ambivalence surfaced in the "lousy" feelings he had after popping a video in the VCR, looking for a scene that particularly aroused him, and masturbating to orgasm. "Sometimes I even say, 'you sick bastard,' to my reflection."

Like most men, Sam had particular tastes in pornography. On the one hand, he had never used a phone sex service and was certain he never would. "I do not understand the appeal of phone sex. I can't see anyone being stupid enough to believe that the girls at the number are (or even look like) the girls in the ads, or that they actually are doing the things they are describing on the phone."

When asked what turned him on the most, he said women smoking and anal penetration.

> I probably got the idea that smoking is sexy from a friend named A. Without a doubt, I have fantasized about her more than any other person. I was shocked to learn that others who know her consider her average or even less than average in appearance. To me she is the sexiest woman alive. She never considered me as anything more than a friend, probably because of my religious affiliations at the time. Last time I visited I left with, "We'll have to go out sometime," but neither of us ever contacted the other again.

A nonsmoker himself, Sam was surprised to learn through the Internet that many people find smoking a turn-on. It is the topic of discussion on a Usenet newsgroup called alt.sex.fetish.smoking. A frequent comment there is, "Wow, I thought I was the only one."

> From what I have been able to see, most people in this newsgroup don't smoke. Smokers probably see smoking as a part of the daily routine, and therefore don't attach any sexual significance to it. Ads glamorize smoking. In the movies, if a character is promiscuous, she is likely to be a smoker. Parents portray it as something only adults do. Many I am acquainted with consider it sinful. All in all, there are a lot of messages in society attributing similar attributes to these two, very dissimilar, acts.

Sam's latest sexual fantasies tended to consist of "replaying scenes I have seen in porn flicks, [and] remembering women I have seen smoking, both in real life and on TV. I only fantasize about women I have seen smoking or engaging in sex on film." Garden variety bedroom scenes in mainstream films and television shows had little effect. "When you're hooked on heroin, a glass of beer doesn't do much for you."

Sam's interest in anal penetration did not conform to the antiporn notion that men want only to humiliate and exercise power over women. He was most drawn to images of "a man receiving it from a woman with a dildo or bending over for a transsexual. Gay porn has no appeal, though the thought of having a feminine partner, who has a penis, excites me greatly." Sam engaged in solo anal play before he discovered how to masturbate to orgasm at the age of 16. As to why being anally penetrated by a woman should hold such appeal, he could only speculate that it had its roots in the "dysfunctional" feelings he had about his sexual identity during adolescence.

Sam also got hooked by particular performers. "Sometimes I have been captivated by the physical beauty of a porn actress, and will obsess over her for several days." The "actress" didn't have to be strictly female, either:

> One of the strongest times I simply saw a picture on the box, she was fully clothed and not engaging in any sex acts. The title was "Fire and Ice," and the actress's name was Stasha. She is a transsexual, but I don't think this had anything to do with the attraction. When I first saw the box I thought the "she-male" sticker was a mistake—this person couldn't possibly have once been male. What made her so memorable was that she had such an incredibly gorgeous face. Facial beauty is always the cause when I obsess over someone.

At the time he began the survey, Sam was struggling "to eliminate lust from my life." He had entered a 12-step program and thrown out or deleted from his computer all the pornography he owned. But he soon dropped out of Sexaholics Anonymous because he suspected it only works when a person has hit rock bottom. "While I do not like the effects sexual addiction has upon my life, at this stage it poses no immediate threat to my marriage or job."

Sam mentioned his interest in pornography to his wife fairly early in their marriage. "She considers it naughty behavior, but not intolerable." She even accompanied him to the video store, although she looked through the regular movies while he was in the adult section. Since Sam had never been unfaithful to his wife, and he was in no danger of losing her or his job, I asked him why he considered himself a sex addict.

> They are not threatened *at this stage*. In Nevada [prostitution is] legal, and I find the prospects highly tempting. That's the next step, and this is a progressive problem. Being unable to stop despite sincere efforts, needing stronger and stronger material to satisfy the need—this sure sounds like addiction to me. I have also heard many times in SA meetings where a man whose depravity is much deeper than my own will describe an earlier time in his life, and that description will sound a lot like where I am now. Spiritually my life is at a point of stagnation anyway. It would probably be so even without the addiction.

Despite the stress porn added to his life, Sam's opinions on social policy differed from Henry's. "Porn is destructive to many," he granted, and "those who would encourage its use should be stopped." While he acknowledged that an outright ban would be the only way to stop the adverse effects, he did not support such a ban:

> I do not think that the gain is worth the cost. Most societal problems could be alleviated by giving up freedom. I would rather live as a free man in a dangerous world. Sometimes the cost of security is just too great. If a citizen's group wants to restrict sexually oriented businesses to some obscure part of town, away from children and the public eye in general, they can count on my support. If they want to forbid such businesses from advertising, and make them operate from a completely unmarked storefront, I will also approve. But if they want to shut down the adult bookstore and completely cut off access to hard-core material, I will vigorously work against them. The flashing neon lights of San Francisco are in bad taste, but on the other extreme, Salt Lake City was wrong to force all the XXX theaters out of business.

While Sam had experienced a need for greater, more dangerous, and more unusual pornography, "I don't think the majority of guys with me in the 'Adults only' section of the video shop are, or will become, sex addicts." Why? Because he did not regard porn as the root cause of his addiction. "I would blame porn for exacerbating it; however, I would blame growing up in a family in which physical affection was rarely seen for causing it." So he concluded: "Porn should be available to those who choose to view it, just as alcohol should continue to be available, despite the fact that a drunk man is much more likely to beat his wife."

Sam sensed in himself a yearning toward some ultimate goal that, while expressed in a warped manner with regard to pornography, nevertheless led him toward the spiritual plane he sought.

> Hopefully I have discovered an alternative to hitting rock bottom. At some point I expect God to do something in my life which will effect a change such as I have never seen before. Pornography will then be as cross-dressing is now, something which once was a strong compulsion, but no longer has any appeal. In the meantime all I can do is pray that He will act soon, and fight the temptation to take the next step (into a Nevada brothel).

Pornography as Therapy

For every man in my survey who told a story of the tremendous burden of pornography—and there were not many—there was another who described how it had changed his life for the better. We have heard plenty of negative stories in the past—the 1986 Meese Commission, among others, went on a hunt for them. Men Against Pornography, a New York group, is reported to be collecting accounts from men who have "recovered" from pornography addiction for a "12-step" style book from a "post-feminist" perspective.

But in the past decade, even Ann Landers began to acknowledge that porn can be therapeutic. Here are the tales of a few men who found it so.

STEVE'S STORY

"Steve" was no great fan of pornography. "I'm insatiably curious about a lot of things, but to put matters in perspective, if you measure by the number of books owned, my interest in pornography is very low—about one-tenth my interest in poetry and music, and one-hundredth my interest in science fiction. I've watched a total of about 30 minutes of porn video, and found it excruciatingly boring." Pictures didn't work for Steve either because, "If there is one thing I find most arousing, it is sex described from the inside, not the outside: the character's thoughts, motivations, and feelings."

Steve characterized his parents' attitude toward pornography as "indifference." When he was 13 and one of his friends at a boys' boarding school showed around a nudist magazine called *Health and Efficiency*, with nude men and women posed to look like statues and paintings, "we all oohed and aahed over it," but he was not particularly aroused. "Of course, we were taught in school the Hellenistic aesthetic: that the nude was a thing of beauty, and that, if anything, the nude male was more aesthetically pleasing than the nude female."

When girlie mags with women in more suggestive postures began to make the rounds, "we laughed a bit at the commentary. My main recollection is that I paid more attention to the smiles than the tits." Steve never left any "pages stuck together with dried semen," as he put it; "My masturbatory fantasies went on in that most amazing of sex organs, the mind, and were more often narrative than visual."

Between the ages of 14 and 20, Steve read "most of the standard works": *Fanny Hill, Moll Flanders, My Life and Loves, The Decameron, Lady Chatterley's Lover, Lolita, The Soft Machine, Special Friendships* (a "magnificent homosexual Bildungsroman" by M. Peyrefitte, recommended by the school chaplain), and *Spring Awakening*. William Burroughs's *The Soft Machine* was still banned in England at the time, so he went to the Bodleian Library to read it. "It came with a big yellow sheet of paper instructing me *not* to leave the book unattended, and to return it to a member of the staff before I left. And I had to read it in Duke Humphrey's Library, which is a beautiful old medieval room sparsely populated by theologians. A fun afternoon."

I was curious that a chaplain would have recommended erotic material; I asked Steve to explain. "He was sane and compassionate. He saw a bunch of adolescent boys, thrown together at an all-male boarding school, and allowed to flounder in confusion about their sexuality. From time to time, he pointed us at books that tried to explain what was happening to us and that some of the crazy stuff was the result of a crazy environment."

Lolita did change the way he looked at the world. "I first read it when I was about the same age as its heroine, and its impact was slow and subtle. The book is a novel of character, the character being its protagonist, Humbert Humbert. Before reading it, I would never have believed it was possible to write such a book about a pedophile." Steve believed that rich portrait helped him a lot when, at age 15, he was first propositioned by an adult homosexual—"in the Underground Station at Oxford Circus, as it happens. My first reaction was one of compassion, and I tried to turn him down firmly, but otherwise in as calm and nonjudgmental a way as possible. I knew he had run a terrible risk, and in a strange way, he had run it on my account. And I remembered Humbert."

Nevertheless, if Steve were asked which books affected him the most in adolescence, Anna Sewell's *Black Beauty* or William Golding's *Lord of the Flies* would be much higher on the list than *Lolita*. In his twenties he subscribed to *Playboy* for two years, "but (I kid you not) found the reviews, articles, and interviews the best part. And the cartoons, which I still think have a unique charm."

Steve's responses to quite a few questions in the survey were "no, not particularly," or "it would be easier to list what I don't enjoy" because visual materials were so unappealing to him compared to written ones, and "I'm a very low-volume consumer of pornography anyway." He recalled a gap of about 18 years when he never looked at porn, though he read general literature that others might consider pornographic, such as Burroughs's *The Wild Boys*. I suspect the questions tried his patience at times, because he often resorted to wit. When asked if there were elements in pornography that excited him but had nothing specifically to do with nudity or sex, he responded, "Hamsters. Yes, definitely hamsters. . . . No, seriously, I don't think so."

Other than teaching him to deal gently with a pedophile, how did erotic materials play a positive role in Steve's life? "Rather strangely, it was at the suggestion of a professional therapist that I began again to read porn a little more often." Steve and his wife went to see a couples therapist when their marriage of several decades was foundering. Because sexual dysfunction was a factor, "The therapist suggested that I think about what sex and sexuality meant to me, and write my thoughts down. The rationale behind his suggestion was very simple: 'If you don't like how you are, how would you like to be?'"

Steve found it hard to write directly about his needs, so he chose to compose a fiction in which "one character would stand for myself, so to speak, but at a psychological distance." He studied some pornography to refamiliarize himself with conventions of the genre, and, in the space of three years, bought about eight books which he said was as much as he had purchased in his life.

> I chose to write this in the form of a story ("show, don't tell," as the books say), with two people behaving as I thought mature and honest people should behave. I added personal notes to the story, giving my attempt at psychological analysis.

At the next therapy session, his wife responded: "I feel no closer to the author for having read that." Steve and his story were subjected "to what I perceived, and still perceive, as anger, ridicule, and contempt. On that day, I learned the full meaning of Yeats's line, 'Tread softly, because you tread on my dreams.'" Although the therapist was sympathetic, he did not handle the incident well, in Steve's estimation. "First, he pretty much watched as something in which I'd invested a lot of myself got ripped apart. I can take that. But secondly, what the therapist had proposed was that we should *both* write about this topic. And only one of us had. It seemed to me that a better therapist would not have let me get 'set up' like that, and would perhaps have insisted that both parties play by the rules. Of course, you're getting here only one side of a complex story."

Although the process seemed disastrous at the time, and the couple eventually divorced, Steve felt that his efforts had accomplished their immediate goal: "to make me understand, and then articulate, my views on sex, sexuality, and sexual relations. I found it helpful and empowering. I have also decided not to be unhappy about those views." Later, he wrote more pornography as a literary exercise, "mostly to see whether I could." This differed from what he had written for therapy: "In the one case, I was concentrating on me, or on surrogates of me. In the other case, I was thinking about the characters, trying to make them plausible, to produce what C.S. Lewis calls a 'sub-creation.' My unreliable opinion is that the literary exercises are far better as literature. One of them was even funny, which means it is a long way from anything I wrote as therapy."

Steve agreed that his experience did not support the notion that exposure to pornography is addictive and leads to ever more violent and kinky obsessions. "On the contrary, the evidence I have is that pornography can be a healing and life-affirming thing, leading to greater self-awareness and self-acceptance."

For him, pornography "is a part of life, a part of art, a part of the world. It is a major literary genre, and anyone who claims to be literate should have at least a sparse acquaintance with it. Because it is often the honest expression of the human spirit." Steve recalled Cicero's quotation of Terence: *Homo sum; humani nil a me alienum puto.* A loose translation might be: "I am human; therefore nothing that is human is alien to me."

Perhaps the best argument by anyone in the survey that objectionable content may lie largely in the eye of the beholder came from Steve:

I once met a smuggler of pornography; that is, of banned, disgusting, obscene books. It was on a boat, and he had a case of this stuff. The boat would be met in the night by an accomplice who was a local fisherman, and they would transfer the cargo, take it ashore, and distribute it. For this vile deed, both of them faced the death penalty if caught. The place was the Adriatic Sea; the country in question was Albania; and the dirty book was the Holy Gospel of our Lord and Saviour Jesus Christ, according to Saint John. I learned two lessons. One, that "pornography," or "filth," or "subversive literature"—whatever name you call the dog before you hang it—is a social and political construct. Any overlap between the literary genre of pornography and official smut is mere coincidence. The second lesson was that there are people—organized criminals—who believe in what they do. They aren't just out to make money. An obvious example from U.S. history is the Underground Railroad—an organized conspiracy for the theft of property and the disposal of stolen goods abroad, to take the viewpoint of the Dred Scott court.

I suggested a reader of his remarks might object to equating the Bible with pornography. Steve responded:

I assert the analogy. The Fourth Gospel opens thus: "In the beginning was the Word." In the ultimate analysis, my support for free speech is religious, for I see all speech as a manifestation of the Logos, the redemptive aspect of the divine. The lesson [of the Adriatic smuggler] has stayed with me. May it always do so.

GERALD'S STORY

Roughly once a month, usually when his kids are off with their mother for the weekend, "Gerald" takes a pornographic video out of hiding and spends an hour or two watching it. Why? Because his doctor prescribed it.

Gerald has been pleased with the results. As a matter of fact, "I think I probably should do it more often." The prescription came about because of a herniated lumbar disc, which Gerald had suffered from most of his adult life.

> I used to run a lot, and when I ran, I ran on pavement. I would have excruciating back pain, lower back pain, and I would have sciatica, where the nerve runs in the back of my left leg. If I walked or put pressure on it, I would feel a jolt of pain. I would be incapacitated for one, two, or three days. As I started getting older, especially in my mid thirties, the episodes started coming a little more frequent, and lasting longer. When I went to see my doctor for a regular checkup and told him about it, and basically he encouraged me to do more exercising. There's not a whole lot you can do about it unless you do surgery or some sort of physical therapy.

Gerald got by like this for years, but eventually his left leg became numb most of the time, and he couldn't enjoy his running. In his 39th year he had an episode that was so severe that his doctor scheduled him for physical therapy two weeks hence. After one week passed, he woke up one morning and "could not pee or poop." A neurologist confirmed that the disk had ruptured and there was extensive nerve damage.

> The next morning they did the surgery. They did what they call a micro-lumbar-lamanectomy. After a few days, I started seeing the urologist, and one of the first things he did was have me learn to catheterize myself, so that I can drain my bladder. And it's difficult, the idea of putting a tube through your penis, just gives a lot of guys the heebie jeebies. Gave *me* the heebie jeebies! But I had to do it in order to get relief.

The damage killed his sexual response as well.

> The back surgery also apparently affected my testosterone production. I really wasn't interested in sex! I wasn't interested at all. I would watch a

sexy program on TV, and I would see something that I would respond to [mentally], but nothing was happening below. And it was kind of frustrating: Something should be happening but it's not. And so it really affected me emotionally.

Fantasy would not cut it either. "If I used my imagination, it still didn't do anything. It was like I had to see something very graphic." Two or three weeks after the surgery, Gerald's urologist told him to get to work rebuilding his sexual responses.

I told him I didn't have a girlfriend or anything like that, and he said, "Well, I don't care how you do it. Rent pornographic movies or hire a girl. It's something you need to do. If you don't have someone, rent or buy pornographic movies and masturbate." Because the purpose is to get the blood rushing back into the penis, and it's one of those things where, because there's extensive nerve damage, if I didn't use it, there was that possibility of losing it.

Gerald followed his doctor's orders. He was not a newcomer to porn consumption. He had seen his first *Playboy* on a newsstand about age 12, and a year or two later was buying the magazine himself. "I looked a lot older, and back then a lot of stores weren't strict about selling them. They were basically selling them to anyone." In the seventh grade, Gerald and a friend went to the quarter arcade in a seamy part of town.

I saw this clip, I saw this woman playing with herself, and I found it disgusting. [He laughs.] I found it kind of sickening, kind of "ooh, yuck!" 'Cause I had never seen anything like that before. It just literally grossed me out. When I went to see my first X-rated movie, I think at the time they did not show full insertion, or anything like that. They showed a woman getting naked and engaging in the acts, but no penetration or closeups like they do now. It was exciting. I started going there a little bit more frequently.

By the age of 16, Gerald was visiting strip bars across the border in Mexico. "That was when I first saw a live, naked woman. They wore tassels and g-strings. It was very exciting for me." But despite all the visual stimulation, Gerald never once masturbated through high school. "I didn't even know what it was until later in high school." And when he did find out, he resisted trying it. "Somehow the idea of touching my penis and trying to masturbate just did not appeal to me at all. I don't know where I got the attitude that it wasn't okay, but I never masturbated. I basically would just suffer with the erections coming."

It was also around age 16 that Gerald joined the Pentecostal Church.

> At the time I considered all sexual thoughts, feelings, sensations to be the devil. And they were evil, and they would bring me along the direct road to hell. I remember riding in a crowded van one time, and the van lurched forward and this girl suddenly fell onto me, and when I grabbed her my hand grasped her breast, and it was very thrilling to me. And I really paid for that. That was the devil throwing her at me, to tempt me. On the one hand, I had these strong sexual feelings, and at the same time I'd get depressed if I had sexual fantasies about "Sisters in Christ." And I had to suppress that, and it was difficult.

By the age of 19 Gerald became disaffected with Christianity. He saw a pornographic movie that featured Harry Reems and ejaculated without even touching himself. "I ejaculated inside my pants. And it was amazing to me. Because it had never happened. That was very key to my starting to masturbate. It was kind of like, I could really enjoy these magazines!" But that wasn't the end of his confusion. Gerald blamed the sole source of his sex education for some early mistakes.

> It warped how I viewed women for the longest time. It came about in one relationship in college, where I was making love to her in the way I had seen it portrayed on the screen. I was sexually manipulating her clitoris or vaginal region with my fingers, and apparently I was just too rough. And I didn't realize that I was hurting her, because she was, you know,

making the sounds that I had heard on the screen. And she had to tell me it was hurtful. And when she told me that, it really hit me: I'm doing something wrong here.

Gerald was fortunate that his partner was able to tell him the following morning, rather than keeping it to herself and dumping him. "I learned how to be gentle, how to bring her with my fingers, with my hand, manually after that."

Gerald was "horny as all get-out" in his early twenties, and used pornography a lot. After getting married, he stopped. "We'd watch one or two [movies but] she didn't care for them." He characterized his wife's attitude as "the classic one":

She should have been enough for me. I think she thought that after I read a magazine or viewed one of these movies and wanted to have sex with her, it was to engage in some sort of fantasy with what I saw on the page or the video. And basically, reading the magazine and watching the video would just make me horny. And I couldn't convey to her that I'm not thinking of some other woman when I'm having sex with you! One time she was very upset, because I had just received a catalog in the mail and was looking at it, and she said "You're thinking of those women, and not me." I think she wanted to be the exclusive woman in my life, the one who turned me on.

I asked Gerald if he thought there was any truth to his wife's belief that she was in competition with something else.

I think she was partly insecure. From what I've read in the literature, some women do feel they have to compete with these women in magazine ads and so forth, and they're afraid of losing their men to that. But for me, when I get a magazine, I appreciate it, but it's like, for me this is fantasy stuff. This isn't real. You know, the chances of me going out with a *Playboy* model or getting to meet an actual porn star are like el zippo. It's fantasizing, I just use it as an enhancement, that's all. It's not like I'm replacing you.

Nevertheless, Gerald largely did not use pornography during the five years of his marriage.

After his divorce, he bought two porn videos, watched exotic dancers and talked with them ("they were very down-to-earth, very normal types of people"), and even dated one. He also got into on-line computer chat rooms, although Gerald preferred to watch more than participate. "I'll kind of watch the conversations going on, see how someone's desperately trying to get the woman to respond."

But in his 39th year, the lumbar disc ruptured and his urologist said get a woman or get some porn. The mission was not merely to make himself sexually potent again: Gerald was numb from the waist down. If he pinched his leg, he couldn't feel it. He could feel the pressure, he could sense *something* there, but it would not be a pinch. He couldn't feel his toes or feet, let alone his penis. "For a while there I was limping, but then after a sensation started coming back it felt like sand in my shoes."

Masturbation would help get blood rushing into all the areas below his waist. At first he tried renting videos, but even driving the car to the store was an unsettling experience because he had no sensation in his buttocks, so he purchased a few:

> When I initially started masturbating, it took a long time. It took like twenty or thirty minutes. Just before I can ejaculate. And sometimes I couldn't ejaculate. And it was the oddest sensation, because the size would be maybe an inch and then gradually it started getting a little bigger. Like maybe an inch and a half or two inches. So now it's about three inches. But it's such an odd sensation, because I remember initially, I couldn't really feel it, I could just feel the pressure.

Gerald's urologist urged him to get back to his normal routine as soon as possible, so after t · months he returned to work. "Somewhere around six months after my surgery I started noticing a little more appreciation. My body would get a little bit more responsive. Even if I saw a sexy scene on TV, I would feel a sensation, a tingling, in my penis. It's nothing like what I would have from the past. In the past, I would get a hard-on."

Gerald estimated that 90 percent of his orgasms currently were assisted by pornography. He turned to it when his children were away. On those occasions, he worked with the videos for several hours in order to orgasm several times. Sometimes when his kids were in bed at night, he'd slip in a video: "I'd say that would occur like maybe once every two weeks. It's not that frequent. I think there's a consistent pattern, now that I think about it. And that pattern is, when I see something that's sort of sexy on TV and I kind of feel a sense of a tingle, then it's kind of like, I want to encourage it!"

When Gerald spoke to me, it had been over a year since the surgery. "I can tell that it started gradually getting a little bigger. It's still not up to normal, and it's been over a year. But now, at least I'm responding. I can see progress."

I wondered if any urologists were prescribing pornography for women. Gerald laughed.

DAN'S STORY

"Dan" saw his first *Playboy* around the age of 11 when a classmate showed off his father's collection. It was a strange feeling to look at the magazines, and although Dan was aroused, he did not make use of such materials, then or later. His parents were supportive of his sexual fantasies as a teen and "encouraged me to talk about them." He thought they were probably neutral on the subject of pornography because they didn't have any problems with nudity or sex: "My parents aren't Christians, so they have a very worldly but thoughtful perspective about such matters." Dan became a Christian at the age of 16, however, and "after that I became very conscientious about that sort of thing."

> Even before then, I could tell something wasn't right about porn, but after I became a Christian, I generally tried to avoid it when possible. I wasn't too impressed with my friends [who] gravitated toward that sort of thing. They seemed to be obsessed.

Since his faith taught him that lusting after women was a sin, Dan did his best to avoid it. "Once I married, I had sex a lot and I lust after my wife, which is ok." If he happened across pornography by accident he would tell her and she was "very disturbed. My wife really didn't like the idea of competing with another person for my attention and would ask if she (my wife) looked as attractive to me." In general, Dan said, "I would say it's better not to bring such things up."

Despite having relatively little experience with pornography, Dan was certain it had had a negative effect on him:

> It has generally lowered my opinion of women. It has promoted thinking of women as sex objects, rather than "persons." I think porn belittles the complex beauty women have in and out of bed. Porn makes it seem that the bedroom is the center of activity. A good sex relationship starts *outside* the bedroom.

Twenty-seven at the time of the survey and a doctoral candidate, Dan felt oppressed by pornography, and though he avoided it completely for himself, he *had* sought out sexually oriented films and stories for his wife.

"Being on the pill for several years had really messed her up somehow. When she stopped using the pill she still didn't get that old feeling back." His wife wasn't very interested in sex at all and had difficulty climaxing. "I decided I had to do something. I wanted to increase her sexual interest." He noted that his wife was not the kind of person who would come out and say, *Gee, I think I have a low sex drive problem*, so "I perceived it as a problem, and simply came up with a solution. Thus I encouraged her to read sexually explicit materials."

First he tried video porn. She didn't like it because "the acting sucks and there isn't the passionate plot." In addition, "She doesn't like the short, stupid jock type that is usually portrayed." But mainstream films with erotic content did help to acclimate Dan's wife to pornography:

> She would get more excited if she saw a film like *Basic Instinct*, although it's not porn per se. At some point, we wound up buying a porn video (with several different "stories"). She seems to be pretty picky, and I don't make much sense out of what she likes and doesn't. She found one or two segments that she likes and sometimes masturbates during it (either with me there, or with me not there—and then tells me about it). She likes one Peter North episode where he is a Navy officer and an attractive female somehow seduces him (very rapidly). I think she identifies herself with the female in the scene, [or] she finds Peter North very attractive in that episode; it's hard to say why exactly. Perhaps it has a sophisticated romantic atmosphere that helps too. She has also masturbated to *Basic Instinct*.

Dan estimated his wife might turn to "that sort of special thing" maybe once or twice a month. "It certainly isn't a regular part of our sex life, but it is one occasional part that is exciting." In addition, erotic stories (including ones in porn magazines) were effective in building her interest.

> I got her some *Playgirl* magazines, and eventually talked her into getting a subscription. She likes the "Fantasy Forum" contributed stories the most. I think she needs to have "dynamic" rather than "static" images. The material needs to have a story or some sort of action in it. Women like dirty novels and similar books. They also like highly romantic/passionate short stories and movies. I encourage my wife to use such "porn." Some of the best sex we've had has been after she has spent a few hours reading such material before I come home.

In the course of finding the tools that worked best, Dan noted other factors:

> I also find that one or two drinks of alcohol help her concentrate more on sex. We can have good sex without these things, but it's not uncommon

for her to be distracted with thoughts about work, house chores, etc. My wife just doesn't have the same level of sexual passion without "porn" on a consistent basis. Her sexual fantasy is being a stripper/prostitute—I think that's the sort of thing she thinks about when reading/seeing these materials. You would never guess that if you met her; she projects a very different personality—one of a sweet, innocent, proper person.

Dan accepted a double standard which caused his wife to feel jealous and threatened if he looked at other women (especially in pornography), while he never had that response when she aroused herself by looking at other men:

It is very important for an average, American, psychologically healthy woman to feel loved and appreciated by her spouse. Men can't relate to this feminine "need" as much (at least less so) because they are men, after all, and not women. To a woman her appearance is very important; if her spouse is looking at other women, to her it is logical that she must not be "good enough" to keep his attention. This can be very damaging to a relationship. I would prefer if my wife became erotic at my mere presence, but that isn't the case (every time). I try to be neat and attractive, but if someone is more handsome than me, it's really no big deal. Then again, my wife only uses porn occasionally. If she used it every day or seemed obsessed with it, I would want her to slow down, because then I would be worried about whether she might not remain faithful to me. So there is a limit even to what I will tolerate.

Public Policy:

Should Society Control
the Use Of Pornography?

To approach the issue of how pornography is viewed by society and the law, I asked the men, "Is there anything wrong with consuming pornography, in your opinion?"

"I think it's basically benign," wrote a 29-year-old technical writer. "I don't think it warps people's brains any more than commercial advertising, religion, or any other contact with society does. The people who say 'Pornography Made Me Do It' are the same people who would be manipulated by the most basic propaganda in our society."

A 48-year-old public administrator in Canada agreed: "I have read some of the antiporn literature, but it has never been convincing. I have never seen anything that I would consider violent or overtly exploitative; I have never even seen it for sale."

Several men thought that watching pornography was problematic, but only under certain conditions. "I have no real concerns about porn unless it becomes the main or only outlet for one's sexual functions," said a 45-

year-old married man. A physician wrote, "There's nothing wrong with consuming it, especially in moderation and in the context of adequate personal relationships." He also felt that "the misogynist attitudes often displayed in porn are certainly not good role models for people."

"There is nothing inherently wrong with consuming porn," said a married chemical engineer, "as long as you keep fiction separated from reality. If you let it affect your perception of women, men, sex, and so forth, you have a problem." He was not concerned about most men's ability to do that.

A fan of bondage observed that "porn can be an excessively time-consuming obsession, as can most other things in life. If it is not that, then I think there is nothing wrong with consuming it." The only objection a 39-year-old married programmer could raise was "the area of town I have to go to just to see a good porn flick. Also, usually the theaters are very old movie houses. While it is neat to be in these huge old houses, a cleaner, more kept-up place would be nice."

A much smaller group of heterosexual men voiced stronger concerns. Several warnings related to content. A 43-year-old married schoolteacher thought "it can create some very unrealistic expectations of women. If you have no real contact with any real women and this is what you expect, you have really been misled."

A 33-year-old Englishman felt the issue of porn's possible harmfulness had to be laid aside in the face of more universal concerns about sexuality. Like many men, he felt that attacking pornography caused more problems than it solved:

I don't see porn as intrinsically harmful, even within a relationship (although I am dubious in the latter case). I don't think the debate whether porn encourages sexual deviancy is worth arguing about. Some people with dangerous sexual interests use porn, and in some cases such use probably acts like a safety valve, in other cases it probably encourages the problem. However, the underlying problem is that people have not learned to resist their sexual urges, not that they can get their hands on porn. I believe that the demonization of porn does far more to encourage such dangerous behavior than porn itself. And I believe this extreme rejection of porn arises only because of a more general problem people have dealing with their own sexuality and sexual urges.

Another man argued that pornography could not be isolated from other media that degrade women: "The only thing harmful about porn to women is the same that is harmful in all media. Women are frequently denigrated in the media. That does influence peoples' attitudes towards women." In the case of pornography, he went on: "It may make persons have more open attitudes about sexual behaviors, possibly even unusual behaviors. But what can be bad about persons having more open attitudes about sex?"

Gay men were more likely not just to reject the defensive position (no, using porn is not wrong), but to embrace a positive one (it's *good* for you). A 23-year-old Canadian student said, "I am not worried that people will have too much porn. On the contrary, I think there should be more. Canada and the U.S. have a problem dealing with sex and nudity as fun, admirable, and artistic." A 42-year-old gay professor celebrated porn as just another harmless option in a smorgasbord of sexual choices:

I don't see anything wrong with porn, with masturbation, even with quickie anonymous sex. Sexual expression can take on many forms—just as can our need for food; people's tastes differ as do their needs and abilities. Just as sometimes a MacDonald's hamburger and fries is OK, so might a quick hand job be OK. Other times you want a good home-cooked meal—or a long snuggly sexual session with your partner. Other times you might want Chinese food or a session of something sexually a bit exotic.

"I believe that the widespread assumption that exposure to 'stereotypes,' 'bad examples,' and 'messages' causes 'undesirable behavior' is sociological bullshit," a 32-year-old college instructor wrote. "I was sheltered from any and all images of homosexuality, and look how I turned out." For gays, rejection of pornography by people whose values they did not share—people who tended to reject homosexuals as well—was to pornography's credit:

> I consider myself a Christian; I was "saved" in a Baptist church when I was 7 years old. The radical religious right's persecution of homosexuals is at the bottom of my disillusionment with the church. I am not disillusioned by God—only with those who profess to speak for him. The fact that pornography is scorned by organized religion, if anything, makes it more attractive to me. [library director, 38]

Only five men, all heterosexuals, said there was definitely something wrong with consuming pornography. Two based their objections on personal experiences. Two cited religion. Two raised feminist concerns. Said a married 45-year-old:

> My main moral concern is that the consumption of porn creates a market for producing it, which may lead to the sexual exploitation of women (and men). I wouldn't want my daughter to become a porn star, so in fairness I shouldn't contribute to a situation that would cause someone else's daughter to become a porn star. (I would say the same about my sons, if I had any.) I also think that consuming porn can increase one's preoccupation with sex, which probably is not a good thing. I have more or less avoided porn for most of my life, with the occasional sampling. My reaction to porn is much like my reaction to gambling, or video games, or smoking, or any other compulsive activity. It's something I normally avoid, but I don't feel totally depraved for sampling it once in a while.

Several men who thought pornography was harmful also implicated the larger culture. "I think what has a much more degrading effect are magazine ads which are much more pervasive and much more dishonest, than actual porn where you are using it purely for a sexual purpose," argued a 31-year-old literature professor.

Gay men were slightly more likely than straights to consider the possibility that porn was harmful to women. "My gut response is from my religious training," said an ex-Catholic; "yes, it is degrading to women. But I don't follow the opposite logic for male porn—men who do it are not being exploited because they give their consent and enjoy what they do." "I do think that pornography is harmful to women!!!" wrote a 32-year-old counselor, "not because it's porno but because of the way heterosexual men view and use women. Men have a real difficult time when reality and fantasies (and women) come into play."

Still, the number of gays who shared that point of view were fewer than those who saw little or no harm. "I've heard women claim that porn is harmful," said one. "But then I have heard some women claim that gay porn is harmful to women too—because there are no women in it." A 33-year-old said: "I think it is really just a vocal group's vision of what they see as sexually acceptable—and they're trying to tell us all what types of sex and sources of arousal are appropriate. I think many women simply don't understand men's interest in porn, so it is written off as dirty, unacceptable—something watched by people who have some sexual or personality deficiency."

Most men rejected any causal link between using porn and mistreating women. "Rapists may be heavy users of pornography, but only because they already have problems which make it difficult to relate to real women," a 32-year-old in public relations said. "Porn use is a symptom of what makes them rapists, not the cause."

Quite a few men accepted that pornography "could" play a role in misleading men to abuse women, though none cited evidence from their own experience. Only a couple who regarded themselves as sexaholics or addicted to pornography suggested that it had been harmful in their case. "My view of women (and my viewing of women) has been affected by my consumption of porn," said a man whose wife was divorcing him because of his activities. "When taken to excess, then it becomes a problem," said another man who was separated from a wife who regarded porn as evil; "I say this because when pictures, thoughts, and ideas get into your head, they never get out."

Other men argued that it was misguided to blame pornography if some consumers misused it:

> I think [porn is] harmful only to the extent that people allow themselves to be "harmed." Just as alcohol, chocolate, guns, and many other obsessions become harmful only when misused. Men who misread the messages of pornography, who take its conventions seriously, are most likely maladjusted in other ways, and pornography is not to be blamed for the misbehavior of such men. Any thoughtful guy can see how pornography is not like life; if he pays more attention to the lessons of the former, then he's just stupid.

In discussing the pornography industry and whether or not it exploits women, quite a few men suggested that performers were not being exploited if they received payment. "The women who work in pornography are paid for their work, just like any other job," one said; "A woman who trades on her appearance or her sexual talent is not being 'exploited' any more than a woman who trades on her brains." A 28-year-old married man said, "The people involved make good money and I don't believe any of them are forced into it. It's interesting to note that the women in pornography earn a great deal more money than the men do!"

One man who said he had carefully studied the arguments about pornography's harmful effects in the feminist press said, "I have consistently found these arguments to be lacking in analysis, lacking in evidence, and lacking in even basic reality testing. They seem to me to verge on dogma, and to be entirely disconnected from the reality of pornography and human sexuality." For example, "opponents of pornography believe that the producers effectively decide that women will model, and then impose that decision by force." On the contrary, he argued, "the pornography industry is mediated by money, not force. And that means that each model decides, for herself, on the day of the shoot, that she's willing to model in exchange for the money that she's being paid."

Others were less certain. "Obviously porn in which actual violence is done would be harmful to those men and/or women involved," a 22-year-old single Canadian remarked. "I know that many porno actresses are really desperate, runaways, uneducated, who would rather be doing something else," said another man, "Yet I'm glad that at least they can make some money off this huge industry taking advantage of our silly male weakness." A literature professor admitted the suicide of porn star Savannah after her face was disfigured in a car accident gave him pause. "I'm sure she was a very troubled person. I don't think pornography led her to [commit suicide], but it's got to be a really hard life."

Even when men acknowledged that some women suffered from their experiences in the pornography industry, most would not blame porn per se. As one suggested, performers may be vulnerable to abuse because they get caught in a crossfire between the legal marginality of the industry, the firm social disapproval of it, and the market demand:

> Explicit erotica has been considered "pornography" by most modern western cultures, hence its production has either been illegal or highly restricted. But there has always been a demand for erotica; most will not admit it openly, but many secretly seek out and indulge in erotica. There is a vast underground demand coupled with both the social and legal restrictions. This has created a market that is willing to pay to get whatever they can discreetly obtain. It has also created an industry dominated by those who are not deterred by social mores or skirting the law in order to make a buck. With such people running the industry, there is bound to be much unethical behavior—pressuring young women (and men) into performing sex on camera in return for money. This condition has also kept the quality of erotica very low. So it is not erotica that is harmful. It is the unnatural suppression of sexuality that creates a harmful situation.

Another man noted that while some women had undoubtedly been coerced and harmed in the making of pornography, many others like Nina Hartley, Gloria Leonard, Annie Sprinkle, and Candida Royalle chose the work freely and enjoyed it. "I think the women who are harmed in the production of porn are usually subject to other forms of abuse which are actionable, such as forced prostitution, sexual assault, or battering," he went on. "And those abuses will not stop if we ban pornography."

Several men believed the growth of amateur porn was proof against the claim that women would never perform sexually for a camera if they had sufficient economic alternatives and were not forced. "I know from the amateurs I know who produce their own porn that they get off on being exhibitionists, and weren't pressured into it," said a married 43-year-old accountant. The symphonic musician agreed:

> There are thousands of these amateur tapes! How is it possible for all those women—people like those who live next door, video-ing their own sexual behavior for anyone to see—to feel degraded? Many of them must feel turned on by acting out in front of the camera.

"I've never heard opponents of pornography raise this issue," remarked another man. "The people who receive, distribute, and sell amateur videos make money from the product. However, the people who appear in them do not. Whatever it is that motivates these people to display themselves, it isn't money. Some people find it easier to take on a multi-billion dollar industry than to accept women as sexual beings."

A few men did feel that the industry was definitely harmful to women. "I haven't read Linda Lovelace's story, but from what I've heard the porn industry sounds pretty rotten," said a Canadian professor. A 20-year-old political science major said, "I believe there exist many cases in which women are coerced or otherwise forced to participate in the production of pornography." He was opposed to restrictions or censorship of pornography based on its content, however. A man who was not opposed to such control was Henry, who claimed to have been sexually abused as a child:

> I have read a couple accounts by people who used to be in the industry. The production of pornography is physically harmful to many women who are involved. The harm comes in the form of drug usage, being used by the producers to enact male fantasy, and denying what I believe to be the inherent insanity of multiple sexual interactions without emotional attachment, not to mention the beatings reported by a few and the incred-

ibly degrading acts committed to force some women to obey. The damage may not be bodily damage. I believe it is emotionally harmful to everyone who participates, men and women alike. I think it is quite a serious matter to use one's body as a machine without thought to the emotional issues. There is plenty of evidence today that women and men do not know what it means to be male or female anymore. To reduce femaleness to a multiple orifice receptacle for penises is criminal. To reduce maleness to sustained erection is ridiculous.

A man who had written porn novels under a pseudonym had ambivalent feelings about the industry:

I don't think reading, writing, or looking at it is harmful to anybody. I do think manufacturing it may be harmful to some of the participants, especially underage girls or naive women with few skills and doubtful prospects. The atmosphere surrounding the creation of these films must be fairly cynical and full of drugs and other kinds of unsalutary temptations that are better avoided by everybody. I also wonder what happens to many of these women later in life. Their work span must only last a decade. Then they have to find something else to do, with not much to prepare the way. I wish more of the money I spend on it went to them.

"If anyone is exploited, it's men," claimed a p.r. man, "but whether they are stuffing their wages into G-strings just to get a pretty girl to smile at them, or they are authorizing $4-per-minute charges to their phone cards in exchange for dirty talk, they are doing it willingly." The Canadian professor who avoided porn felt the same: "I think it's more harmful to men than to many women. We're the ones who waste our time and money on it. Who is harmed by heroin—the poppy growers or the junkies?"

About a fifth of the men in the survey took the trouble to suggest how the possible harms inherent in pornography might be alleviated. Their recommendations can be summed up as: better quality porn and improved social attitudes. "Once people learn that it's OK to consume porn, market demand for 'good' porn will help quell 'bad' porn," wrote a chemical engineer. A 22-year-old who believed porn was often degrading to women also felt pornography could be employed to "remove sexist ideas from people's heads, if more sexually explicit material picturing women as equals to men were released and made publicly available."

A few men suggested pornography might improve if more women took the time to watch it:

> They would find there are many kinds of it, and some kinds may even be appealing to them. By getting more women involved in the making of porn, as writers and directors as well as performers, they have more input and control over the product.

Several men called on the makers of porn to do more: "Making the industry more respectable would give the performers more rights," said a married professor.

Since a clear majority of the men in the survey believed pornography had done them little harm, and in many cases had done them some good, I was curious to see whether they worried about its effects on other, presumably more vulnerable or less balanced citizens.

"I'm not concerned about the effects of pornography since I really don't believe that anyone has ever been harmed by it," said a 41-year-old grad student. A 48-year-old Christian widower added: "It's much more likely, I think, for someone to get screwed up because of sexual repression and suppression during their growing years."

A 21-year-old gay student made an even stronger statement:

> American society as a whole is screwed up about lots of things and one of them is porn. We're so bombarded with messages about what's wrong and morally disgusting, and I think it's a load of crap. We're too uptight about little things that wouldn't be problems if we didn't make them problems. The only worry I have about the availability of porn is that someday the radicals are going to get it banned and it *won't* be available.

Quite a few men who said they had no concern about others went on to address the issue of porn consumers who are a problem to society. "To be sure, there are people in society that cannot separate fantasy from reality, but I believe they are mentally ill, and pornography didn't cause their illnesses."

Several others expanded on this theme:

> People who are already unstable or inclined to rape are going to consume porn in unhealthy amounts.

> My take on these concerns is that rape comes out of some other sick need, and has much more to do with violence than sex—so porn has little to do with it. One testimonial I recall hearing was from someone who got off on the thought of drowning someone. He loved seeing scenes of people on TV who were drowning (movies that depict it, etc.). This really got him off. We could eliminate all the porn in the world, and this guy would still have something to get off on.

A 67-year-old gay male took a cynical view of the supposed link between pornography and violent behavior: "I can understand how those facing prison might grasp at any straws to survive." But a bisexual software engineer, 25, voiced discomfort with some written material he had seen:

> Distressingly often, I'll run into a story on the net that has to do with torturing and raping children or something similarly vile. And I know that there are people in the world who do these things for fun. And I know that the people who write and enjoy these stories are probably from the subset of the population from which these creeps crawl. That sends shivers down my spine. My suspicion is that the existence of such porn is just one of the symptoms of the fact that such folks are around, and doesn't do much of anything to increase or decrease their numbers or their active sadism. Still it gives me the willies to know that someone out there is really getting a kick out of it.

A few men approached the question from the standpoint of adult rights and responsibilities. "All adults should be free to engage in the perversion of their choice, provided there's no coercion involved, and they keep it to themselves," said a 38-year-old man. "I do have one friend who too openly enjoys pornography and masturbation, and talks about it in inappropriate settings." Remarked a 42-year-old professor:

> I feel that the right to read/think/watch what you want is pretty much paramount and should come before the tenuous links between what someone reads and their behavior—or soon Marx will be banned (as would the Bible—some of the stuff people do in the Bible is *nasty*).

A 41-year-old man in education administration defended the right to view porn despite his own addictive experiences: "I am a recovering alcoholic—if it were up to me I would ban alcohol and drugs. But that would only benefit me and deprive others for whom pleasure is derived from those substances. I can't hold the liquor companies and drug dealers responsible for my disease and the effect of alcohol and drugs on my life. The same would go for pornography."

Several men who granted that pornography might have some negative effects in society nevertheless were convinced that censoring it would be worse. "There [is] a complex relationship between the level of violence in a society and how that is reflected in its art," said a Canadian government employee who avoided pornography for ideological reasons. "I doubt that porn *causes* any violence, but I think that it reinforces it, and probably gives permission to some men to be violent. I believe that censorship, however, causes more problems than it cures." A 31-year-old gay man in graphic design said, "I do worry about those who are significantly affected by viewing such things—stalkers, serial whatevers, Christian groups, etc. What bothers me is those adversely affected often draw unnecessary attention to casual consumers like myself."

Not surprisingly, some men expressed concern about children and pornography. They objected to children either appearing in or seeing pornographic materials.

Children merely viewing porn, at least up to a certain age or without some context, was less worrisome, but many men expressed concern about that too. "I worry how the younger folk seeing these things for the first time, especially if they've never had sexual relationships themselves, think and feel about the things they see on the screen," said a 35-year-old programmer.

"Hard-core porn should probably not be available to anyone under, maybe, 14 or 15," a 27-year-old single man wrote. "Not because there's anything ethically wrong with it, but because you need to be at a certain maturity level to put it into perspective." A Navy veteran, 31, took a harder line: "I think it should be withheld from children [because] it tends to ridicule self-restraint and encourage an undisciplined life."

Several men, knowing from experience that parents have virtually no privacy from their children, did their best to make pornography inaccessible. "I take steps not to expose my children, and I certainly use it in a private way," said a Canadian public servant. "I have a lock box so the kids won't stumble upon it," said the father of two small girls. A man whose 7-year-old daughter knew the mechanics of sex and babies remarked, "I don't think she *really* understands it. I don't have anything hard-core in the house for that reason." However, he didn't think a few old copies of *Penthouse* on the premises were likely to shock or harm her.

Surprisingly few men addressed the contradiction between their belief that pornography might be harmful to young children and teens, and the fact that most of them had been exposed to it when *they* were kids. If porn were indeed harmful or confusing to children, then it should have had a similar effect upon most of the men in the survey, but few said it had. This struck me as odd, particularly in view of the fact that pornography apparently had the least effect upon boys who saw skin magazines at a *very* early age, say 5 to 8. Boys that young often found it puzzling or boring, and tended to lump pornography with all the other quaint things that adults like and do, rather than regard it as something with special power and fascination—unless the adults around them made a big fuss. Many men had been exposed to some form of pornography at age 9 to 11, yet many believed children should not see it before 12 or 16. So it would seem at least some of them ignored the facts of their own experience and parroted public notions about not mixing children and porn.

Jack was a rare exception: "I wish that I had not found what I had, at least not when I was so young. I have no idea how I would have turned out otherwise, but I can't help feeling that I might have been a little 'mentally healthier' if I had waited till I was 13 or 14 at least, before finding porno and having to learn how to masturbate to it."

Erotica vs. Pornography

In the debate over the proper place in society for sexual materials, many commentators make a distinction between pornography, which they oppose, and erotica, which they do not. The most famous attempt to separate the two was made by Gloria Steinem in an oft-reprinted essay that first appeared in *Ms.* magazine. Observing that the roots for the word "pornography" meant "writing about prostitution or female captives," and erotica came from "eros," or passionate love, Steinem wrote:

> Look at any photo or film of people making love; really making love. The images may be diverse, but there is usually a sensuality and touch and warmth, an acceptance of bodies and nerve endings. There is always a spontaneous sense of people who are there because they want to be, out of shared pleasure. Now look at any depiction of sex in which there is clear force, or an unequal power that spells coercion. It may be very blatant, with weapons of torture or bondage, wounds and bruises, some clear humiliation, or an adult's sexual power being used over a child. It may be much more subtle: a physical attitude of conqueror and victim, the use of race or class difference to imply the same thing, perhaps a very unequal nudity, with one person exposed and vulnerable while the other is clothed. In either case, there is no sense of equal choice or equal power.

For Steinem, one style characterized erotica, the other pornography. If there is a clear and pertinent distinction between pornography and erotica, I was curious to see whether it was evident to the people who were most familiar with the former. More important, was the distinction significant enough to warrant treating them differently under the law?

A great number of men believed porn could be separated from erotica by the nature of its sexual content, but they disagreed about which sexual content could be considered erotic as opposed to pornographic. Some thought erotica omitted actual intercourse. "I think porn shows people having sex and erotica shows sexually stimulating pictures of people while not having sex," was the opinion of a mechanic. A divorced Australian man agreed: "Seems to me that pornography is the actual depiction of individuals or groups engaged in sexual activity of some kind whereas erotica is a mere suggestion of sexuality and is hence totally different."

But other men felt erotica could include intercourse by approaching it in an indirect manner. As a 27-year-old Unix administrator described it, "Porn deals with close-ups of penetration while erotica may deal with a view of the whole scene and include penetration but not at highly-magnified levels." Nearly as many men described the difference in terms of how erotica and pornography approached sexuality in general, rather than which sex acts were shown. "Erotica is art that uses sex and sexuality as the main subject in the depiction," a 37-year-old married man suggested, while "pornography is a graphic depiction of sexual behavior." "*Generally speaking*, pornography exploits sexuality whereas erotica explores sexuality with sensuality," remarked a 32-year-old divorced man who liked porn. "If I am correct," ventured a 24-year-old student, "porn is just hard-core sex, erotica is soft, lovemaking sex. Easier on the ears, too."

"In my view erotica is softer, 'fuzzier,' and perhaps more romantic," a New Zealand native theorized. "I guess sometimes I think of erotica as being soft core and more literary, and a flowery style," said a literature professor. A 21-year-old gay music student listed examples: "'Erotica' has a tenderness to it that 'porn' doesn't quite. 'Improve your marriage' videos for couples are erotica. *Playgirl* is erotica. Some Catalina gay films are erotica. Most Falcon gay films are porn. *Honcho* and *Blueboy* are porn. I think it's a subtle difference: everyone sees it differently, and many people don't see it at all."

Several men said erotica was distinguished by its heavy use of imagination, and stimulation of the mind more than the eye. A married bisexual in academia felt that "the imagination is a much more realized and integral part of the experience" in erotica. "Erotica has to do with sexual love," a Canadian professor, married twenty-two years, said: "If its appeal is between the ears, it's erotica; if it's between the legs, it's pornography."

Others thought erotica involved more context, more of a plot to surround the sexual activity. "I see erotica as having a plot line with sexual content (perhaps strong, and strongly stimulating, at times) and pornography as being sex for the sake of sex—that is, its reason for being (raison d'être) is purely to stimulate a person psycho-sexually," said a 48-year-old widower. A 35-year-old office worker put it this way:

> I think pornography focuses almost exclusively on the sexual acts themselves, while erotica provides more of the human, psychological *context* in which the sex takes place. That's what can give it an extra charge—that these are more seemingly real people with emotions, rather than just bodies connecting the plumbing. An erotic scene can take place with no sex and almost no nudity at all. I think of that incredibly sexy scene in "The Age of Innocence" where Daniel Day-Lewis is riding in a carriage with Michelle Pfeiffer, and he removes a glove from her hand and kisses it. That was incredibly erotic because of the intensely charged atmosphere between them, built up over the course of the story and those characters' relationship. But an erotic scene could also be just as down-and-dirty as basic pornography, too. It simply has more of a frame to it. Erotica can include pornography, but pornography doesn't usually contain the erotic.

A few men thought the differences lent themselves to particular media—that pornography tended to be visual and erotica written. "My first reaction would be that erotica is only words," said a 32-year-old virgin. "Would I consider *Penthouse*'s letters pornography or erotica if they were in a magazine that had no pictures *at all* in it? I guess erotica." "I associate pornography with visual images and erotica with written images," agreed a 24-year-old library clerk. A 30-year-old homosexual working in education also said he saw "a difference between erotic fiction (with no pictures) and porn."

A couple of men simply noted the distinction in the way erotica and pornography are treated by society. "Erotica has a crawlspace in the mainstream that penetration-dependent porn is not likely to acquire," noted a 26-year-old in desktop publishing. "You can get erotica at Waldenbooks, but not *Swank*. Otherwise the distinction is murky." A man who had written porn novels made the same point more dryly: "Erotica, I notice, is something publishers call a book when they want to get it into a respectable bookstore." Another man complained of a double standard in the U.S. with regard to graphic material: "*National Geographic* magazine can show naked children, some with small breasts, and get by with it, but let someone else do it and they are in the slammer."

Even while drawing distinctions, a number of men admitted the differences were muddier than they seemed. One who thought erotica "is more romantic and highly suggestive" added that "there is so much crossover that it would be impossible to draw a line." A 23-year-old postgraduate student thought, "The distinction between porn and erotica is one of degree, with one only being a more explicit version of the other." The 44-year-old gay computer analyst remarked, "One person's erotica is likely to be someone else's pornography, and vice versa."

Many of the men who said there was no appreciable distinction between pornography and erotica felt that any perceived differences were subjective, semantic, or class-based. A 32-year-old in public relations directed his remarks toward people like Steinem: "'Erotica' is a politically correct term that antiporn people use to label the pornography they approve of. There really is no difference." A graduate student in mathematics cut to the chase: "The people who try to differentiate between erotica and pornography are usually just censors."

Quite a few men remarked on the class aspect. "Erotica is for intellectual, cultured, rich people," a biochemistry graduate student remarked; "Sort of like the difference between being crazy and being eccentric. Depends on how much money you've got or which social circles you run in." A 38-year-old married man felt the same: "Erotica is pornography that appeals to the intelligentsia. It has some artistic pretensions. Otherwise they are the same." A Spaniard echoed the sentiment: "A Spanish movie director says that pornography is erotica for unwealthy people. It's true. I grew up more in a porn way than in an erotica [way]." A 43-year-old married man offered an analogy:

> Erotica is coffee-table book porn. A pretty cover on the same thing. Marla Maples marries Donald Trump, an obvious jerk; a girl on E. Colfax sucks a cock for $15. Marla Maples is to erotica as the girl on Colfax is to pornography. A poor pervert is a pervert, a rich pervert is eccentric, and so on. Bottom line: same content, different marketing and packaging. If it makes your dick hard, it makes your dick hard.

"'Erotica' is what you call pornography if you want to hang it in a gallery, isn't it?" a law student asked rhetorically. A public administrator in Canada was well aware that his nation's legal system saw a clear distinction between erotica and porn, "but that is more in the mind's eye than reality. Erotica is often used as a term to denote pornography with artistic intent! This of course is crap; it is merely part of the time-honored distinction between 'high' art and 'low' art." He added, "I use the terms interchangeably."

A 30-year-old Australian said, "Porn is seen as the 'dirtier' or 'obscene' side of erotica, but what's erotic for one person may not be for another, and obscenity is a *highly* subjective term." "Both 'pornography' and 'erotica' are value-laden terms," observed a 27-year-old Englishman. "'Pornography' has always meant 'the bad stuff' while 'erotica' has always meant 'the good stuff.' Probably the most interesting thing I've always gotten from the pro/antiporn debates is that no two people ever seem to have the same definition of 'pornography' or 'erotica.'"

The best illustration of the semantic and subjective confusion over sexual imagery was offered by Steve, the 49-year-old British male who had little interest in pornography but saw no harm in it:

> No, I see no distinction, not even an aesthetic one. The only difference is in the speaker's mind: "pornography" is a "boo word" and "erotica" is a "rah word." To give a concrete example: During a debate on pornographic images, the proponent of censorship gave as an example of the utterly obscene, indefensible, and unacceptable, "pictures of women having sex with animals." As it happens, I own a reproduction of such a picture. The original is in the Spiridon Collection in Rome, and is entitled "Leda and the Swan." The pervert who painted it was Leonardo da Vinci.

Despite the differing opinions on whether erotica and pornography could be distinguished from each other, very few men thought the two should be treated differently by society or the law. "No, I don't think the law should distinguish between them but then I don't think the law has a place in regulating the reading/watching of its citizens," said a 23-year-old postgrad student. A 43-year-old gay male said simply, "I would repeal obscenity laws."

More men felt that, from a practical standpoint, to make a valid legal distinction was an impossible task. Said a man who invoked Orwell's *1984*, "If an individual wants to contemplate a distinction between erotica and pornography, that's their business. However, if society, and especially the law, wants to draw such a distinction, and then treat the two categories differently, then the two categories must be objectively defined. I do not believe that there is any practical way to do this." "Though I think there is a distinction," a 27-year-old single man remarked, "it is far too subtle, too personal, too subjective to be defined by law, and so [they] should be treated the same way." Even if society tried to make a legal distinction, a 20-year-old Canadian student indicated, "Makers of pornography will start to classify their work as erotica and the two begin to merge. So I don't think there is a distinction between the two and there shouldn't be one."

Some men felt the law should treat porn and erotica differently. "I don't think erotica requires as much regulation," remarked a married Canadian professor who avoided porn. A 29-year-old mechanical engineer expressed some concern about violent pornography, while a 34-year-old technical writer felt existing laws should be more strictly enforced: "Restrictions seem to be getting lax. By the time my son is an adult, soft porn and erotica may be freely flowing from commercial television and other media, as it does on the Internet. I don't think that's a very appealing concept, and I think it should be curtailed." A 60-year-old man suggested different treatment by society, but not by law, probably worked best: "Yes, I think the two should be treated differently by society, but I'm not sure how we organize a normative structure to handle all of this. I think informal norms can go a long way, rather than turning to laws."

A professor in France described the issues in Europe:

> Nobody should care about erotica as a problem. Advertising *is* erotica (at least in France). As far as pornography is concerned, there are laws; some are OK, some are hypocritical. In France you may not represent a member of the church in porn movies. And this is a true problem, as for instance watching nuns making love is the Italians' kick. It is lawful [apparently he meant available] in Italy, where pornography is curiously prohibited (but sold publicly), but unlawful in France, where pornography is permitted. Now on the other hand, European laws should nowadays be the same all over Europe. So what is the next step? French freedom of lovemaking, but with no priests involved, or Italian abstinence, with nuns banging themselves all over the place? Ask a lawyer!

More than one man who advocated more control of pornography admitted that either he did not know how to accomplish this, or it simply wasn't going to happen. A 56-year-old professor, who defined pornography as depictions of sex with an unequal power balance, said, "To the extent that pornography perpetuates uneven distribution and control, I believe it should be controlled. But who decides what its effect is, and

how should it be controlled? These are questions I have no answer for."
A married Black man said he thought erotica and porn should be
treated differently (although he seemed to like both), "but they won't
be. In the eyes of society and the law, a naked body is a naked body."

Most of the men, however, were closer to the 28-year-old employee
of an alternative sex magazine who said he saw a distinction, but not
one around which laws could be fashioned. As to whether the difference warranted their being treated differently, he said, "I don't believe
they should be. One would think that we would be able to take off the
white collars so long after Plymouth Rock."

Given that most men thought pornography was not harmful to
women or men, and that society and the law should treat it no differently from erotica, did they feel it should be controlled at all? Perhaps
surprisingly, nearly three-quarters of the men in the survey thought
pornography required some control.

By far the largest concern was exposure of children to pornography.
Quite a few men said this was the *only* control they sought. Despite
wide agreement on the necessity of controlling when or if children and
minors could see pornography, there was quite a bit of *dis*agreement
about what shape that control should take.

Several wanted to keep pornography away from anyone under 18.
"Pornography shouldn't be sold to minors," said a 37-year-old single
man. Another man who thought no one under 18 should either appear
in porn or view it, explained, "They're not ready for it yet." A gay man
who did not specify an age said, "pornography is something intensely
adult and should be viewed by people who have the maturity and life
experiences to understand that pornography is a fantasy, not a slice of
reality. Generally speaking, I believe young people don't have the maturity to understand the difference." Some of these men admitted, however, as a 24-year-old engineering student put it, "Of course they will
still be able to somehow or another get their hands on something
pornographic, but it should be a little hard to get."

As I have noted, these recommendations were at variance with the
men's personal experiences. Almost all of them had been exposed to

pornography when they were younger than 18. Whether they felt their own early exposures had harmed them in any way or they were merely echoing public consensus was not a question I asked them directly, but such contradictions demand further examination in the public debate over pornography.

Several men suggested that age restrictions on pornography could be eased *if* there were better and more widespread sex education. "I think that sexuality should be encouraged at an early age, but it should not come without some sort of contextualization, some sort of education as to its function and role(s)," remarked a married bisexual male. "Without context, many pornographic images are degrading, violent, at least confusing. I think that age has something to do with wisdom, but I also think that education should be encouraged at an earlier age—not just the birds and bees, but how sexual relations affect people, what such relations mean, etc."

Parents should exercise more control over what their children see, some men felt. "Parents should be able to control access to it by their minor children," said a married law student with two kids. What was ironic about this common attitude is that many children apparently are first exposed to pornography they find among their parents' effects. This was happening long before the advent of the Internet, which has gotten so much attention in recent years. In a sense, pornography from the Internet may still seem "out there," an alien phenomenon, in a way that pornography found at home may not be. If a child finds porn in his parents' closet or drawers, he or she more likely interprets this as a sign of general interest, if not approval, on the part of parents and/or society than if the material comes over the wires and airwaves from a distant and unknown location.

Very few men thought there should be any restrictions on pornographic content after the age of 18. The few who did referred to degrading, harmful, or violent pornography, as well as kiddie porn and bestiality. Despite their seeming specificity, even these objections did not present a united front. Several men expressed concern about violent imagery without saying it should be banned or controlled. A 56-

year-old married professor said, "I have some concerns about kiddie porn, bestiality, and torture, but it is much better to view these things than to do them. If porn can act as a substitute for the real thing, then it should be allowed." A 22-year-old Canadian software engineer wanted to outlaw "porn featuring *actual* violent acts, or featuring children in violent or sexual acts because the *making* of such porn should not be encouraged."

A small number of men favored controlling pornography by keeping sales outlets segregated to certain parts of town. "I think it is important to keep away from children, and also restricted to certain areas, so families and people who hate it can stroll about on the street without having it rubbed in their noses," said one. "It shouldn't be displayed where it can make people uncomfortable," the 56-year-old professor agreed.

Among those who avoided pornography for political reasons, a Canadian professor said it should be available only in special stores with discreet advertising, and off limits to minors, but "I don't think it should be censored." A federal officer in Canada said "Written stuff should be unregulated; other laws concerning coercion are probably adequate in the field of film. Children should not participate in any way."

Men who identified themselves as addicted or once having been addicted to pornography had mixed feelings about control. One said, "Children should not be involved in porn, *period*. That includes porn depicting children, involving children in the sale or distribution of porn, or providing it to children." He also thought "other forms of degrading and harmful porn should also be banned," but he willingly admitted that "it's hard for me to be objective." However, a 39-year-old virgin whose "whole life has been subsumed by pornography," which tended "to accentuate my alienation from people, especially women," wanted to see availability "loosened up for adults." Though his life might have been better if he had not had pornography, "I cannot make a judgment as to the positive or negative effects of porn on others." He agreed that pornography should be "rigorously kept from the experience of children," however.

Only Henry, who believed he had been molested by men in his childhood and was fascinated and appalled by his father's hard-core pornography until he forswore it in high school, called for total sanctions. "I think pornography should be outlawed and its production and distribution vigorously pursued and prosecuted with large penalties and jail time. Neither my wife nor I believe pornography is worthy of protection under the First Amendment, nor do we believe it is protected under the First Amendment."

A few men said pornography should not be controlled at all. "I think pornography should be available freely and without restriction," said a British student, 21. "It's only today's society which has caused our repulsion to all things sexual. If society wasn't so hung up about its own sexuality, it wouldn't have these problems. Those who were interested in certain sexual practices could get on with them quite happily, and so could everyone else."

Although he offered many other arguments against the control of porn and the notion of its harms, a 35-year-old programmer, married with two kids, said, "The simplest reason that I am opposed to restricting pornography is that I like it. This is not a frivolous argument. One of the basic principles underlying our society and our legal system is that people should be left alone to do what they want. The law restricts people's actions only to the extent necessary to protect the rights of others." A 33-year-old bisexual male picked up the argument from there: "If it were something dangerous, I might feel differently. Since I think porn is benign, I see no reason to control it. In fact, I'd rather see my children looking at porn than watching murder and violence." A 23-year-old gay man said information may be controlled in matters pertaining to national security and concluded: "Porn is not a national security issue."

Several men felt that trying to control pornography would create more problems than it solved. "Controlling porn is a Pandora's box, where someone is making decisions for others," said a 43-year-old accountant, married 13 years. "While the acts in certain porn (kiddie porn and so-called snuff films) may be illegal, once you allow interference with any type of information (print, film, electronic, magnetic, opto-magnetic), you are trying to accomplish the impossible." A 49-year-old software engineer in Britain, no great fan of porn, said, "Absolutely not. 'Control is never a means to any useful end; it is a means only to more control'—William Burroughs, in *Naked Lunch*, and perhaps my favorite quotation from a pornographic book."

Two men who supported no restrictions on pornography of any kind said even minors should have open access. "My feeling today is that porn should be handled like any other stuff: porn movies just like regular movies, porn magazines just like other magazines, etc.," said a bisexual software engineer, 25 and single. "Even age requirements seem silly to me. What exactly do we gain by prohibiting little Johnny from reading 'Busty Babes in Bondage'? A lot of prudery and superstition has been given classier names and just sticks around in disguise." A 21-year-old computer consultant, heterosexual but "bi-curious," felt the tension and secrecy sparked an interest that just wouldn't be there if porn were out in the open: "Even with children, do you think if pornographic magazines were not hidden off in the back shelves, a child would ever attempt to 'get away' with looking at them? How many children, if shown *Debbie Does Dallas* as well as *The Mighty Morphin Power Rangers*, would choose to watch *Debbie* a second time?"

The childhood experiences of at least some of the men in the survey suggested he was right. Many who first saw pornography at age 3, 5, or 8 had very little interest in it and forgot about it until puberty struck, *unless* someone else (such as excited playmates or horrified adults) made a big deal about it. Pornography appeared to have little or no natural allure for at least some small kids; it was the behavior of other people around it that got their attention.

Perhaps with that in mind, a 27-year-old bisexual man with male preference sounded a clear call for openness:

I do not feel that pornography should be controlled at all. Since sex is the beginning of life, it should be celebrated in life. People's (read [as] religious zealots') attitudes to sex make me sick. Why we as a society depict the human body as something that should be covered up and shamed, and why something as basic as sex should be hidden in darkened closets and bedrooms, is totally beyond me. I feel that hiding sex from people (during the development of self and others) has a direct correlation on the number of violent "sex offenders" in our society.

Pornography and Violence

Antipornography activists routinely link pornography with violence. Porn depicts violence against women, they assert, and it inevitably leads to violence against real women. How do men who like pornography respond to these assertions?

"*What* violent acts?" asked a 32-year-old. "The producers of porn magazines and videos are careful not to depict anything that a crime victim might say in a lawsuit might have inspired a violent crime. I have *never* seen violence against women depicted in an adult video, or in magazines. Even men-on-men violence is very rare." He noted that to listen to antiporn activists, "you would think that most pornography was about violence, rape, and molesting children. Anyone familiar with porn knows this is completely false." Stories written mostly by amateurs, posted to the Internet, and therefore not purchased or sold for commercial gain, were a different matter: "There are stories about rape and sexual torture to be found, and they are very much a turnoff for me."

A 41-year-old computer programmer noted that violence of any kind was rare in hard-core porn, somewhat more common in soft-core, but still light in comparison with the violence in mainstream films and literature:

> There is very little violence in visually oriented hard-core pornography. I have personally seen one bondage-S&M video which had very mild violence. I'd give it a PG for the violent content: It had nudity but no sex. The rest of the hard-core videos that I've seen had absolutely no violence, just sex and nudity. There is of course some violent hard-core pornographic literature—see some of the writings of the Marquis De Sade for examples. These are not readily available; you usually have to special order them. None of the adult book shops that I've been to carry this kind of stuff. (My copy of De Sade's *Juliette* was special ordered from Barnes & Noble—not an adult book outlet!) Once in a while I will get aroused while reading a violent passage in *Juliette*; there was a sadistic passage or two in Anne Rice's vampire novels that gave me an erection, as well. Usually I prefer hard-core sex and nudity to this sort of tripe. While violence in hard-core pornography is rare, this is not the case in soft-core pornography. The Anne Rice vampire books that I've mentioned several times are an extreme. Even the much milder violence in Bret Ellis's *American Psycho* is quite extreme for soft-core. More typical for soft-core pornography is a level of violence comparable to the movie *The Maltese Falcon*, i.e., a PG-13 level of violence. The emphasis is still on sex and nudity.

A minority of the men in the survey acknowledged being aroused by violent depictions of sex, particularly in certain carefully defined and limited contexts; some had been inspired to act out quasi-violent scenarios; and the vast majority agreed that a person can consent to violent sex. But not a single one could point to an instance in which he personally saw evidence to support the thesis that consumption of pornography *leads* to violence.

A 41-year-old man who liked photos of naked women and couples such as those in *Penthouse*, as well as soft- and hard-core videos and what he called the "'good' sadistic sex" of Anne Rice's vampire novels, offered himself as an extreme counter-example to the antiporn thesis. "I'm about as non-violent as you can get," he said. He hadn't hit, pushed, slapped, or shoved anyone since the age of 14 when he shoved another boy who was a brat. "Everyone in the neighborhood except the boy's mom went out of their way to praise me—nevertheless, I felt very badly about it." Since then, he said, he had been assaulted at least six times, and "I have never raised a fist even in self-defense. I'd much rather run than fight."

A 28-year-old computer student felt the same: "I am an avid consumer of pornography, and I think I'm about as gentle a person as you're likely to find. I literally feel bad when I have to kill an insect, and I certainly wouldn't strike anyone or do violence to them unless I were defending myself." As to the issue of pornography's effect upon others, he said:

> There is a "lot" of pornography out there, and I suspect if it really did cause people to become more violent, we'd have considerably more violence than we do now. I live in a community of about 40,000. I estimate that there are roughly 700 videos in the store I use most often, and there are two other stores which have a few hundred each. Many (over 50%) of these porn videos are rented at any given time. Even with all this pornography circulating in the community, we have a very low incidence of rape and sexual assault. If I remember correctly, there were three rapes in our community last year.

"It's far more likely that feminists themselves provoke men to acts of violence!" another man joked. "Seriously, car chases, gunplay, fisticuffs and so forth are way more prevalent [in regular movies], and there's no serious movement to ban them."

"There may be some correlation [between porn use and violent behavior], which I have not seen evidence of," granted a 43-year-old accountant, "but I have no reason to believe there is an *ad causum* relationship." A 20-year-old Canadian student interested in a career in sex counseling challenged the link on the same grounds: "Just because there is a correlation between two factors, like pornography use and violence, does not mean that one causes the other. Feminists want to prove that pornography causes harm towards women and when you want to find a certain result, you'll interpret the data to give that result."

One man said even if a link could be shown, it wouldn't matter: "People having cars increases the chance of car accidents. Does this mean that when 99.9% of people can drive their car for a year without killing anyone, we should ban cars because of the .1% of people who are incompetent or unlucky? Of course not. It means we should deal with the .1%." He suggested the "tiny minority" whose propensity for violence might be activated or heightened by porn should be rehabilitated with psychological assistance or given "long-term jail sentences to protect the rest of us."

A number of men not only had no personal proof to back up the feminist thesis, but said they believed the opposite to be true. "I have never seen this and believe just the opposite," wrote a 37-year-old bisexual, married for 15 years. "Repression breeds violence. The more sexually liberated countries of Europe have far less rape." A 33-year-old software support specialist, married eight years to his only sex partner, agreed that "pornography can act as a cathartic experience and reduce one's propensity for violence." He then added: "One wonders why Andrea Dworkin doesn't go around killing and raping, since she spends so much time reading/watching and then writing about that devil porn."

A few men found the "porn leads to violence" thesis plausible but admitted they had never seen any evidence to support it. "Not myself," a 47-year-old Canadian who worked for the government responded. "I generally sympathize with the victim [but] I think the relationship between art and action is much more complex." A happily married oncologist said, "I am sure that some people who have violent fantasies or are prone to violence might be influenced this way. Note the kid who did the arson thing in response to Beavis and Butthead. There are a lot of weirdos in America."

A gay 31-year-old pilot said he didn't have any experience to back up the theory, but "concerning the human mind and sexuality, I do think this is possible." He went on to suggest, however, that pornography was only a small part of a "perpetual motion machine" in the media that concentrates on the human tendency toward violence. "When this portrayal is viewed by people who cannot separate themselves from or control their violent characteristics, it just adds to it." But to say a man is inspired by violent pornography to commit a crime "puts an unlikely amount of authority on pornography," he concluded.

Several men said the content or influence of pornography was beside the point. "I believe if you have a propensity to commit a violent act, then no amount of pornography will increase your violent acts," said a gay 27-year-old computer support technician. He had seen no connection between porn use and violence in any of his friends, straight or gay.

A 26-year-old writer and administrative employee said: "I've seen football players and other athletes bully people and beat them up. So why don't feminists attack the multibillion-dollar sports industry? Surely there's a more direct connection in people who beat people up professionally becoming violent than people having sex on film."

A casino security supervisor suggested the sources of violence lie deeper:

> I think the propensity for violence against the opposite sex comes from youth, perhaps from birth. I have seen young boys, as young as five or six, assaulting girls in a sexual manner. I would assume these same youths grow up to consume porn as part of their lifestyle. This would seem to support the feminists except out of the same age group we find boys heavily exposed to violence from westerns and crime movies and TV shows who do not employ violence in real life. The difference, I think, is that the westerns contained a message of respect for women and children.

Most of the time, men felt pornography could only reinforce a viewer's established tastes and tendencies, rather than influence him in a new direction. As a 22-year-old doctoral student in physics put it:

> I think that violent porn meets a kind of spiritual resistance in people who are opposed to violence (so it is perceived as a negative example), but that it reinforces the attitudes of people who aren't opposed to violence by putting it in context of sexual pleasure. I haven't met anybody who liked violence, so I can't really quote my experience. My own resentment for violence has strengthened after I was exposed to depictions of violence. However, I think people who like violence will like it more after exposure to a "positive" depiction of violence (showing violence as good or pleasurable), including that in porn.

More than one man recalled reports that pornography drove men such as Jeffrey Dahmer and Ted Bundy to their crimes. A 21-year-old math student who had had no sexual contact with others cited Bundy, "the killer/rapist whose criminal career supposedly sparked to life when he found a bunch of pornographic magazines in a dumpster." He worried that "pornography is really a way to vicariously dominate women—i.e., have them pose nude at one's command, as if they were some kind of sex slaves." But, he added, "I haven't gotten any more violent," and "I have not seen [evidence of the theory that pornography leads to violence] in my own life."

A divorced, 32-year-old computer consultant discounted Bundy as an example of any link between pornography and violence. "Curiously enough, while many use Ted Bundy as a case in which pornography 'forced' him to do his vile deeds, it should be noted that Ted Bundy once claimed Satan himself compelled him to his atrocities. Moreover, when police searched Mr. Bundy's car, they didn't find pornography in it, they found cheerleader magazines." His conclusion? "In my view, people who 'blame' pornography for their actions are only seeking to avoid personal responsibility for their actions."

Other men accepted a potential gray area somewhat short of the certainty that porn causes violence. There is room for confusion among some consumers of porn, especially if they're young and inexperienced, suggested a 23-year-old bisexual male who had been active both in women's studies and in men's groups:

I think pornography can serve as a confusing element in how one conceptualizes violence, sex, or both. In other words, I know men who have said that they thought that if a girl said no to sex, she was just asking you to push harder and then told me how pornography reinforced this attitude. Or I know of other guys who respected the decisions women made about sex, but somehow felt they were missing something because porn suggested an aspect of male/female relationships which they weren't experiencing.

Like all the others, however, he added: "Personally, I've never felt that porn has increased my propensity for employing violence, mainly because I have a strong aversion to violence."

Perhaps the firmest dismissal of the porn-causes-violence thesis came from an Englishman, a software engineer with five children:

I reject the implication that there is some sort of "argument" about pornography put out by feminists. I do not grant them even that minimal level of intellectual honesty or respectability. The "arguments" I have read are a palpable tissue of lies, distortions, non sequiturs, special pleadings, and outright gender-biased hate speech. I don't believe even those making them actually believe them. To me, they are simply another example of the "Big Lie" technique of the late unlamented Herr Goebbels—that if you yell it loudly enough, and phrase it extremely enough, somebody will believe it. On the other hand, I have read both the report of the (British) Royal Commission on Pornography, and a condensed version of the U.S. report (by Ed Meese, wasn't it?). These were two serious, detailed, and meticulous studies, and they both concluded what in both cases the majority of the investigators did not want to conclude: that there is no evidence whatsoever that the consumption of pornography is harmful; that there is no good social grounds for regulating it; and that the harm that is sometimes caused by its production or distribution is a direct consequence of its marginalisation by society. I will not accept, now or ever, the right of any other person, especially women, and especially feminist women, to define or control my sexuality. There is nothing to debate: my body; my self.

Can Violence Be a Turn-On?

When men were asked if they had ever been sexually aroused by violence in pornography, there was less unanimity. A clear majority, almost two-thirds, said without qualification that they never had found violence arousing. Many added it specifically turned them off. But a minority said that porn which included violence had aroused them.

Much of the disagreement was due to differing interpretations of the term "violent." The survey did not define it, nor did it distinguish between consensual or non-consensual violence, which was the crucial point both for men who said they were not turned on by violence and for those who said they could be. "I have been excited by some fantasies which involve S&M," a 34-year-old English software developer and doctoral student said, "but I do not regard these as violent in that they presuppose 1) consent and enjoyment, 2) ritualized infliction of strictly controlled and limited pain, and 3) unrealistic and unbelievable fantasy."

Remarked a 38-year-old man, married 15 years: "Depends on whether you'd consider bondage and dominance to be violent. I've had several partners, including my feminist wife, who enjoyed light bondage and simulated rape. Depictions of those definitely are a turn-on. My experience is that the strongest women are most stimulated by being dominated."

A 36-year-old male pointed out that much of what appears violent in pornography is actually a very controlled form of fantasy play:

> I get turned on by pictures of classic role-playing such as "bondage," "S&M," including people being whipped, etc., and "forced" although it is really fake and they are playing; it is consensual in nature. It even feels good in real life to play around with this type of stuff a bit. This is not what I'd call "violence."

Wrote a 23-year-old bisexual who preferred women:

Violence can be erotic, but I think it's important to distinguish between consensual and non-consensual. I know I like some violent things to be done to me that turn me on. So, as far as porn goes, there are violent scenes that turn me on because I have a fascination in the physical sensation of pain—I find the tension between pain and pleasure very erotic. But it all has to be in the context of consent. If I see a rape scene where the victim is saying "no, don't do this," I don't like it and it doesn't turn me on. But most of the "rape" scenes in porn have the victim excited and asking for more. If the acting job or picture is convincing, then it's a turn-on because I really believe that the person does want that to happen to them.

Another man recalled an instance of violence in a soft-core film that eventually turned him on because the character's display of pleasure was so convincing:

I just saw a movie that was made in Hong Kong called *Sex and Zen*. There was a scene where a fairly depraved rich woman commanded the hero to beat her with a bull whip. At first, I was not interested at all. I thought: okay, there's something for everyone in this movie, now let's get on to the next thing. But the whipping scene went on too long for me to ignore it; I had to sit and watch it all and take an attitude. And after the initial uninterest tinged with disgust, I began to connect, faintly, with the wild pleasure that the female actress was portraying in the course of being whipped. I watched how her long brown hair flew and floated, the way she arched and undulated her body, her seeming ecstasy, and I kind of liked it. Do you understand? I was connecting to her pleasure, not indulging any of mine. I was starting to experience the action as she seemed to experience it, not as I would have.

Closely related to the idea of the consensual use of force was the appeal of being the object of such force—focusing on the person who chooses to be the "victim," rather than upon the person who "imposes" the violence. The key word here is "submission"; some men said the "submissiveness" of one of the performers fired their libido, rather than the violence *per se*. A 34-year-old Englishman wrote: "When I have observed depictions of violence in pornographic materials, any additional arousal, apart from the nudity, has been from the elements of submissiveness portrayed, rather than any elements of violence suggested."

The question of consent has been a thorny one for feminists who oppose pornography. Because the activities that occur in pornographic films—let alone in such jobs as nude dancing and prostitution—seem unimaginable to many commentators, feminist criticism has taken some odd twists in order to "prove" that women cannot *actually* consent to such acts. For instance, it has been argued that limited professional and financial options drive women to this kind of work to such an extent that they do not have free choice.

When and how can a person be said to have (or to lose) free choice? Is it possible to consent to being the object of violent activities—including sex that includes pain, for example? Although most men in the survey agreed that a person can consent to violent treatment, there was considerable disagreement about just what that meant.

Many simply said that consent to anything was theoretically possible, although they had no personal experience of, or interest in, violent sex. "If some people enjoy S&M, why not? It's their business," said a 32-year-old French Canadian. "Sure, anyone can, man or woman," a 44-year-old gay computer analyst commented. "People do the strangest things for sexual gratification. Women can be just as rough as men."

"Yes, obviously," an English software engineer agreed: "S&M clubs exist; there are advertisements in the porn magazines, and this evidently is part of some people's makeup. However, let's put this in perspective: You're in a lot more danger of coming to actual harm playing football or other violent contact sports."

Somewhat more firmly than others, a 42-year-old professor of computer science said that in theory anything is possible for grown adults:

> I think that in a free society adults would be able to consent to many acts that are now illegal. I see nothing wrong with someone consenting (on the assumption that it is somehow *informed* consent) to be the object of violence. I can see no reason to distinguish between genders. Can a person

make informed consent to be killed? I'd like to think so. Can a person make informed consent to be tortured? I'd like to think that too. I know of people who find it sexually satisfying to be beaten (even quite severely). If they can give informed consent and can pay the medical bills, that is (I think) their decision.

Some men added that consenting to violence was utterly mystifying to them. "I suppose that one can consent to violence being done to them, and I am sure that there are people for whom this is sexually fulfilling," a 24-year-old audio engineer said. "However, I have no idea why, and would never want to participate in such a thing."

Perhaps, several men theorized, people consent to being the object of violent sex only when they're not normal. "Yes, they may consent; in my humble opinion they're nuts, that's their problem," said a 29-year-old Navy vet and mechanical engineering student. "Those women probably already have had a rock-bottom self-image or a spirit broken by someone in their past," was the opinion of a 34-year-old technical writer. "I suppose that certain sick people can consent to pain," the symphonic musician said. "I consent to a moment of pain when I donate blood, but that's not for sexual reasons. What's that bumper sticker say? Pain Sucks!"

A man who had been sexually abused by women as a child had a more gentle and ambiguous view of such tastes:

I think she can invite it—and if she can invite it, I think she *can* consent to it—but this would happen if that's the only way she thinks she can get her needs met, and I think it does happen, quite often. It's pathetic and tragic. It isn't right. But it does happen. And it isn't the violent partner's fault, necessarily. As for men, it works both ways. There are guys that really get off on being brutalized by women, emotionally and physically, and there are women who love dishing it out.

Some men recognized a mixture of fascination and repulsion with violent sexuality in both themselves and society at large. "Sure, I guess men and women can consent to be the object of violence," a physician said. "I don't know why either would." He thought the sex in the movie *9-1/2 Weeks* was "pretty awful that way" and the relationship "clearly screwed up." On the other hand, the book and movie had both been popular, he obviously had read and seen them, "so what does that mean? (But I recognize it's not acceptable)."

A few men based their affirmative response on the fact that they knew people who did such things. "Sure, absolutely, I've met people who really go in for things like that," a 25-year-old bisexual said. "Go figure." He observed that pain and pleasure can be mixed in odd ways. "Had a one-night stand recently where she kept telling me to bite down hard on her nipples even after I'd gotten to the point where I was afraid of causing tissue damage or biting the damn things off. Seemed violent to me." Observed a 38-year-old man who had been married 15 years, "I've known women who liked spankings and anal sex, both of which seem inordinately painful to me! Anyone can consent to anything, I suppose."

Others based their "yes" on personal experience. A 21-year-old self-described masochist described his own activities:

> I'm really into pain, for some reason, as a form of stress release. It's something I can control, usually. The "razor blade thing" is a form of masochism where I have a girl pretty much play with razors on my skin. I'm not talking about exposing internal organs or anything, just designs or whatever comes into their head. I guess I learned about it from watching cuts and wounds bleed when I was a kid. It sort of fascinated me. When I found out the tremendous exhilaration gained from doing it to yourself or on purpose, I got hooked. It doesn't have to be a sexual thing every time, but sometimes when you're with the right person and you're totally exposed, both physically and emotionally through pain, things just sort of click. The pain starts as a big rush of adrenaline. That's the initial response from the body as well as the arching of the back and tension in all the muscles. It's very sensual. I guess it would be comparable to watching your partner's reaction to giving oral sex. I really get off from watching a girl writhe in ecstasy and get all tense and arch her back. It's sort of the same thing.

When the pain stops, then there's that cool rush of burning feeling going to the spot where it happened.

In sum, men who said *Yes, a person can consent to being the object of a violent sex act* employed nearly the same rationale as the few who said *No, he or she cannot.* Maybe pornography consumers and antiporn feminists believe much the same things about human nature and what it can or should be; they just happen to use different language about the same phenomena, or they envision very different activities when they use shared words like "consent" or "violence" (which can mean anything from armed, forcible rape to friendly bondage and spankings which are mutually chosen). Some feminists have gone so far as to suggest that to stare at a woman in public is a violent act (or an aggressive and invasive one, at least).

Men who admitted to being aroused by violence also voiced highly ambivalent feelings about the content as well as their reaction. Sam, who yearned to devote himself to a spiritual life but felt addicted to porn, said, "I am aroused by seeing pain inflicted, a fact which disturbs me." He added, "My confidence in my own humanity is somewhat reassured by the fact that real suffering on the part of an unwilling victim repulses me."

Another man, who had been sexually abused by several women, had mixed responses to expressions of violence in sexual material:

Yes [I found it arousing]. It was the forcefulness of the way the man was imposing himself on the woman and her expressions of pain and violation giving way to arousal and orgasm—this was in an audio tape. It became disgusting to me and I threw away the tape. I was so ashamed of myself that I really looked at why I had that arousal around the violence. I've healed from it. But I think I was using the arousal as a way of acting out my anger at the women that sexually abused me when I was a child and couldn't resist their sexual invasions of me. I'm healing from that, too.

A 22-year-old physics grad student who reported one serious sexual relationship in his life, described his complex reaction to violent pornography, which incorporates most of the reactions to violent porn we have seen:

> Yes, I have been turned on by acts of violence in porn. It is difficult to say what exactly was arousing in these depictions. Certainly the sexual context was playing a role; I would say that reading a scene of violence, I anticipated the sexual acts that would follow and perceived them as the real content of the scene. However, I feel aroused also by the display of power. Usually I would be appalled, though, because almost all the scenes (which, incidentally, involved mostly violence against women) would show physical suffering, and that would destroy the illusion of "playfulness." I think that the audience is supposed to identify with the dominator, rejoicing in the feeling of power (including sexual power) over the submissive. This feeling itself is repulsive to me, even though I can share it.

Thus, like most men he was repulsed by the violence, but like others he was turned on. Perhaps he was turned on mainly by incidental elements (the sex and the anticipation of it), rather than the violence itself.

But most men insisted they were not at all aroused by violence. "No, no, no!" said a symphonic musician, married 26 years, "I hate violence, in everyday life, in mainstream movies, in pornography, in everything." In his household rating system, only a "PG-50" movie made the grade. *Schindler's List* was one movie that did not rate a PG-50, "and I went for many reasons [he is Jewish] and put up with the violence." He said he would never see *Reservoir Dogs* or *Pulp Fiction*, or even the "erotic thriller" *Exotica*. "In my experience, an erotic thriller means two minutes of nudity and 60 minutes of violence. I have never been aroused by scenes of violence in pornography, and I doubt I ever will."

"I suspect I would be so repelled by the violence, there's not a chance in hell that such behavior would be eroticized," agreed a 60-year-old married man. "Also the repulsion would cancel out any other elements of the situation being a turn-on." A 39-year-old programmer called violence a "strong turn-off. In fact, I don't really like it when the women spank themselves. Sex is not about hitting and hurting." "I find it sickening even if the violence is obviously acting," said a 47-year-old journalist from New Zealand. "Violent acts do not turn me on," agreed a 38-year-old Australian, "in fact I would avoid it vehemently." The French professor of philosophy agreed: "Never, and when in some movies 'actors' play rapes, it turns me down! Violence to women is something I cannot stand (neither to men, as a matter of fact)." Many other survey participants made comments in this vein.

When asked if they had ever committed a violent act against a significant other, three-fourths of the men surveyed said they had never been violent toward a significant other, and less than a quarter could report any kind of violent act. A few cited an extenuating circumstance such as self-defense (they hurt their partner in a reflexive move during a fight when the other person was the aggressor), or "violence" in the form of consensual sex. Some men had overcome earlier psychological handicaps: Although they had witnessed, been victims of, or performed violent acts while growing up, they managed to avoid them as adults.

"Despite the occasional desire, I have never hit anyone I was involved with," said a man whose personal history included a mother who had struck both him and his sister when they were children. "Never," the 28-year-old computer student, married seven years, declared; "It is unconscionable. I cannot imagine myself being violent against anyone, particularly my wife." A 22-year-old Canadian software engineer who reported violence in his family as he was growing up declared, "I never have committed a violent act toward anyone, at least not after the age of 12."

The men were asked whether the general level of violence in their lives had risen during the time they were using pornography in large amounts or on a regular basis. They were asked to assess the levels not simply of physical violence, but of arguments, tensions, and misunderstandings. A 22-year-old software engineer in Canada, who was working on a bachelor of science degree and cited one sex partner in his life, summed it up for most of them:

My consumption of porn has been pretty steady over the last 8-9 years, so it's hard to say. Certainly I have had little or no physical violence in my life. I haven't noticed any increase in tension or arguments, or misunderstandings either. If anything, my life is much easier and happier now than before I started using porn. (Not that I'm implying a causal relationship; it's just that there are too many other factors worth considering.)

A 24-year-old audio engineer echoed that position: "I tend to be a very calm person and porn only seems to have a calming effect on me, perhaps because it more often than not relieves any sexual tension."

If there was stress or violence in their lives, a few men said, it could not be blamed on their use of pornography. A divorced public administrator, 48, declared, "There was no violence in my relationship(s). Arguments, tension, misunderstandings, god yes, but to blame this on pornography (which generally depicts pleasure/enjoyment?) is rather farfetched. 'Sorry we had the wretched misunderstanding yesterday, darling. It's the pornography.'" "Work," a 26-year-old administrative employee observed dryly, "is a much more direct cause of emotional and physical violence."

Plenty of men argued the opposite of the question posed by the survey: They believed that pornography use and violence were inversely related. "Actually, sometimes I think pornography has reduced tension, because it is a way of obtaining sexual release, if that means anything," wrote a 21-year-old virgin, "and in this sense helps to clear my head." A 33-year-old bisexual computer consultant (preference for women) agreed: "If anything, the 'violence' decreased, probably because I was able to blow off extra tension using porn and masturbating. This tends to make working out difficult relationship issues easier."

A married man suggested pornography could serve as a refuge from tension and fights:

Sometimes during periods of distance when my wife was actually being physically violent towards me, I had to retreat from her and perhaps use more porno, masturbate more, but that's backwards from your question;

i.e., it seems that my being subjected to physical and emotional violence by her led to more viewing of porno, instead of the other way around! She likes to slap, and pinch, and kick. No, she won't go to a counselor. She just blows up at some things.

A couple of men said the level of tension or violence had escalated in their lives, but they could not attribute this to pornography. An equally small number of men said that violence or tension increased somewhat in their lives during the time they were using pornography, but they found no reason to blame the porn for that. A 22-year-old physics grad student allowed that "tension and frustration" had increased in his life, but like many of the other men, he believed the relationship was reversed: "When tension and frustration increase, I tend to consume more porn. There is no physical violence in my life, and my propensity to violence didn't change."

The only "violence" anyone could attribute to porn use was consensual, exploratory, and directed at the self, as in the case of the 21-year-old enthusiast of razor blades. Several men said that while violent or quasi-violent sex acts held some appeal, they would never pursue them unless their partner expressed interest too.

"I suppose I'd like to act out some violent scenarios, such as spanking or bondage," said a married man with two kids. "But I never have. None of my partners ever expressed interest in these things, and I never suggested it. And despite my interest in these things, it never occurred to me to search for a partner who was also interested in them." He added that, "however you view my wants, they aren't the result of things that I've seen depicted in pornography. They come from deep inside me, and largely predate my exposure to them in pornography."

"I've had fantasies about wanting to rip a woman's clothes off," a biochemistry grad student related. "I even had a fantasy where I wanted to jump out of a closet and do that to a girlfriend. But I've never had a desire to do anything in terms of forcing them into something that they wouldn't want to do."

A physician who had said "I do not enjoy the violence in pornography, and wish it wasn't there," said something a little different later:

> The only semi-violent aspect in pornography which is somewhat arousing
> is when an attractive, strong guy is with a woman who is reluctant to have
> sex, kind of forces himself on her (not violently, but clearly coercively) and
> she is overwhelmed by attraction, arousal (of course she was always fight-
> ing this), gives in, and enjoys it. Again, this is not so much violence as coer-
> cion. I do not do this myself, because I do believe it is not only un-PC, but
> not right. No means no means no. Now, occasionally I may have tried to
> seduce my partner when she has expressed lack of interest, but again, even-
> tually no means no, and I have never been violent or physically coercive.

If anything in this man's description of an arousing situation seems
improper or brutish, let alone "un-PC," we might remind ourselves that
it describes the sort of encounters that routinely take place in romance
novels written for, purchased by, and read by women in the millions,
and apparently regarded as "highly romantic."

"I doubt I would ever propose such a thing, unless it were to be acted
out on my body," said a married man. He recalled a friend telling him
about a woman who, in the middle of their first sexual encounter, told
him to hit her. I can't come if you don't, she told him; well, I can't come
if I *do*, he replied. The evening was a washout.

Quite a few men suggested any urge toward violent sex usually consisted of the desire to be the "victim," not the perpetrator. "I think I
have wondered about getting fucked by a guy with a huge dick, and liking to think I'd enjoy it," a 36-year-old publicist said. "But I've never
done this."

Some men who had fantasized about or actually indulged in violent
sex, added that they could not be certain they got the idea from pornography. As a 38-year-old man put it:

> Yes, I have had the desire to act out violent sexual scenarios, in the case
> of bondage, dominance, and simulated rape—although whether those
> impulses are attributable to porn or not is debatable. I think every male
> has such fantasies, to some extent. In terms of importing such acts into
> real life—only after determining that a woman wouldn't be offended by it.

"I enjoy spanking," said a 24-year-old, married history student, but, "even that is only because of partners who have enjoyed it, not because of porn." Asked to explain, he said:

> We were having sex doggie-style, and I smacked her butt. I guess it's more like swatting than spanking. More startlement than pain. She moaned, and I could tell she was turned on. She never asked me to do it at all. Every now and then I throw in a little swat, and she responds well. Occasionally she is not feeling playful during sex and will politely ask me not to do it.

A 22-year-old Canadian software engineer who had had one sex partner said:

> The most violent scenario I've acted out is bondage of arms and/or legs tied to the bed. The bonds were always so loose that I or my partner could have slipped out at any time, and were more for fantasy than anything else. It was fun, but we haven't done it again. It wasn't *that* much fun. I'm not even sure we got that idea from porn; after all, everyone talks about tying limbs to the bed during sex.

Often, violent sexual play occurred only when the men let their partners take the lead—either because they were afraid to volunteer their own fantasies, the idea of violent play had never occurred to them (at least with a particular partner), or they just simply felt it was more proper to leave it up to the other person. Several men said they were not interested in violent or quasi-violent scenarios themselves, but had obliged sex partners who were. "No," responded a 40-year-old British man who had been married seven years and had occasional girlfriends. "On the other hand, my wife likes to be dominated occasionally, and porn at least provides a few role models so that I know how a dom is supposed to act." His wife liked to be spanked and whipped. "I don't take any direct pleasure in this, only the anticipation of what will happen afterwards. I certainly don't like pain. I've intimated a few times that it might be fun if she tied me up, but the only time she tried it (with another male present) I couldn't take it seriously and simply regarded it as a challenge to escape as soon as possible." He allowed as how the presence of one of his wife's occasional lovers might have affected his reactions. "Another bout with just her and myself might well fall just as flat, but I'd like to try."

A classics professor recalled, "the one time that there was sort of a fantasy rape scenario—and I would only want it to be as purely consensual fantasy play—was instigated by the woman. We were making love; it was completely silent, that was the thing. And she just suddenly was very passionate, but she started like, mock pushing me away, as though she had suddenly switched into this fantasy." He understood that he was supposed to respond forcefully. "Because, you know, she would've just said stop." So the encounter played out and seemed to work. "It was fine, it was really good. We didn't really talk about it afterwards."

A 36-year-old computer software specialist also indulged in "violent" playacting partly in response to his wife's OK:

> I've learned that it feels good sometimes to be direct and forceful and "take what I want" and that my wife digs it too when I do it to her. We play games about "rape." She has given me "rape rights" or something like that—I'm permitted to grab and force her whenever I feel like it, which is often amusing and I enjoy it and she seems to also, so this is even better than fantasies, in a way, because I get to go sort of inside how *she* feels, and she's *not* a faceless nameless fantasy zombie. Of course there are times when she does not go along with it. Sometimes I try and persist, other times not. Sometimes she wants to be taken outside of herself, she gets obsessed with something that's bugging her and I feel like I should just totally thrash her around (sexually, not violently) to take her mind off it, and it usually works. Perhaps I learned some of it by watching examples. But part of it comes from her and what she likes, which has nothing to do with pornography.

He said his wife probably didn't derive her ideas from pornography. She "started out thinking it's totally disgusting and still basically thinks so, and fights with me on occasion about porno-related subjects."

With the right partner, and an understanding between the players, violent sex can be fulfilling for certain men and women. A 35-year-old computer programmer said, "I'm not a violent person by nature and the thought of hitting someone for my pleasure was entirely foreign." Once he grasped that it served the pleasure of a particular woman, however, he accepted the idea:

> I view it sort of like any other thing you might do for a lover because you know it pleases them. For instance, some women like having their ears nibbled, others don't. So you might nibble on the ears of a lover who likes it to please her whether or not you derive any pleasure yourself because you know that if she's enjoying herself generally, so will you. Whipping a woman who accepts that by mutual consent isn't much different conceptually from nibbling on a woman's ears by mutual consent.

He explained the crucial issue of consent and how it works in BD/SM situations:

> One of the things you learn initially when you start getting involved with B&D, S&M, etc., is the subject of consent. First, you never do anything without some form of consent. Clearly someone who has a real gun to their head will consent to damn near anything but it isn't valid as far as I'm concerned. The second thing you learn is how to remove that consent when things have gone beyond your point of tolerance. You use a "safe word"—that is, a word or phrase that you can use, that isn't likely to be said in a "scene," that indicates to anyone else involved that you should stop immediately and that you really mean it. Saying "stop" or "no" in a fantasy rape might be construed as being part of the scene; saying "aardvark" can't be and would clearly tell your partner to stop.

Although this man said, "I get no pleasure at all from hitting a woman; I don't even get aroused and often find that any hard-on I had disappears," he could enjoy such an act when he knew the woman enjoyed it. He learned that if you give someone what she wants, she is more apt to give you what you want: "For instance, the first person I did S&M with, who taught me about it and safe words and such, gave me one hell of a blowjob while I was spanking her—better than the one she had given me earlier without the spanking. She was much more aroused, much more into the sex, and it enhanced everything." After that training, he could pursue a more elaborate scenario:

I watched a kidnap/rape scene in a movie once—and then shortly thereafter, I was meeting a lover in New Orleans for a weekend and I decided to do something similar to her. I knew already from previous get-togethers that she was into pain and bondage and we'd talked about a rape scene once. She had said that she liked wrestling and being held down and such and I asked her about spanking and the like. She admitted that she'd fantasized about it but never done it and we eventually decided to explore it together. So, since we were meeting at the airport, I told her that if her flight came in first, where to meet me. I then grabbed my luggage, came up to her, held an obviously toy gun to her and started giving her orders. We got into a taxi, got to the hotel, checked in, went up to the room (all the while I was holding the gun or had my hand in my pocket on the gun) and then I tied her to a chair in the room and started telling her about selling her into slavery to a white slaver, etc., and then "raped" her. There was a lot of verbal play—telling her I was going to sell her into white slavery but wanted to sample the goods first, things like that. Then there was grabbing her hair and pulling it, forcing her to go down on me. Grabbing her breasts, ripping her clothes off, slapping her face when she resisted, etc. About 2 hours later, we came out of the "scene" thoroughly spent and with smiles on our lips. She apparently knew most of what I'd planned in advance—in part from hints I'd dropped, in part from things I told her to make the set-up work (where to meet in the airport, that she should ignore me if she sees me before I see her, etc.). When I showed up with the toy gun I confirmed what she already suspected and she went along willingly. Apparently, she also wore clothes that she didn't mind getting ripped. We both enjoyed it.

The 75% Problem:

Child Sex Abuse
and the Porn Industry

To get a stronger sense of what the men thought of ethical and moral concerns raised by critics of pornography, I asked them to consider a concrete example. In full, the question read:

> Feminist critics of pornography assert that as many as 75 percent of the women who are filmed or pictured in pornography have been victims of child sexual abuse or incest, and conclude that the purchase of porn supports and encourages an industry that thrives on the sexual abuse of women and children. How do you respond to this?

Their responses were far more varied and contradictory than they had been to the other questions about violence.

Although nearly two-thirds were skeptical about the 75 percent figure, only a few rejected it out of hand. "First, my jaw drops," said a 38-year-old married man. "Then I laugh. Then I start to explain that they are confusing causes with effects. Then I remind myself that arguing with True Believers of any stripe is hopeless, and I shut up."

Many doubted the figure because of its source. "Feminists, like their conservative allies, regularly make up and massage statistics to support their agenda," was the opinion of a 41-year-old graduate student in math. He classed the 75 percent figure with other forms of "urban folklore," adding: "I'd like to see the evidence for their claims."

"Ms. Dworkin and her comrades have never been able to substantiate these sorts of assertions," wrote a 29-year-old law student, "since they don't have the patience for any kind of rigorous study of the problem."

A gay 42-year-old assistant professor of computer science supported the heterosexual males: "There is a faction of feminists who exhibit a very strong dislike of sex, for whatever reason, and who seem most particularly to be offended by male sexuality and by male attitudes toward sex. They seem to want to control and quash sexuality except that which is somehow feministically(?) acceptable."

A 25-year-old software engineer wrote:

> My first response is that when I was a women's studies minor at college, I did a lot of checking up on feminist statistics when studying for class or working on reports. I found that an alarming percentage of them were totally wrong, and most of the rest were deceptive. So when I see "as many as 75%" were "victims of child sexual abuse or incest," I read that "as few as 5% saw a copy of *Playboy* before they were 18" and ignore it. Feminist statistics have lost all credibility with me.

A 56-year-old professor said, "I question whether there is any relationship at all. The porn industry has many strong women like Nina Hartley and Brandy Alexandre who are proud of their involvement. If I honestly believed that pornography thrived on the sexual abuse of women and children, I would stop using it."

"It is true that many got into pornography because they were runaways and abused sexually and such, but I think that 75% is kind of high," said a man of Bangladeshi descent. "I could have sworn I read somewhere that it was more like 45%." He was of the opinion that many women were drawn to the work "by the money and the thrill of the sex," and cited an acquaintance who had recently started medical school:

> She is from a middle-class family. So how does she pay her bills? She strips at a local gentlemen's bar and also does the strip-a-grams and lap-dancer calls. Because school takes up so much of her time, she only can work Fridays, Saturdays, and Sundays. Stripping is one of the few jobs she could find that paid enough in three days to help her pay her bills. L. actually hates what she's doing, but being a doctor is what she wants to do and she is willing to do whatever it takes.

"I think there may be some truth to this," said the business manager who once published porn novels, but "I think it's way less than 75%. It's very clear to me that some women like to show off their bodies and like the fact that men want them, and are less inhibited about it than others. I don't think this is necessarily because they were abused as children. I think it is a very large jump to assume that pornography is intimately connected with this problem, or staffed predominantly by its survivors. I think a few sad stories are not enough."

Other men took a different tack. Rather than question the 75 percent figure outright, they noted that if it had no context, then the high level of abuse it suggested among pornographic performers was meaningless. A 35-year-old bisexual, married two years and working on a masters, said it was "An impossible observation to comment on without some sort of contexting, some sort of comparative curve. I'd be interested to know what the sample group is and how it might compare to, say, fast-food workers as a control."

Another man who brought up the absence of a control for comparison accepted that the figure might be accurate. "Conservative estimates currently state that three out of four women—across societal stratification—have been sexually abused at one or more periods in their life. Given this, the statistical correlate between women being survivors of sexual abuse and pornography is ludicrous." Accurate or not, he continued, "One may as well state that, since 75% of all married women were molested as children, marriage supports the abuse of women and children."

Several men, straight and gay, said antiporn feminists tend to exhibit a sexist chauvinism by focusing only on women as victims. A 26-year-old gay man in personnel asked, "What about the *male* models?" Another gay man, 42 years old and an educational administrator, expanded on this point:

I don't know how the [75 percent figure] can be documented or proven. However, in regards to the assertion that the purchase of porn encourages an industry which thrives on the abuse of women and children, I would assume this is also true with men to some degree. Objectification of individuals into objects for sexual gratification is a type of abuse of the human person, just as much as physical abuse.

Even if the source and validity of the 75 percent figure could be established, men questioned its significance. "I respond to this by referring them to the fallacy of *post hoc ergo propter hoc*—temporal succession does not imply causality," remarked a 27-year-old computer analyst. "Maybe—*maybe*—some women get into porn because they were abused. But that does *not* mean that porn causes abuse."

"I see no causal relationship," wrote an assistant professor of computer science:

I'm not sure it even makes sense on some level. Does the recycling industry thrive on waste? Yes, but does the recycling industry cause the waste? No. The people employed by the porn industry should be informed consenting adults. It is not the business of the pornographers to examine the past life and childhood of their employees.

Men also argued that the sex industry cannot be said to depend on the abuse of women. "Unlike a law firm, which would encourage young people to go to college and 'lead a proper life' to culture them into the firm, I doubt that there are scouts out there for the pornography industry encouraging parents to abuse their children so that they might one day become porn stars," a 21-year-old computer consultant wrote.

"I don't believe the porn industry thrives on the people they film," wrote the mechanic, "They thrive on the consumer. Supply and demand." A math grad student agreed: "The only thing the porn industry thrives on are those, like me, who need a little help in jacking off."

Several men suggested the enemies of pornography were being unfair to isolate the porn industry from the sexism, violence, and objectification in society at large. A public administrator in Canada said, "From what I know, pornography is only one part of a very large industry which includes dancing, live shows, escort services, etc. There is also the crossover from porno to legit entertainment. I suspect that many are attracted to it for financial gain, status, and all of the legit reasons anyone goes into public entertainment."

A 37-year-old divorced man noted other sources of information and entertainment which depend on battered and abused women:

> The industry may attract abused women. Other industries probably do also. I would expect that the women who work in rape help lines, psychology, social work, and the police all have disproportionately high numbers of women who have been abused. Do these industries "thrive" on the abuse of women? I think not. Everyone has a cross they bear. For some it is child sexual abuse. Our crosses lead each of us in various directions in efforts to solve the issue involved. The differences are only in the details.

Several men attacked the feminist case by analogy. A French professor of philosophy commented, "You may argue that buying a car supports the workers' poverty and bad education, or that buying cigarettes supports a lethal industry. But also, that is really far-fetched!" Posing the rhetorical question, "If a person chooses a career based upon their poor self image, are the people who use that worker's product responsible for the worker's self image?" A chemistry teacher offered another analogy: "By the logic of Dworkin and MacKinnon, people who watch Richard Pryor movies and listen to his tapes are encouraging the racism that gave rise to his anger, and, by extension, his comedy. By their logic, the cure for racism in America would be to no longer watch Richard Pryor."

A 43-year-old accounting and software professional offered several analogies to suggest the ways in which the feminist critique puts the cart before the horse. He argued that the illicit status of pornography and the sex trades encourages the abuse of women who work in the industry, not the work itself:

> Illegal immigrants are also subject to abuse and violence. On the other hand, persons in "respectable" and legal businesses have a number of remedies available to them. Second example: The government grows (limited) amounts of marijuana for medicinal and research purposes, which is distributed to end users. Other people grow, manufacture, and distribute other drugs, which are illegal. Of the two groups, one is associated with crime; the other group is associated with government pensions and normal lives. Of the two groups, which would you rather belong to if you were a victim of workplace assault or harassment? People in illicit or disreputable businesses do have diminished legal rights. Final example: Newspaper headlines— "Stripper found dead in Minneapolis" . . . "Prostitute claims she was raped." Sensational, sells papers, but the general attitude is that they deserved it. "Mother abducted and raped"—the consensus is outrage against the perpetrator, and the community pitches in to help solve the crime.

In other words, if a woman works in a marginal, disrespected, or illegal profession, she is less likely to report abuses to the authorities. She is also less likely to be believed and served by the legal system. This man's argument did not apply strictly to the question raised—whether the pornography industry fosters and supports abuse of children who later enter the industry—but it did raise questions about whether the sex industry is inherently abusive.

Some men said antiporn feminists do not respect the motivations and rights of women who work in the sex industry. While the activists claim to speak for all women, men offered proof that they do not. Several attacked the assumption among antiporn feminists that working in the pornography industry is so inherently degrading that every woman in the trade had to be suffering and unhappy. A 32-year-old computer consultant, divorced after two years of marriage, said: "One thing I'd like to see the feminists answer is how 25% of the women involved in pornography *aren't* victims of abuse, yet still have no qualms about making love in front of a camera and doing the ritual 'come shot.' Just a point of curiosity I'd like to see them explain without reducing the argument to some sort of 'they don't know how subjugated they are' nonsense."

A resident of Nevada—the one state where prostitution is legal—suggested his region offered contrary evidence to feminist assumptions:

> The fact that Nevada's brothels never lack for employees tells me that women willingly enter into prostitution for personal reasons: sex, money, whatever. If women are that willing to enter prostitution, it seems they are just as willing to make porn. The money is as good, they get screen exposure, and they don't have to have as many johns to earn the same amount. Given the tremendous rise in amateur videos over the last few years, I would either have to conclude that the feminists are right and 75% of women are victims or I would have to conclude that women like sex too. My experience in talking with a wide variety of women leads me to believe that women like sex. Yes, organized crime rings have produced porn as a source of income and money laundering. Yes, women get addicted and children are abused. But most porn is produced by private enterprise to make money and fulfill a demand by the public.

Steve, for whom pornography had provided a small bit of psychological salvation, asked: "Could it be that pornography is a way of coping with bad sexual experiences? Of recovering one's autonomous sexuality? Of healing?"

A 28-year-old newsletter editor/publisher, married for seven years, said he knew such a person:

> I know a couple of women involved in the business. The one that does movies may indeed have been sexually abused as a child, I do not know.

What I *do* know is that she is doing the movies for the money and because she enjoys having people watch her. She is not doing this against her will, no one has pressured her into doing this. She sets her own rules, including who she will fuck on camera.

The sex publishing employee also suggested that far from being only an isolated option for downtrodden women, sex work might be a way they find their way back to self-confidence and a feeling of self-worth and attractiveness (to say nothing of economic independence):

Is there a reason abuse survivors flock to sex work? Is it possible that some of these women do so in order to gain a sense of control of one's own sexuality? I can name one person who is an abuse survivor who worked as a stripper for a while, and solved many of her personal issues through it (and also paid her way through college), then moved on. She doesn't do it anymore, and credits dancing nude in front of unknown men with regaining a sense of control over her own body and destiny. Where does she fit in? Does this mean that buying *Juggs* magazine helped subsidize her road to recovery? Should we encourage porno use for such purposes? What these questions lead towards here is my personal belief that porn is a tool like anything else. It can make money, it can gratify, it can hurt people.

Candida Royalle, a former porn actress who became a director and producer with Femme Productions, a woman-owned company that makes couples-oriented pornographic films, recalls an incident that supports this theory:

Three Daughters, for example, became a very cathartic experience for the actress, Siobhan Hunter. She was one of the Mayflower Madam girls, who had worked as an escort to put herself through medical school. The scene we were shooting was supposed to be a very tender portrayal of her first time and we were shooting in a green room, and the actor had a moustache. All of a sudden, Siobhan started freaking out. She said, "This is reminding me of my actual first sexual experience. It was a green room, with a man with a moustache, and it was a horrendous experience, and I'm starting to freak." So I sat her down and I talked to her, and I told her that my first experience was done with someone I loved, but that it was also a dreadful experience. I told her that I use the movies as a form of catharsis—as a way of redoing it, in a way, and making it better. I thought she could try to use this the same way. The man she was working with had so much genuine feeling for her, that is exactly what happened. They did the scene together and at the very end, while the cameras were still rolling, she sat up, they were hugging, and she started crying. If you see the scene, you'll see tears on her face. It was such a release for her.

The man who gives up on arguing with True Believers said whatever motivates an actress or model for pornography is irrelevant. "Virtually all of these women are doing it voluntarily, for the money. Maybe they have drug habits to support, maybe they're easily led, maybe they genuinely exult in sex or exhibitionism. Frankly, who cares? They are adults with free will. What they do with their bodies is their own business. Why they do it is no concern of anyone but them." As the math grad student pointed out:

Actors and actresses in pornography are adults who are fully able to give or refuse consent. They are responsible for themselves and their actions. It seems curious to me that feminists are claiming that the actresses in pornography are poor helpless weaklings who are unable to speak for themselves. This is exactly the kind of patriarchalism they pretend to detest.

If abuse of women is not inherent to the trade but primarily fostered by its marginal status, then it naturally follows, more than one man argued, that we—especially feminists who demonize the industry—should direct our energy toward supporting the rights and welfare of women who work in it rather than scorning or pitying them and trying to destroy their livelihood. Men called it foolish and hypocritical for feminists to target pornography when its suppression would probably drive it underground and worsen the working conditions for the women who work in it. As the man who made the marijuana harvesting analogy put it:

> I think the best solution, for someone who truly wants to eliminate victims from any line of work, is to insure that any line of work in which women (and children and men) are employed is made completely legal, with the responsibilities and rights thereunto, and held in the public's mind as being as honorable as any other.

A 33-year-old man in the eighth year of marriage to his only sex partner agreed: "If women truly wanted to help those women they would make it acceptable for them to take jobs in pornography."

In contrast to the skepticism expressed by the men above, about a fifth of survey participants found the statistic plausible, or accepted it as true, including a Canadian man who happened to work for the government as a statistical officer. "Of course, existing laws make coercion in sexual matters illegal, but current cultural reality makes conviction unlikely. More likely that the woman would be arrested for being immoral, than that the male exploiters would be arrested for forcing them into it, as is the case with prostitution."

A 23-year-old bisexual in higher education who had experimented with bondage, hot wax, and anal insertions at the request of his female sex partners, said he believed the statistic partly because he considered himself a pro-feminist male:

> I agree [with the statistic and rationale]. That's a lot of the reason why I stopped using/getting porn. I think the exploration of sexuality and the actual photos don't hurt people directly—they maybe confuse them or support harmful beliefs—but there are a lot of abuses in the porn industry. There should either be more regulation and enforcement, or it should be exposed for what it does to women and children. I definitely would encourage consumers to stop buying products that they know are contributing to abuse.

A systems programmer whose wife was divorcing him said, "I don't doubt that many of the women depicted were abused. I don't know how accurate the 75% figure is. I suspect that most of these women are dysfunctional in some way and have been lured into porn in order to survive. I don't have a problem saying that porn exploits women. The vast majority of it clearly does." On the other hand, he said, "Many great artists were dysfunctional and they have created great beauty." Whether anything in pornography could be called "great beauty" is certainly open to dispute, but this man's reference to Van Gogh implied that if we accept the feminist reasoning with regard to abused women in porn, we should forgo the purchase, enjoyment, and reproduction of the work of an individual such as Van Gogh or Dostoevsky.

A Mexican gay man who fantasized about being raped accepted the statistic, owing to:

> the second-class citizenship status that society has cast on women. Men see young girls and the first thing they think about is what it would feel like to stick it in her. We men can be very "basic" animals/grunts when it comes to getting off. Along with that throw in the power trip, masculinity, greed, and of course, self-confidence, and you have men and women with lots of hangups. I think most of the women who subject themselves to the porn business have a very low self-esteem resulting (directly or indirectly) from "abuse," be it sexual, emotional, or otherwise.

A 34-year-old technical writer, separated from his wife, said he accepted the statistic "at face value." This perhaps tied into the standard he maintained of staying away from pornography because of how it represented male-female relationships and influenced his thinking and values; but it might also relate to the fact that he reported an older boy coerced him into masturbating him to orgasm a number of times when he was about 9. However, this man did not accept an inherent link between porn and abuse, nor would he endorse a crackdown on pornography:

> The porn industry is a result of the nature of men to seek sexual gratification or stimulation. Therefore, if you get tough on porn producers and distributors, the market will simply go underground, as with drugs and prostitution. If you want to get tough on the porn industry, you have to address the consumer's conscience. You'd have to instill a certain set of values, which cannot be done by the government. It has to be a grass-roots effort, starting with the family, moving to churches, schools and businesses.

He concluded that "there will always be sexual abuse, unfortunately." And there will always be a demand for porn. But the two were not necessarily linked: "My attraction to porn is not connected to my own sexual abuse as a child, in my opinion. But others may think it is so. I would not challenge the assertion in other people's cases."

"No doubt most women working in porn are not in it because it's their first choice career," wrote a physician. "I do have problems with that. I think the feminists are right. Most porn I consume tends to be 'up-scale,' which I suppose could include more 'porn artists by choice' but that's probably a rationalization, and many of the women are probably not there by choice. By the way, the same is probably true of the men. It does not stop me from using porn. If these allegations were borne out, I might stop using video porn, and stick to literature, which doesn't harm or abuse anyone."

In the context of much greater inequities and abuses of women, Steve argued that whatever happens in the pornography industry is a symptom, and therefore of minor concern:

> It would be dangerous to linger on the abuse of women and children in the porn industry when there are so many other abusive relations in society with greater priority. Many other male-female relations are founded on abuse, e.g., the division of labor both in and out of the household; business abuses people by tying their economic welfare into unstable and uncontrollable financial systems; industry abuses people by treating them as a commodity (labor) to be hired and fired as dictated by the movement

of money or the demand of shareholders; political parties abuse people by presenting them with little or no opportunity to determine the nature of the legislation by which their lives are regulated; religions abuse people by encouraging complacent and smug "virtue" in those for whom such "virtue" is easy at the expense of compassion, forgiveness and charity for those for whom it is not. The abuse which exists in the porn industry is a reflection of all these deep problems in current society and the industry will not change nor will it disappear until these problems are tackled. If I do not buy the argument that there is nothing perverse in the sexual interest fed by pornography, [then I also] reject that it is such perversion which causes these problems. On the contrary, the selfishness and short-sightedness which manifests itself in all these problems is what has perverted a normal, harmless interest in sex into the abusive industry it has become.

A Look Behind the Statistic

In her testimony before the Meese Commission, Andrea Dworkin said, almost in passing, "The women in the pornography, 65 to 70 percent of them we believe, are victims of incest or child sexual abuse." Later, while campaigning in Minnesota to pass civil legislation against pornography that was authored by herself and MacKinnon, Dworkin raised the figure to 75 percent.

As best as I have been able to establish, Dworkin's source was a study by the Delancey Street Foundation, a self-help residential facility in San Francisco that treats prostitutes, criminals, and drug addicts. Staffers interviewed 200 street prostitutes and found that 70 percent were under the age of 21, nearly 60 percent were 16 or under, and many were preadolescents. The study investigated the women's background, whether they had been the victim of assault or juvenile exploitation before becoming prostitutes, their self-concept and plans for the future, but not specifically pornography. The authors of the report decided to document the pornography angle, however, after many of the women brought it up themselves.

In brief, 73 percent of the women reported having been raped, and 60 percent reported incidents of juvenile sexual abuse. Nearly a quarter of the women who had been raped said their attackers made allusions to pornographic materials, on the order of "I seen it in all the movies. You love being beaten." Ten percent of the women said they had been used as children in pornographic films and magazines. Thirty-eight percent said sexually explicit photographs had been taken of them when they were children for commercial purposes and/or the personal gratification of the photographer, all when they were under the age of 16. In addition, 22 percent of the women who reported cases of juvenile sexual exploitation said the adult had used or shown them pornographic materials before the sex act. The authors of the study noted that all of this information came from unsolicited remarks—the women volunteered it without being asked directly—so "it is assumed that the actual response to this question would be notably higher."

Sobering as these numbers are, it is hard to see how Dworkin could have derived her figures from them. None of the findings approaches the 75 percent level, save for the number of street prostitutes who had been raped at some point, perhaps by pimps, boyfriends, and johns after they were on the street rather than abusive relatives in the home. The rate for involvement in the manufacture of pornographic materials barely surpasses a third. Some of the men in the survey done for this book have referred to erotic photos taken of girlfriends and spouses, but all under conditions of consent, and not likely shared with anyone else, let alone sold commercially. The abusive relatives and pimps who made pornographic records of the San Francisco runaways may also have kept them for their own pleasure, or for blackmail purposes, not sale.

If one adds up all the separate categories—used in pornographic films and magazines before age 13, posed in sexually explicit photographs, exploited sexually with porn nearby—the total is 70 percent, but only if one assumes no overlap between the categories, which there certainly must have been.

The numbers may not even apply to all prostitutes. Call girls who are self-employed or receive their referrals through an escort service tend to have much more control over their time, which clients they see, and which sex acts they perform. Rates of violence are undoubtedly lower among this variety of sex worker as compared to more vulnerable women on the street, who tend to be younger and homeless, and may well comprise a minority of "working girls." According to Gail Pheterson, researcher, clinician, and co-founder of the International Committee for Prostitutes' Rights, "street prostitution accounts . . . for less than 15 percent in the United States. . . ." Thus, the less-than-75-percent figure for street prostitutes in San Francisco probably drops even more when extended to all prostitutes.

Remember, too, that the street prostitutes featured in the Delancey study were women who used drugs. In this and perhaps other ways they represented the very dregs of their profession.

Finally, Dworkin either does not understand statistical analysis or willfully ignores the study's findings. It suggests that between 10 and 40 percent of street prostitutes in the San Francisco area may have been used in the making of pornographic materials. One cannot reasonably extrapolate those numbers to the nation or the pornographic industry as a whole. Say 90 percent of all pornography sold in the United States originated in San Francisco; then perhaps the 10 to 40 percent of the street hookers photographed might constitute the largest portion of the whole.

But the majority of commercial pornography in the United States is *not* made in San Francisco. According to the Meese Commission report, about "eighty percent of the American production of this type of motion picture and video tape takes place in and around Los Angeles. . . ." The Commission said this was probably attributable to the number of technical personnel and performers "who are, have been, or wish to be employed in the mainstream motion picture industry." The chances that these include a lot of street prostitutes are low.

In their conclusions, the authors of the Delancey study were careful to note that "It is very difficult to establish conclusively the causal relationship between pornography and sexual abuse of women." They added that their findings "can neither confirm nor reject the 'catharsis model' of pornography, because they are based on the victims' rather than the assailants' responses. . . ."

Nevertheless, Dworkin not only exaggerated the numbers in the study but asserted that they proved something its own authors would not claim. She seems to care less about truth than stirring her listeners to action, even if that means unleashing unproven claims supported by slipshod methodology. It is not hard to see what prompted the more vitriolic and contemptuous remarks that some men in my survey directed toward feminist arguments and their use of statistics.

The Public Debate:

What Did Everyone Get Wrong About Men Who Use Pornography?

The gulf between critics of pornography and its fans seems unbridgeable. Not only do the two sides disagree about its effect on society and individual consumers, they cannot even agree on what pornography *is*. Where one side finds objectification, subordination, degradation, and violence against women, the other sees beauty, fun, women's pleasure, female power and assertiveness, and fantasy largely separated from the real world.

The case against pornography rests upon a series of assumptions that have never been tested against the point of view of average male consumers:

1. Men—at least men who use pornography—cannot separate fact from fantasy.
2. For men, the women in pornography represent all women.

3. Pornography shows precisely what men want, both from pornography and from sex.
4. Pornography teaches men about sex.
5. Men turn to pornography only when they are lonely and unhappy.
6. Pornography is addictive.
7. Porn consumers inevitably crave more kinky and violent content.
8. Pornography causes men to become violent.

If we compare how the users of pornography responded to my survey about these assumptions, the case against porn becomes not only questionable, but absurd.

Men Cannot Separate Fact from Fantasy

Foes of pornography maintain that men cannot distinguish between the fantasy of pornography and the reality of their sex lives. "Men believe what turns them on," MacKinnon writes. The film *Deep Throat* "was a success because it felt *real* to men," she goes on. "The experience of the (overwhelmingly) male audiences who consume pornography is therefore not fantasy or simulation or catharsis but sexual reality: the level of reality on which sex itself largely operates."

MacKinnon also writes: "Pornography is often more sexually compelling than the realities it represents, more sexually real than reality." I am unaware of any research that placed a porn magazine next to a nude, willing woman and asked male test subjects which they would choose (or simply which they found more real), so I can't imagine where MacKinnon got this idea.

If she were correct, men in my survey would not have found pornography unrealistic. But complaints filled their responses to the question of what they liked and disliked. They hated genital close-ups, they were tired of cum shots, they didn't like women hooting and hollering in false ecstasy (especially if they looked bored), they thought the men were unattractive and treated the women poorly, they hated the lack of romance and buildup to sex. Their complaints indicated the porn could have been done differently, and therefore did not simply reflect life. When asked what they wanted to see more of, many men said "more realistic scenarios," which suggests they didn't mistake fantasy for reality at all. Some who acknowledged that pornography was fantasy felt it wasn't sufficiently *un*real, as in the case of the gay journalist who remarked that pornography is supposed "to create an illusion in which the 'real world' is suspended and everyone has the chance to 'make it' with an attractive, healthy man (or woman)."

A simple example of porn's unreality is the "cum shot." Obviously, most men rarely pull out and ejaculate in the air or on their partner's body during sex, or there would be much less demand for condoms and birth control pills. So pornography does not reflect reality in this instance, and men do not copy what they see in porn. The cum shot is a convention, much like the moments in musicals when people inexplicably burst into dance and song—and a convention not highly prized by many viewers, to judge from the remarks of men in the survey.

Several commentators have tried to argue that enjoyment of pornography is somehow different from pleasure with any other form of entertainment. Susan Cole writes, "there are real women in the pictures, and . . . an erection, any way you look at it, is not a fantasy." Well, no, it is not. An erection is a physical *response* to a fantasy, like sweaty palms and a racing pulse during a horror movie. When we perspire and our heartbeat accelerates, an observer might say that physiologically we are on the verge of fight or flight, but this is not what we intend or actually do when we watch a movie like *Psycho*. MacKinnon argues that the physical response of an erection means that pornography is an incitement to act, like racist literature or telling a trained attack dog to "kill"; but if she knew how many erections the average man has in his lifetime and never acts on (morning erections, hard-ons at the movies or when a woman smiles and pays one a compliment at work, or those embarrassing and unbidden erections in adolescence due to fluctuating testosterone), she would admit how ridiculous her attack dog analogy is.

Diana Russell is certain that "the argument that consumers of pornography realize that such portrayals [of rape myths] are false is totally unconvincing." As proof, she cites three books or articles by *women* (including herself), as well as studies of college and high school students that suggested they were more inclined to believe rape myths after watching erotica. Of course, no one talked to men who customarily use pornography; no one consulted older, mature men for their perspective; and no one seems to have addressed the role of "experimenter bias" in these studies—the extent to which students might have guessed what the researchers expected to hear.

Taking sides appears to be more valuable to some theorists than obtaining hard, fair, and objective evidence. MacKinnon approvingly quotes researcher Edward Donnerstein's reputed comment that "We just quantify the obvious"—a disturbing admission of bias—while Russell castigates him for "copping out" because he objected to the way his work had been used by antiporn feminists.

In Susan Griffin's formulation, "the pornographer . . . never admits to his hatred and fear of eros. . . . The traces of the chauvinist's feelings come to us, therefore, only by inference and allegory." In other words, it would do no good to ask men about pornography, because they can't be honest. So Griffin accords greater weight to her own fantasy about what goes on in men's minds than to whatever men might have to say for themselves. She smoothly concludes that "the pornographic mind is identical both in form and in ultimate content to the Nazi mind," whatever that means.

In what men seek from pornography there is a tension—and a collaboration—between realism and fantasy, the true-to-life and the ideal. The two aspects both oppose each other and work together toward a delicate balance for maximum effect on the viewer. Or rather, they often *don't* work together, which is why so many men, so much of the time, are less than pleased with the pornography they see, as my survey has indicated.

On the one hand, men want to see attractive people, beautiful women, muscular men—people who look better than the average, people to whom one might never have sexual access. On the other hand, if the performers are too perfect, that can be too distancing and intimidating.

On the one hand, men want to see people performing at their very best: screwing with skill and endurance, performing oral sex with convincing technique and verve, approaching sex in exotic settings with great imagination and no clumsiness or misunderstandings. On the other, they don't want everything to be so amazing and perfect that it takes the fantasy totally out of reach, the viewer cannot pretend he is voyeuristically seeing "real" people having "real" sex, and it's crushingly obvious that such an event could never happen to him in real life.

On the one hand, viewers like the women in pornography because they respond to everything that happens, no matter what it is, when it's proposed, or how it's performed. On the other hand, it is important to male viewers that the women really do seem to be enjoying themselves, that they are utterly involved in the sex for their own pleasure too, and not just serving the interests of the male actors and onlookers.

This tension or interplay between realism and fantasy hardly sets pornography and its users apart from other forms of entertainment. Readers of romance novels want lovely plots and perfect bodies, but enough humanity and not too much perfection that the story becomes totally unbelievable. Action movies feature "real" heroes who have personal problems and make mistakes within the "perfection" of split-timed capers and escapes. "Realistic" stories by Dostoevsky or Hemingway still depend on rare events in people's lives (like war or murder), helpful coincidences, heroes and heroines of uncommon virtue and vice, to hold our interest. Green, red, and yellow kryptonite were elements of reality that kept the stories of otherwise invincible Superman interesting.

If someone were to publish an utterly realistic novel about the life of a grocer or a receptionist, few people would likely want to read it. If offered an utterly fantastic and perfect tale of true love among the wealthy and privileged, not many more would jump at that. Are we attracted by the realism or the fantasy? The answer, of course, is both.

If the balance is pushed too far in either direction, much of the potential audience evaporates.

Some men look to pornography to tip the balance more one way or the other. They are drawn to homemade amateur pornography—where the sex is not perfect and the players not particularly handsome or gorgeous—because the realism and passion is what turns them on. This is not packaged sex, with a stupid script and a cheesy soundtrack, and actors who may have coupled many times before but don't have any particular feelings for one another. This is real sex between people who are either well acquainted or hungry for sex, and/or willing to perform for a camera *without* being paid. Or so it would seem. Some viewers on the other hand prefer more fantasy: utterly perfect, unattainable bodies in exotic settings with quality camera work, fantastic plotting, and superb physical technique.

Sometimes the balance wavers between "perfect" mundanity and "perfect" uniqueness; that is to say, some men prefer to see loving, romantic, vanilla sex between happy couples, while others push toward the frontiers of kinky sex, bondage, scat and water sports, incest and power domination. *Why* they are drawn to such content can vary as well: some seek it because it's what they like and do in their actual sex lives, others because it's something they would *never* do but find intriguing to watch—just as the rest of us are mesmerized by murders and war stories on television, or by a car wreck on the freeway, but would not wish these things to happen to us in real life.

To Men, Women in Pornography Represent All Women

The notion that men will take the "lessons" in pornography and apply them to real life requires that men see the performers in porn as indistinguishable from the real women in their lives. Several commentators state this as fact. "Pornography purports to define what a woman is," says MacKinnon. Cole writes, "In the real world, real women are seen as pornography. Thus, they cannot rise above what men think they really are, especially if the 'fictions' of pornography (which are advertised as the real thing, and which real men seldom see as fictions) give men sexual pleasure." Note the passive voice: "are seen" by whom? Cole's passive construction slides over the critical aspect of who is doing the seeing and is therefore an attempt to hide the fact that she does not really know, because she has not talked to anyone who enjoys pornography. She does not tell us how she knows "real men" seldom see pornography as fiction. Writes Griffin, a woman on a pornographic magazine cover "has become all women. . . . This picture of the body of one woman has become a metaphor . . . for all women's bodies. Each sale of a pornographic image is a sadistic act which accomplishes the humiliation of all women."

Since some women are already on record to say they aren't humiliated by such depictions, the situation obviously is more complicated than MacKinnon, Cole, and Griffin believe. The truth is, men know only too well that not all women are like the ones in pornography. That is one of the things that makes it appealing: that the women in porn do not behave like most of the women the viewer knows. As Nancy Friday explains in her book about men's sex fantasies, the "heart of fantasy's enchantment" is: "No matter what men may do to/with their imaginary lovers, her reactions are just the opposite of [the disapproving] mother's—*she loves him for it* [Friday's emphasis]. 'Yes!' she shouts, 'more!' A fantasy woman does not reproach her man for letting other men peep at her, for wanting to share her with another guy, for dreaming of her having sex with a dildo or a dog. Fantasy gives men the love of women they want, with none of the inhibiting feminine rules they hate."

What Friday also found was that male fantasies tended to be built on reality, not vice versa. They were not divorced from real life like the faceless males who ravished women in the fantasies *they* recounted to Friday. "Most of the fantasies in this book are built upon memories of real women. . . . I find this ironic: it neatly turns the tables on the usual idea that only women want (I hate this phrase) 'meaningful relationships' while men revel in anonymous one-night stands." Friday recognizes what this suggests about men's interest in pornography. Whereas women told her they fantasized about a demon lover who "is never seen with photographic clarity," men reacted in the opposite way: "hence the great popularity of the nude in girlie magazines. The more a man can see, the closer the dream is to reality, the more specific, the more real the woman—the more exciting."

In other words, the male viewer is not using pornography to create reality; it's the other way around. He loves pornography for how closely it emulates reality *at its best*—although it obviously is not real. The pornographic woman is at the peak of her attractiveness, and utterly responsive to him. The few real women in his life who acted this way (if he's been lucky) were in love with him, or at least highly attracted to him. That is the great secret Nancy Friday discovered when she quizzed men about their sexual fantasies—the great secret that has thoroughly eluded all the antiporn commentators—and this is why she titled her book about male sexual fantasies *Men in Love*.

"In pornographic books, magazines, and films, women are represented as passive and slavishly dependent upon men," declares Helen Longino, thereby demonstrating her ignorance of the common pornographic scenario where women take initiative and control. The threat from "mysterious female sexuality and capability" means that "pornography asserts that women have neither, that women are (often literally) castrated, helpless, incapable," Susan Lurie assures us. She is clearly unaware that pornography celebrates women's pleasure, and that the S/M sub-genre often depicts a female punishing a man, binding him, or whipping him for being "bad"—perhaps for not satisfying her, or for having lustful thoughts in the first place. (Lurie also does not explain what "literal" castration of a woman might be, or whether anyone's seen it in pornography.)

You would think if there were nothing but humiliation, degradation, and violence in pornography, no self-respecting woman would have anything to do with it. Yet critics of pornography paradoxically complain that self-respecting women routinely force themselves to resemble the models in porn.

"Ordinary women wear makeup," Griffin observes. "Ordinary women attempt to change our bodies to resemble a pornographic ideal." But Griffin compares these ordinary women to images of Marilyn Monroe and "the extraordinary film star"—mainstream cultural ideals, not specifically pornographic ones. Griffin also does not explain why the use of cosmetics predates the widespread availability of pornography by centuries. She does not explain how pornography could play a greater role in women's lives than the magazines they buy for themselves—*Vogue, Mademoiselle, Cosmopolitan*—which contain advice on beauty, diet, cosmetics, and clothing, and even cosmetic surgery tips. *Cosmo* "teaches women, step-by-step, how to become sex objects," Lisa Steele observes, and "*Vogue* and *Bazaar* . . . offer in-depth instruction in the narcissistic pastime of turning oneself into a living sculpture. . . ."

Surely women have absorbed most of these lessons from sources other than pornography—and absorbed them far more than the men in their lives could ever have pressured them to do. "No one has shamed my body like women have," a woman told Naomi Wolf. Another recalled her teen classmates saying "I was on the Itty-bitty Titty Committee" and teasing her with "You're a sailor's dream: a sunken chest." She concluded, "Boys would never say that. Just girls."

"Any woman who has stolen a glance at her spouse's *Penthouse* has to wonder whether she can live up to what he finds sexy there," worries Cole. But that's the woman's fantasy—that her man would expect this of her. Does he flagellate himself when she admires Tom Cruise, Brad Pitt, or Paul Newman? Usually not, because he knows she has chosen him for many reasons, not just his looks. Why would the endless images of Cindy Crawford, Claudia Schiffer, and Naomi Campbell on the covers of *her* magazines concern her less than the women in *Penthouse?*

Where women's attitudes and self-image are concerned, research seems to implicate women's fashion magazines more than pornography. Alison King reports a study by C.L. Krafka that suggested that female subjects who viewed pornography the researchers thought dehumanizing and degrading did not report greater sex-role stereotyping, lower self-esteem, or inferiority about their looks. A study led by T.F. Cash, however, found "women had lower self-esteem after viewing models in mainstream magazine advertisements."

This should not be surprising, since the variety of women's sizes, shapes, and ages in women's fashion magazines may arguably be far more limited than in pornography. A commentator who has only seen a few copies of *Playboy* or *Penthouse* would not know this, but Laura Kipnis, who surveyed some of the less well-known publications, describes them in her book, *Bound and Gagged. Dimensions* is a magazine for "fat admirers," and features "quite fat lingeried models. . . ." Full nudity is not a factor, but the magazine's transgressive quality may be read from the fact that, according to Kipnis, it can be found only in hard-core porn stores. *Over 50* offers "vistas of antediluvian flesh." With the advent of amateur sex videos, a greater variety of ages and forms have naturally become available in action, as well.

As they so often do, women presume to speak for men in this area: "Readers feel short-changed when a woman does not look and act the part of the *Playboy* model. It is an insult to their masculine capacity to get what they want," declares Judith Bat-Ada, although she doesn't say how she knows this. She contends that this process leads to child molesting: "It makes him hate her. And it makes him turn to the younger female daughters in the family." Perhaps it might in those rare cases where it happens, but can we impute this process to all users of pornography? What inspired men to molest their daughters before there was *Playboy*?

When MacKinnon complains that "We spend our money to set ourselves up as the objects that emulate those images that are sold as erotic to men," I believe she puts the cart before the horse. Is it not perhaps the other way around: that women in pornography are made up to look like the cool, expensive, and unattainable goddesses men see in public, but become warm and available in private fantasy? So few women have extensive knowledge of the contents of pornography that it has to be porn that copies life, not the other way around.

Pornography Shows What Men Want

"Pornographers . . . know what to make, and the distributors know what to sell," Susan Cole declares, as if the mere fact that something is on the market is proof that the consumers want it and would not choose something else were it available. Are Pintos, Edsels, red dye #2, and thalidomide what consumers wanted? They were on the market and people bought them, so they must have been. Freud never asked what do men want, MacKinnon observes; "Pornography provides an answer. Pornography permits men to have whatever they want sexually. It is their 'truth about sex.'"

I am afraid it is not. Many of the men in my survey did not often get what they wanted from pornography. They couldn't understand why there were so many genital closeups and so little plot and romance. They hated the ubiquity of cum shots and desired more variety in bodies, hair color, and sexual behavior. They were annoyed by the repetitive formula of kiss-fellatio-cunnilingus-anal sex-intercourse-cum shot (mix to suit) and wondered why so many performers looked bored.

MacKinnon claims that pornography "eroticizes the despised, the demeaned, the accessible, the there-to-be-used, the servile, the child-like, the passive, and the animal." That does not sound like many of the women I have seen in pornography, or the ones the men in my survey said they liked most. MacKinnon wants to pretend that "women feel compelled to preserve the appearance—which, acted upon, becomes the reality—of male direction of sexual expression, as if male initiative itself were what we [women] want, as if it were what turns us on. Men enforce this. It is much of what men want in women."

Everyone would like to be served at times, *everyone* wants to be desired—which requires assertiveness and initiative on the part of someone else. Women whose sexual relationships with men are fulfilling have their needs served by their male partner. If men wanted only power in sex, they wouldn't experience performance anxiety, impotence, or premature ejaculation (or feel guilty when they do), because these are symptoms of not being able to satisfy one's partner—or the fear of it. If domination and power were all that mattered to men, they would care only for their orgasm, and not their partner's. The fact is, many men do care very much about women's pleasure, both in life and in pornography, where it is the focus of so much attention.

Pornography Teaches Men About Sex

Susan Cole worries about "young male adolescents who are learning lies about what women want." She adds that for many adolescents, "pornographic materials are the only form of sex 'education.'" But if parents, schools, and the rest of society leave a yawning gap in a child's knowledge of sex, it is not pornography's fault that it partly fills the gap.

Even young girls go to pornography for information they so desperately need. Older sisters, female playmates, and babysitters looked at and showed pornography to some of the men in my survey. A woman told Naomi Wolf that when she was a teenage babysitter, "It was an all-points bulletin search for the sex stuff as soon as the parents were out the door." Sara Diamond writes: "Porn remains about the only source of explicit information on sex for young people. I can remember hours poring over my parents' blue novels or rifling secretively through *Playboy* at the corner drugstore. I wonder how many other feminists have emerged, critical perspectives intact, from an early flirtation with pornography."

Yet Peter Baker insists, "Young men do not find it hard to understand what pornography is and what it means. Even before they see any pornography, young men have already received and internalized a great deal of false information about the roles and sexualities of men and women." Baker, a researcher, journalist, and counselor of men who have had difficulties with porn, believes the men he has counseled are representative of all men. True, pornography lies to men about women, but it lies about men, too, and male viewers recognize this. They know they are not like the men in porn, and most of them reported they quickly got over their insecurities over those differences. Why should they think the women in porn are any more true to life?

The real issue is not what a person sees but how well he listens to and is considerate of others. If a young man takes away the "lessons" of pornography and clings to them even in the face of conflicting input from his real-life experiences with other people, then the problem is not pornography but the man's poor social skills. Would abusive and insensitive men's treatment of the people in their lives be significantly different if they had never seen pornography? I doubt it.

Even in antipornography literature, one may find evidence that men respond to training. In her report to the Meese Commission about experimental research on the effects of pornography upon the "average individual," Edna Einsiedel reported that researcher Daniel Linz's "debriefing procedures" after showing college males a series of R-rated slasher films and X-rated nonviolent films "were found to be generally effective in reducing negative effects."

In other words, even if young men's opinions are swayed by explicitly sexual or violent material, they respond well to discussion later. Opponents of porn seem unable to see the significance of this. Instead, they claim there is only one kind of pornography (violent and degrading), that all men respond to it in exactly the same way, and that no man can possibly think things out for himself afterward, let alone be persuaded by reality or a lover to change his mind. As Laura Kipnis dryly observes, "The argument that pornography causes violent behavior in male consumers relies on a theory of the porn consumer as devoid of rationality, contemplation, or intelligence, prone instead to witless brainwashing, to monkey-see/monkey-do reenactments of the pornographic scene."

Men Use Pornography Only When They Are Lonely and Unhappy

"It is also not surprising that men tend to use pornography when they are feeling worst about themselves, usually lonely," Baker declares. If one has been counseling men with problems, as Baker has, then this would be a fair assumption. But the men in my survey had looked at pornography in a variety of moods, with their friends and schoolmates, and sometimes with wives and girlfriends. A fair number said they tended to look at pornography more often when they were feeling happy.

Baker continues, "Of course, pornography can never meet the real need that men have for close human contact. Many men therefore become caught in a vicious circle of feeling lonely, using pornography in an attempt to make themselves feel better, finding it does not meet their needs, and so turning back to it as the only apparent hope for escaping from the isolation." This had been the experience of a few of the men in my survey, but not many others. Pornography raised their spirits, especially if they watched it with a lover. Baker concludes, "There is something very sad and desperate about men's use of pornography as a substitute for real human contact." Sad, perhaps, but any more sad than clinging to romance novels, gambling, or food to fill a human void in one's life? The crucial question is: Do most men use pornography to fill such a void? Not according to the ones I interviewed.

Baker adds, "many men become obsessed with the size of their penises." This was certainly not the case with most of the men in my survey. A few had doubts when they were young, inexperienced, and easily impressed by what they saw. But most of them appeared to leave such cares behind after maturing and acquiring a little sexual experience in the real world. Certainly no more than one or two could be described as "obsessed with the size of their penises" today.

Pornography is Addictive

Critics of pornography rarely make any distinction between men who consume pornography and all men, or between men who consume pornography and those who become addicted to it. In her introduction to testimony by "pornography's victims" before the Meese Commission, Phyllis Schlafly declares: "These testimonies prove that pornography is addictive, and that those who become addicted crave more bizarre and more perverted pornography, and become more callous toward their victims."

In an essay entitled "Pornography and Addiction," Corinne Sweet asserts that "many men are fully addicted and the extent of this addiction is both widespread and widely denied." She offers no numbers, but immediately suggests that pornography is "legitimated" by such phenomena as the "page 3 girls." The British tabloid *The Sun* is infamous for the smiling, topless, full color pinup that appears on page three every day, along with salacious news stories of sex and violence. Sweet notes that the newspaper sells 4 million copies a day, although what this has to do with men and porn addiction is not clear: One has to assume that women buy the paper too, and that some folks read it for the soccer news or classifieds.

One can sense the same murky insinuations in Peter Baker's worried declaration that the combined monthly sales of all Britain's pornographic magazines—from *Penthouse* and *Mayfair* to *Knave*, *Fiesta*, and *Club International*—is 2.25 million. Apparently the reader is meant to assume each sale represents a different man, rather than the possibility that a smaller number of men buy multiple magazines. And what if there *were* 2.25 million buyers of pornography in Britain: Could they all be addicts and nascent sex killers? One does not get that impression from the Englishmen in my survey.

Admittedly, a handful of all the men I talked to—no more than five—appeared to have a current or past obsession with pornography that could loosely be termed an addiction. But so many more clearly had no such obsession. Until the opponents of pornography can prove that the harmless ones are in the minority rather than the majority who spend billions on erotic materials in the United States every year, one must conclude that pornography is not addictive.

Porn Consumers Inevitably Turn to More Violent and Kinky Material

The notion that men career down a slippery slope from soft-core to hard-core and extremely violent pornography is more common than the notion that marijuana smoking leads to heroin addiction. Writes Corinne Sweet: "There is a cycle of addiction, where users seek out harder and harder pornography, leading, in extreme cases, to 'snuff' films where a woman's sexual murder constitutes 'entertainment.'" MacKinnon's take is, "More and more violence has become necessary to keep the progressively desensitized consumer aroused to the illusion that sex is (and he is) daring and dangerous."

The experiences of many men in my survey simply did not follow this model. Some found what they liked right away and stuck with it for decades. Others investigated the rarer forms of pornography, found them not to their liking, and returned to pleasanter pastures. Many—if not most—had their limits, beyond which they cared not to stray.

Central to the "slippery slope" theory is the assumption that pornography not only includes violence against women, but consists primarily of violence, or solely of violence, and would not be pornography *without* violence. "There is almost no pornographic work without the infliction of pain," declares Susan Griffin, "Pornography itself is a sadistic act. . . . Over and over, pornography depicts acts of terrible violence to women's bodies." "Abuse is not *caused* by pornography, it is part of what pornography *is*," agrees Susan Cole [her emphasis]. This is one place where activists from the religious right can agree with the radical feminist left. "The depiction of rape, child sexual abuse, torture, and bestiality are commonplace," says Beverly LaHaye, president of Concerned Women for America, in a book edited by Phyllis Schlafly.

Porn critics positively savor the gruesome details they say are typical of the genre. Women are "hung by their breasts from meat hooks," Catherine Itzin assures us. They are "fucked, tied up, spread-eagled, having ejaculate sprayed over their faces and bodies," Diana

Russell thunders, and "No one knows what percentage of them are also being beaten up, tortured, raped, or even killed." MacKinnon says, "Electrodes [are] being applied to the genitals of women being called 'cunt' in photography studios in Los Angeles and the results mass-marketed." Cole assures us that "men shove bamboo up women's vaginas," one finds "a meathook in a woman's vagina," and women are "branded with hot irons or gang-raped. . . ." As always, Andrea Dworkin weighs in: "A woman, nearly naked, in a cell, chained, flesh ripped up from the whip, breasts mutilated by a knife: she is entertainment, the boy-next-door's favorite fantasy, every man's precious right, every woman's potential fate."

But criticism does not stop with mere content. Not only is pornography supposed to consist primarily of violent depictions, but it celebrates violence against women. Ray Wyre, director of a residential clinic for child sex abusers in Britain, asserts: "One reason pornography is incredibly dangerous is because 97 percent of all the rape stories in pornography end with the woman changing her mind and having orgasms and being represented as enjoying rape." He offers no citation for this statistic; one doubts he studied "all the rape stories in pornography" and did the math himself. Who did? Wyre doesn't say. Besides, "97 percent of all the rape stories" may be a red herring if the total number of rape stories in pornography is minuscule. In *Feminism Unbound*, MacKinnon states, "Pornography sexualizes rape, battery, sexual harassment, prostitution, and child sexual abuse; it thereby celebrates, promotes, authorizes, and legitimizes them." Leaving aside the issue of how often such acts as rape and child sex abuse actually occur in pornography, apparently their mere existence in porn serves to "celebrate and legitimize them" . . . sort of the way the Fritz Lang film *M* celebrates child murder and TV cop shows applaud robberies and assaults merely by depicting them.

Despite this parade of assertions, consumers of pornography in my survey rarely described mayhem that was anything like the examples above. In the handful of cases where there was some form of violence, few men enjoyed it or identified with the perpetrators of sexual violence.

Nearly all the men who had not seen any violence in pornography also had no interest in finding any. Since at least two-thirds said they did not find violence a turn-on, yet regularly looked at pornography, one may safely assume they were not seeing much violence in porn.

What accounts for this radical inconsistency between the users of pornography and the critics?

Part of the answer lies with emphasis. Enemies of pornography continually refer to the worst, most vivid, most upsetting (and incidentally most rare) pornography to make their case. In the same way, MacKinnon repeatedly writes that "only 7.8% of women in the United States have not been sexually assaulted or harassed in their lifetime" . . . and then one reads the fine print and discovers she bases this on a single study of women in the San Francisco area conducted by her friend Diana Russell, and that the tabulation includes "obscene phone calls, unwanted sexual advances on the street, unwelcome requests to pose for pornography, and subjection to peeping Toms and sexual exhibitionists (flashers)."

When critics of pornography actually try to measure the violent content, the results are weak, to say the least. Catherine Itzin approvingly charts the findings of a study of the images on the covers of porn magazines on the east coast of the United States at the time of the Meese Commission. Although intriguing items such as fisting, leg irons, forcible rape, and corpses leap off her chart, their actual incidence in the pornography studied by researchers P.E. Dietz, Paul Elliott, and Alan Sears was negligible. The above items appeared in one percent or less of the material. In contrast, a subsequent study by Dietz of *detective* magazine covers found that 76 percent involved domination of some kind and 38 percent depicted bondage.

Opponents of pornography also casually assert that violence in pornography is on the rise. MacKinnon writes, "More and more pornography is more and more violent, and arousing," but she provides no evidence. Russell and Karen Trocki are more sly: in 1993 they wrote, "Pornographic materials and mainstream depictions of women have become increasingly violent in the past two decades." This unfairly groups porn, which has little or no violence, with R-rated feature films such as *Thelma and Louise* or *Fatal Attraction* which do contain violence. For authority, they cited an essay by Charlene Senn, which in turn referred to a 1980 study of pornography by Neil Malamuth and Barry Spinner, and a 1986 study of mainstream materials by T.S. Palys. As Bill Thompson points out in *Soft Core*, however, the Malamuth and Spinner review of violent imagery in *Playboy* and *Penthouse* included satirical cartoons of sado-masochism—some with dominant females and submissive males—which makes the "proof of rising violence against women" suspect. Malamuth and Spinner's study covered the years 1973 to 1977, and suggested a rise in "violence" from 5 to 10 percent. That's not an overwhelming amount. Using such a skewed sample to characterize all pornography as violent is as accurate as saying statistics indicate that all Americans may be homosexual.

Palys's examination of videos between 1979 and 1983 found that XXX videos with explicit sex were far less violent than R-rated ones with nudity and simulated sex. Examples of male domination and graphic aggression were higher in the R-rated videos, but they did not increase over time, and the number of violent scenes in XXX actually fell.

Thompson goes on to cite several studies that suggest MacKinnon, Russell, and anyone else who claims violence has risen in pornography are simply wrong. J.E. Scott and S.J. Cuvelier's 1987 study of *Playboy* and *Penthouse*, covering the years 1954 to 1983, found a "violent" image on one page in 3,000, and four out of every 1,000 pictures, respectively. The rate dropped after 1977. A study by researchers at Reading University of European pornographic magazines (supposedly "harder" than American or British) up to 1990, found that "violent imagery" declined 42 percent from 1972 to 1979, and a little further by 1983. "Non-violent but demeaning" imagery climbed 23 percent from 1972 to 1979, and then declined 19 percent through 1983.

What makes the debate about violence in pornography so tricky is that "violence" is open to interpretation. What looks like violence to one person may be play to another. When MacKinnon infers a connection between "sadomasochistic pornography and lynching," it is clear she knows nothing about consensual bondage and S/M, safe words, and the world of people who play at restraint and pain—people like Jay and his lover. Even many of the men in my survey defined S/M as violent, so their point of view was closer to MacKinnon's than to fans of S/M. They regard typical bondage and S/M scenes as perversion, violence, or masculine power over feminine helplessness, rather than as scenarios of utter trust in which a woman gives a man temporary seeming power over her, knowing he will not abuse it. "There's also a lot of power in consenting to that [bottom] position, and in exploiting it to drive your top wild with lust," Jay said. Unlike the casual, improvisatory nature of many sexual encounters, S/M activities often involve considerable planning, with a script, clear roles, and a "safe word" which either party can say to stop the action the instant it becomes too unpleasant or uncomfortable.

A man in my survey who liked to read and fantasize about spanking and bondage but never pursued them with his wife or premarital girlfriends, referred to a Web site that had information. "Being consensual, BD/SM is no more violent than is any contact sport," he quoted. Although feminist theorists hold that a woman cannot truly consent to violent sex, he said, people who engage in BD/SM "talk about why they consent, how they feel about it, and what it means to them. Their reasons are usually very personal, they are often psychologically grounded, and they are all different. The more of them you read, the harder it becomes to credit the claim that all these people are somehow deluded about their own desires."

These issues have been thoroughly addressed by anti-censorship feminists in *Pleasure and Danger: Exploring Female Sexuality*, by S/M lesbians in *Coming to Power*, and in the writings of Pat Califia. Even observers who are unfriendly to pornography know the difference between S/M sex play and real violence. Psychotherapist Louise Kaplan notes, "Most couples who participate in sadomasochistic scenarios are willing . . . to exchange roles. Most often both partners are searching for a good 'top,' a master who is in complete control of his or her sadism, allowing the slave to be assured that his or her sexual excitement will not go out of bounds either." In other words, trust is an essential element of S/M and bondage, as both Jay and the man who pretended to kidnap and rape a lover at the New Orleans airport attested in my survey.

"Many women recoil at S/M because it seems to reflect what history teaches them men want most: to inflict sadistic pain on them," writes James Ridgeway, a journalist and author of *Red Light: Inside the Sex Industry*. "But the surprise of the commercial S/M scene is that it most often finds men on their knees, abject slaves of their steely dominatrixes. Often cross-dressed in women's clothing, they clank around in medieval chains, their cocks and balls ingeniously tied up, their bare asses lashed by whips, as they perform housewifely chores."

In discussing a porn novel called *Whip Chick*, Dworkin wrote: "The portrayal of men as sexual victims is distinctly unreal, ludicrous in part because it scarcely has an analogue in the real world." In other words, Dworkin argues that most porn is real to its viewers, but *this* porn is not. Apparently, men are perceptive enough to see through the utter fantasy of "powerful women" (but does that mean they are not turned on by it?), but the rest of the time they cannot see that the treatment and behavior of women in pornography is mere fantasy. She offers no explanation for the difference, other than that she says so. But other commentators disagree. The late John Preston, a popular author of gay pornographic stories, interviewed "Mistress Holly," the owner/manager of an expensive brothel near Sunset and Vine in Hollywood, and reported:

> Holly speculated that only 15 percent of the male clients of the House of O were dominant in their sexual desires. They are watched carefully [with audio monitors], she said, to make sure they never go too far. . . . "But the vast majority of the men come for a dominatrix. They are men who are usually in charge all the time. They are the type who lord it over their wives, play the father role to the hilt with their children, and are probably giving the orders at work, too. They just can't hold up to that pressure. So they come here and they hand over all their power and all their decision making to the domme."

Kaplan writes that among clinically defined sex perverts, the rate of sexual masochism is something like twenty males to each female. "Mistress Anastasia," a professional dominatrix, told Ridgeway that hurting men and getting paid for it helped heal her past sufferings at the hands of men.

All of this contradicts the antiporn notion that it is primarily—even solely—the domination of women that excites consumers of pornography. "Pornography reveals that male pleasure is inextricably tied to victimizing, hurting, exploiting," writes Dworkin, "that sexual fun and sexual passion in the privacy of the male imagination are inseparable from the brutality of male history." On the contrary, pornography may be the place where men escape from male history and social contexts, to go where women always say yes (instead of the no men hear so often in the real world), and where men do not have to take command and be in control, but instead are commanded and desired. Human sexuality (and pornographic taste) is much richer than Dworkin would lead people to believe.

That some folks do abuse others, physically and sexually, or that they might become sexually aroused by depictions of bondage and S/M sex for "the wrong reasons," cannot be the basis for condemning pornography, any more than we condemn alcohol for fatal auto accidents. Since Prohibition, there has never been a strong public call for a ban on alcohol, but there *is* an expectation that individual human beings will use alcohol responsibly or suffer the consequences. As a woman once wrote, when she was a child she "liked the sex-and-dominance games, which could be overtly sadomasochistic, because I liked the risk and the intensity. . . ." Whether she suffered lasting harm because of such play is anybody's guess: Her name is Andrea Dworkin.

The most extreme form of pornography, and therefore the handiest weapon in the "porn-is-violence" debate, is the "snuff" film, in which a woman is tortured and actually killed on camera for the sexual pleasure of the viewer. According to Beverly LaBelle, the term comes from a movie by that title in which a woman apparently is cut up by a dagger so that the viewer is treated to "chopped-up fingers, flying arms, sawed-off legs, and yet more blood oozing like a river out of her mouth before she dies." When *Snuff* surfaced in 1976, feminist protests shut it down in some cities. The film helped to galvanize the antipornography movement into the 1980s.

The only problem was that it was a hoax: an old-fashioned horror/slasher flick with some nudity thrown in. When Manhattan District Attorney Robert Morgenthau investigated, he discovered *Snuff* was really a 1971 Argentine movie called *Slaughter*, to which some extra scenes had been spliced. A story in the *New York Times* noted that the "victim" was interviewed by a policewoman, and the authorities concluded, "The actress is alive and well." A decade later, Susan Cole admitted the deception was "obvious from a close viewing," but she insisted that "'snuff' movies exist as a genre. Police report that violent abusers *do* film the slow deaths of their victims."

Well, it's true, they do. Not in order to sell it to others, however, but only to please themselves. According to John Douglas, head of the FBI's serial crimes unit:

> They kill or rape or torture because they enjoy it, because it gives them satisfaction and a feeling of domination and control so lacking from every other aspect of their shabby, inadequate, and cowardly lives. So much do many of them enjoy what they do that they want nothing more than to experience it again at every opportunity. . . . [I]n California, Leonard Lake and his partner, Charles Ng, produced videos of young women they'd captured being stripped and psychologically brutalized—offering voice-over commentary along the way.

Douglas refers to the videos as Lake and Ng's "home movies."

Given that isolated psychopaths record their crimes in the privacy of their lair for their own pleasure, one cannot assert that such material is manufactured for the purpose of public sale to Dworkin's "boy-next-door"—who wouldn't want it in any case. Based on that slim but crucial misconception, however, one finds references to snuff in nearly every book and essay by opponents of pornography, often with no citation of an authoritative source at all.

"In Los Angeles, a woman hired through an agency is murdered, and filmed during this murder," and then "men pay huge sums of money to see a film which . . . has captured a real death of a real woman," Griffin says. For evidence, she refers the reader to Laura Lederer's interview with former porn actress "Jane Jones," whose account of snuff involves stories that "came down the grapevine." So much for hard evidence. Similarly, Aminatta Forna assures us that snuff films "are believed [there's that passive voice again: "are believed" by whom?] to be flourishing with the use of untraceable illegal immigrants and Latin American women and children as their victims," but she offers no proof.

In her otherwise heavily annotated book *Gyn/Ecology*, Mary Daly displaces the evidence one degree: "In a notorious underground porn movie shown in New York, an actual rape-murder was done to the unsuspecting 'actress,' and the popular movie *Snuff* simulated this original, capitalizing on the voracious voyeuristic appetite of film-goers." Unfortunately, Daly provides no documentation that would support either the existence of this "notorious underground porn movie" or the inflammatory adjectives "popular" or "voracious" with regard to the imitation. If *Snuff* had truly been popular, you would expect the men in my survey to have seen it, but everyone referred to the film itself as well as the genre by reputation only. That doesn't stop Daly from going on: "This kind of entertainment is enjoyed by judges, physicians, policemen, and other professionals today, all in the line of 'duty,' when women who have been victimized (rape victims, for example) come under their power."

If snuff films were really on the market, feminists would have hunted them down and held them up for gruesome display. Law enforcement agencies would be jumping for joy to possess the most perfect homicide evidence one could ever hope to put before a judge or jury. Why hasn't this happened?

As a professor of law who must live or die by her citations, MacKinnon has worked the hardest to provide backup for such claims. "Information . . . is understandably hard to get," she admits. Why? Because everybody wants to hide this heinous proof of the common man's depravity, or simply because it is so rare as to be effectively non-existent? Apart from quoting Senator Arlen Specter's remarks in the *Congressional Record* as an authority, in several of her books MacKinnon cites a single Orange County, California municipal court case in which a man was convicted of murdering two young girls in the process of making a film. She invariably buries this information in an end note—perhaps because, as she admits, "the film was never found." But somehow this enables her to insist of snuff films that "They exist," and "The intended consumer has a sexual experience watching [them]" (apparently "intended" consumers are as good as real ones). Evidently the Orange County case is also sufficient to support rhetorical questions like "How many women's bodies have to stack up here even to register against male profit and pleasure presented as First Amendment principle?" If no one can be shown to have purchased or sold such material, then profit and the First Amendment are red herring issues.

Less scrupulous commentators than MacKinnon assert that there are snuff films "priced to make [them] available to Everyman," and "increasingly popular as videos in the American home"[!]. Even Cole, who acknowledged in 1989 that *Snuff* was an "elaborate hoax . . . that was obvious from a close viewing," referred to the movie by name in a public panel discussion four years later as "absolutely the ultimate though not the typical pornographic nightmare, featuring the actual death of a woman for the sexual pleasure of the consumer," and reprinted her remarks in a 1995 book. Although she acknowledged thirty pages later that the movie was "a hoax," Cole apparently didn't tell the Toronto audience about this during the panel discussion. As always, she also never made it clear that the vast majority of porn consumers not only wouldn't be interested in such material, but haven't even seen it.

In 1997, journalist and former Israeli soldier and police detective Yaron Svoray published *Gods of Death*, the remarkable account of his search for a genuine snuff film. The trail took him to Thailand, Germany, Miami, Los Angeles, New York, London, Paris, Amsterdam, and the war zones of Bosnia. In pursuit of his goal, he committed breaking and entering, hired bodyguards and a cast of 16 to participate in a sting, rented $150,000 in counterfeit money from a Beirut crime boss, and spent thousands of dollars of his own money—much of it on dead ends and swindles. A career FBI agent told him, "As far as anyone in the bureau knows, there has never been a legitimate snuff movie ever found." An officer in the New York Police Department's child crimes unit said, "I've never seen one and I hope I never do." A 29-year veteran of the Dutch police assured Svoray there was no such thing.

Yet Svoray managed to view a snuff film in a wealthy man's Connecticut home, and in Bosnia he found brutal video footage of sex slayings by soldiers. I believe he saw what he says he saw. But he clearly shows that such movies are closely guarded by their (probably criminal) owners, *not* sold to the public, and that the Bosnian footage of rape-killings of women—like the movie made by MacKinnon's Orange County killers—was incidental to the actual carnage. The video included sequences of blindfolded men being executed and solders firing on crowds of men as well as rapes and killings of women. This violence was not staged for the purpose of manufacturing pornography: The victims would have suffered and died if there had been no camera around or theoretical consumers to buy. Svoray concludes, "There was no snuff porn industry. There was no conspiracy. The darkness was everywhere, everywhere." He adds, "Pornography was not the problem, it was a symptom. . . . Blood sells." Yet I suspect that MacKinnon will cite Svoray in her subsequent books as proof that snuff exists and men want it.

That truly hideous material is out there cannot be denied. But the people who refer to this monstrous footage when they say "pornography" have never bothered to prove that it is what most men like to see. The fact is, most men *haven't* seen it, nor would they want to. Pretending that the most extreme and rare forms of pornography represent the acme of the form—the grail toward which all porn consumers secretly yearn—is like pretending that Jeffrey Dahmer is the person all eaters of fast-food burgers aspire to be. It is a measure of how successfully the enemies of pornography have sold this myth to the American public that so many men in my survey used the word "snuff," even if only to affirm they had never seen it, did not wish to, and in some cases were all for an utter ban on it.

If anyone ever finds some.

Porn Causes Men to be Violent

A more serious charge than the notion that pornography portrays violence is that it causes violence in the real world. Declares Dworkin, "men believe . . . that they have the right to rape" and "men really believe they have the right to hit and to hurt." Not *some* men, not men who are addicted to pornography—just men, period. And in case you thought Dworkin was being careless, she writes elsewhere: "Pacifist males are only apparent exceptions; repelled by some forms of violence as nearly all men are, they remain impervious to sexual violence as nearly all men do."

The argument has two facets: first, that pornography creates a climate of increasing violence in society by inuring its consumers to violence in general; second, that it causes its users to be violent toward women. Opponents of pornography have two methods of making the case. The argument rests partly upon laboratory studies that suggest a connection between the consumption of pornography and increased callousness toward women, greater propensity to rape or to discount the seriousness of rape, and a taste for increasing violence. Second, opponents of porn list real-life examples in which pornography played an apparent role in a particular man's violence against women—a serial sex killer, usually—as well as a few studies that suggest ordinary men have "gotten ideas" from pornographic material and forced their partners to participate.

The primary lab research to which critics of pornography refer has been conducted by Edward Donnerstein, Neil Malamuth, Dolf Zillmann, Daniel Linz, and others. This is not the place to discuss the weaknesses of these studies at length, particularly when they have already been extensively critiqued by others. (See, for example, Bill

Thompson's *Soft Core* and Alison King's essay, "Mystery and Imagination: the case of pornography effects studies," in Assiter and Carol's *Bad Girls and Dirty Books*.)

Suffice it to say that most studies have used college students, who were handy for researchers but might not accurately represent the population at large. Young adults in their late teens and early twenties tend to be sexually and romantically inexperienced. They probably have unclear ideas about what they might or might not do, and what is and is not acceptable behavior. Critics of pornography usually fail to note that female college students in these surveys sometimes show as much heightened aggression, arousal, and callousness as males.

As for examples from life, there are primarily two: killers whose acts and convictions are a matter of legal record, and "average men" who force pornography and porn-inspired sex upon their domestic partner in the privacy of their home. In the first case, antipornography activists often cite a favorite psychopath who owned pornography or supposedly used it shortly before or during the commission of a heinous crime. Susan Cole names Clifford Olson, a child-killer whose dresser drawers were "crammed with pornographic magazines" (though she provides no citation for this claim); the Ontario rapist/killer of Barbra Schlifer who "explained in sworn testimony that he had had a pornographic magazine in his hand when he cut his victim open"; and Paul Bernardo, whose Toronto trial revealed that he had videotaped the rape and torture of two teenaged girls before killing them. Of Lawrence Singleton, a man who raped a 15-year-old girl and cut off her arms, Susan Griffin writes that "He must have read pornography," although she offers no evidence that he did and admits charitably, if ungrammatically, that "every man who has read pornography does not behave as he did." Ted Bundy, the serial killer who implicated pornography in an interview videotaped by the Reverend James Dobson shortly before Bundy's execution, is the most famous specimen; even some of the men in my survey referred to him.

Horrible as such examples are, they require massive assumptions to support a conclusion that pornography "caused" the violence. Not one of the critics bothers to examine the killers' troubled childhoods. Olson was reported to his teachers as a "bully, a thief and a con artist," and he said he had been raped by an uncle when he was four. Bernardo was given to violent tantrums as a child, and ran away from home at age five or six and wasn't missed. Bundy's mother pretended to be his sister and told him his grandparents were his parents. His grandfather Sam Cowell was a workaholic who terrorized his family with temper tantrums, swung cats by the tail, and kicked dogs. Bundy's Aunt Julia told a psychologist who evaluated Bundy that when she was 15 and Ted was 3, he laid knives around her body while she was sleeping. Both Bernardo and Bundy apparently suffered the stigma of "illegitimacy": Bernardo learned at 16 from his mother that he was the progeny of an affair, and Bundy was shocked at 22 when cousins teased him about the truth: that his mother had borne him out of wedlock and Bundy was his third legal surname before the age of five.

To accept the antiporn case, one must presume that the "propaganda" of pornography was somehow more influential in these men's lives than the violence and humiliation they suffered at the hands of real people. "Our research has shown that virtually all serial killers come from dysfunctional backgrounds of sexual or physical abuse, drugs or alcoholism," says the FBI's John Douglas. "I'm not going to tell you that pornography fuels the desires of someone who wasn't already thinking in that direction."

Plus, as Alison King points out, "the fairly strong consensus among researchers is that sex offenders invariably had *less* exposure to pornography than the average male—a point accepted even by the Meese Commission." This seems counter to common sense, but a study by Kant and Goldstein showed that sex offenders tended to grow up in households where there was almost no discussion of sexuality, and the values were traditional and conservative. Many of the rapists Goldstein studied had been discovered with pornography in their teens and severely punished. It would seem that sexual socialization and general attitudes—the context for these particular men's experience of pornography—were greater factors than exposure to porn in itself.

Furthermore, focusing on isolated killers ignores the hundreds of thousands—even millions—of men who look at pornography and never abuse their partners and acquaintances—men similar to most of the males in my survey. It is easy to say killers like Bundy and Bernardo were fans of pornography and leave it at that; few acknowledge that men like theologian Paul Tillich, jazz trumpeter Louis Armstrong, and symphony conductor Eugene Goossens were, too.

"I think it's natural to look at pornography," M. Scott Peck, psychiatrist and author of the multimillion seller *The Road Less Traveled*, has said. "*I* like it." A recent account of American submarine espionage refers casually to "life on a sub where the outside world was represented mainly by stockpiles of girlie magazines and 'crotch novels' with titles like *Cocksure Girls* hidden on board." Despite the longtime association of prostitution and pornography with soldiers, no one suggests that military service is an inherently bad influence on American youth. Most of the sailors on the USS Seawolf either had wives and children or would eventually commit to them. "The fact of the matter is that most people who buy and read pornography are not at all dangerous and never commit antisocial offenses," says Douglas.

Noting the significance of family background, and the fact that researchers such as Donnerstein and Malamuth never investigated their subjects' prior sexual attitudes for comparison in their studies, Kathryn Kelley tested groups of men and found that those who had the most "positive" sexual attitudes displayed the least antisocial effects in response to viewing porn. "Sex-guilt" feelings seemed to influence a person's negative responses the most. To implicate pornography as the primary cause of the activities of violent, crazy individuals who probably would have been violent and crazy even if they had never seen a picture of a naked woman, makes as much sense as banning alcohol because spouse abusers are often drunk when they batter their partner.

Deborah Cameron and Elizabeth Frazer question the addiction model of pornography use and forcefully argue *against* implicating pornography in the crimes of Ted Bundy. If his cause-and-effect stories sounded comfortingly familiar, they write, "it is because feminism . . .

has made them so." Sex killers' confessions come "not . . . from some privileged personal insight, but from a finite repertoire of cultural clichés which the murderer, like everyone else, has come across in case histories, pop-psychology, newspapers, films and ordinary gossip with family, friends and workmates." Cameron and Frazer argue that such accounts *"come from the culture"*—their emphasis—and have become an acceptable new discourse when older ones like devil possession have been discredited. It is not sufficient to accept a story like Bundy's just because it "appears to be feminist."

Ann Rule, who knew Bundy personally and wrote a biography of him, is convinced he was merely spinning another tale with his "eleventh-hour confession" about pornography:

> I wish that I could believe his motives were altruistic. But all I can see in that Dobson tape is another Ted Bundy manipulation of our minds. The effect of the tape is to place, once again, the onus of his crimes—not on himself—but on us. I don't think pornography caused Ted Bundy to kill thirty-six or one hundred or three hundred women. . . . The blunt fact is that Ted Bundy was a liar. He lied most of his life, and I think he lied at the end.

The notion that users of pornography "force" sex acts they have seen in it upon their partners is more difficult to disprove, since it involves mostly law-abiding citizens in the privacy of their homes as opposed to convicted sex criminals with trial records. That this notion is just as difficult to *prove* has not stopped the foes of pornography from making wholesale assertions. When Cole claims that "users force women they know to buy pornography, look at it and/or replicate the activities in the pictures," her only evidence is interviews at a battered women's shelter in Ontario, and Diana Russell's study (discussed below). "For some men pornography becomes so integrated with their sexuality that they will attempt to act it out with their partners," says Baker. This assessment is hardly sinister *unless* one presumes that: A) not a single woman would ever want to do anything shown in pornography, B) men routinely do not listen to what their partners want and do not want, and C) "getting ideas" from entertainment—like wanting to take up ballroom dancing after seeing an Astaire/Rogers movie—is somehow unusual and objectionable.

Other opponents of pornography put it more bluntly. "On paper and in life, pornography is thrust upon unwilling women in their homes," asserts MacKinnon. In another book, she writes, "it is not the ideas in pornography that assault women: men do, men who are made, changed, and impelled by it." She knows this because she knows what goes on in every man's head: "Sooner or later, in one way or another, the consumers want to live out the pornography further in three dimensions. Sooner or later, in one way or another, they do. *It* makes them want to; when they believe they can, when they feel they can get away with it, *they* do." Apparently men are victims too.

But seriously, when MacKinnon writes that "sooner or later, all men want to do what they see in pornography," if she means they want to try some of the sex acts with a consenting partner, and see ecstasy on a woman's face, then the men in my survey would agree. But just before that sentence MacKinnon refers to "murdering a young woman . . . raping her, having vaginal and anal intercourse with her corpse, and chewing on several parts of her body"; and I cannot say a single man in my survey mentioned this as a cherished fantasy.

How can MacKinnon know that men want to "live out" everything they see in pornography? Russell offers as proof a 1971 study by Donald Mosher that said 16 percent of college male students he had judged to be "sex calloused" had "attempted to obtain intercourse by showing pornography to a woman, or by taking her to a 'sexy' movie." However, there was no mention of whether the men were "successful" or the women politely declined and were ushered home safely; or whether the men may have chosen women they judged to be interested in sex, susceptible, or vulnerable in the first place. If the men had sex-calloused attitudes, would they perhaps have used the "blue balls," "sex clears pimples," or "if you love me" method to get sex forty years before? And what about the other 84 percent of the young men Mosher *also* thought were sex calloused who did *not* use pornography to try to get sex—not to mention the ones he believed were not sex calloused at all? The 1992 University of Chicago *Sex in America* survey indicated that between 1942 and 1992 the number of men and women who reached the age of twenty and were still virgins had risen steadily, with the proportion of men outpacing that of women. Clearly pornography is not doing the job its opponents claim.

Russell also cites a 1992 study by Charlene Senn that suggested women exposed to pornography are more likely to have been forced or coerced into sex. But is this a causal link or only a correlation? Perhaps women who are more adventurous, who take more risks, are both more likely to encounter pornography (and even enjoy it), and to enter a situation where they run into trouble with men. In many of these cases, the Senn study found, men were present when the women were exposed to pornography, "which means that most women who consume pornography are doing it because a man wants them to," Russell says. However, neither Senn nor Russell showed that the women *didn't* want to! We all do things (and *want* to do them) because our partner wants to. Russell and Senn assume force or coercion on the part of men and resistance on the part of the women when pornography is present; but they never showed that the forced sex and the pornography figured in the same incident.

In her own study of 930 randomly selected women 18 years and older in the San Francisco area, Russell found that 14 percent had been asked to pose for pornographic pictures at some point in their lives, and 10 percent said they had been upset by someone trying to get them to enact something he or she had seen in pornography. According to her questions, these women could have been asked to pose a number of times and only been upset once: *Why* were they upset? Just because someone asked them to pose, or because of *how* they were asked or *who* was doing the asking?

About 24 percent (or a total of eight) of the married women in Russell's survey who had been raped by their husbands said they had been upset by requests to enact pornography. These are not huge figures to begin with, but MacKinnon, who often turns to Russell's survey for her wilder claims, somehow alters this to 24 percent of *all* the married women in the survey, not just the ones who had been raped by their husbands, and comments, "That is a lot of women."

Well, yes, that *would* be a lot of women—as many as 160—if it were true, but that's not what Russell's survey found. The 24 percent applied only to a small subset of all the married women in the survey: those who had been raped by their husbands (about 33 women). Furthermore, of those eight married women who were upset by their partner's request to do something he had seen in pornography, several women refused and that was that. Some wives had indeed been raped, beaten, or forced to perform anal intercourse or fellatio as an enactment of something seen in pornography, but in some cases the women reported, "It was a proposition; it never happened," "I always refuse," or "I make a mockery of him; I tore them up." This hardly conforms to the notion of men "forcing" unwanted sex acts on their helpless and non-consenting partners.

In my survey, one rarely saw the addictive, overbearing behavior of men depicted in antiporn literature. Almost none of the men I talked to conformed to this pattern: They were considerate and discreet. Their partners adopted a "live and let live" attitude about the men's activities, which the men reciprocated. If the women were not interested, the men rarely forced the issue and kept their own use private. If women expressed curiosity, the men were delighted to share the pornography, but just as quick to put it away if the women did not enjoy it. Often, the men waited for a sign from the women. "My wife will sometimes watch a video with me," one man said. "It's rare, but when it happens, it's generally her idea. She's not very interested in it, but I think she sometimes likes to use it because she knows I like it and that it can excite me."

Even Ted Bundy backed down when his longtime Seattle girlfriend balked. She told police that he suggested they try bondage after he saw it described in *The Joy of Sex*. They did it several times before she refused to do it any more. He was not happy, but he abided by her wishes.

How could there be such a disparity between what the enemies of pornography believe and what the evidence and the men in this survey had to say? As Jen Durbin has observed:

> It's too easy to get a skewed impression of porn if you only read about it. Students who read Andrea Dworkin become convinced that pornography equals pictures of dead Asian women hanging from trees, smiling buxom women meeting a gruesome fate in a meat grinder, ecstatic women fellating revolvers, etc. Students who read Nina Hartley become convinced that pornography is a form of self-actualization for uninhibited feminists.

First, I think crusaders against pornography have a tendency to read more into people's remarks and surveys than is warranted. To open an essay called "Pornography and Rape: A Causal Model," for instance, Russell quotes a man from Shere Hite's survey on why he wants to rape women and what he fantasizes about when he thinks of doing it. But the man never said that he *did* rape anyone, he was just describing his thoughts. Russell doesn't show that he also looked at pornography, and she takes no note of the pages and pages of testimony in Hite's book headed "Many men would not rape a woman." According to Russell, when Hite asked if the men had ever wanted to rape a woman, 46 percent of her anonymous respondents answered "yes or sometimes," which makes it sound worse than it was. Actually, 14 percent said yes and 32 percent said sometimes, so the bulk of the respondents were somewhat tentative about it. Russell continues, "7% said they had fantasies of rape, but presumably had not acted them out—yet." That's a gratuitous "yet." Did it ever occur to Russell to ask women—particularly feminist colleagues who had written about their rape fantasies, such as Robin Morgan—when they expected their fantasies of being raped to be realized? Russell is puzzled that an even greater portion of the *non*-anonymous men in Hite's survey, 52 percent, indicated that "yes or sometimes," they had wanted to rape a woman. Since these men felt no need to hide their identity, perhaps they were simply more comfortable with their fantasies and knew they could control them.

Russell then makes a sizable leap in logic: "Hite's percentages are quite comparable to my finding that 44% of a probability sample of 930 adult women residing in San Francisco reported having been the victim of one or more rapes or attempted rapes over the course of their lives." In other words, because roughly half the men in a non-representative Shere Hite survey said they had occasional thoughts of raping someone, and roughly half the women in a Diana Russell survey had been raped or suffered an attempted rape, the men who think about raping *do* commit rape or attempt it. This is an illogical and unwarranted conclusion, because it assumes thought equals action, and posits a one-to-one correspondence between rapists and victims, when one might easily argue that a small group of men commit multiple rapes and assaults upon a larger group of women. Men's "propensity to rape," as Russell terms it, may be no more prevalent than women's propensity to strike their children—that is, often considered, seldom performed.

Russell properly concludes that "having a desire to behave in a certain way is not the same as actually behaving in that way, . . . [but] it is helpful to have this kind of baseline information on the desires and predispositions of males, who are, after all, the chief consumers of pornography." Unfortunately for her case, *nowhere* does Russell show that the 46 to 52 percent of the males in Hite's survey who occasionally "thought of rape" were the males who looked at pornography the most, or that they had a record of mistreating women or a likelihood of actually raping anyone.

Now and then, the zeal of antiporn advocates leads to outright sloppiness. On the subject of "habituation" to violence in porn, Russell refers to a 1984 study by Dolf Zillmann and Jennings Bryant. She says the study showed "that an appetite for stronger material was fostered in their subjects, presumably, Zillmann suggests, 'because familiar material becomes unexciting as a result of habituation,' (1984, p. 127)." Hence, "'consumers graduate from common to less common forms of pornography,' that is, to more violent and more degrading materials (1984, p. 127)." That sounds pretty convincing, but I couldn't find the quotes Russell attributes to Zillman on the cited page 127, or *anywhere else* in the article!

Russell also gets many of the details wrong. She says it was a six-week study when it actually took nine weeks. She says Zillmann and Bryant's "massive exposure" study showed various pornographic materials to undergraduate subjects for "4 hours and 48 minutes per week" and remarks that this "was not that massive." Even so, she over-reports the exposure by 500 percent, because it was actually only 48 *minutes per week* (thus, four hours and 48 minutes *total* over the six weeks). Finally, Russell says, "Various measures were taken after 1 week, 2 weeks, and 3 weeks of exposure," but the measurements she refers to were taken one, two, and three weeks *after the six weeks of watching pornography were over* (which is why the study lasted nine weeks, not the six weeks Russell erroneously reports). If she can't even get the basic design and procedures of the study right, how can we trust her description of the more complicated matter of its findings?

The remarks Russell attributes to Zillmann are not out of character for him, but it is impossible to see how either researcher could have derived these conclusions from his study. All Zillmann's measurements indicated was that each time the college-student subjects viewed explicit material again, their heart rate and blood pressure did not climb as high as on previous viewings. This suggests they were less shocked and aroused in a general sense (which could mean anything from less sexual excitement to less embarrassment and anxiety in general). *The researchers never asked any of the subjects whether they wanted to see more explicit material,* however, which pretty much destroys Zillmann's presumption of "habituation," or what I have referred to as the slippery slope. Apparently, it never occurred to Zillmann or Russell that decreased arousal and excitement could just as easily indicate lessened embarrassment and surprise, and ultimately a lack of interest, as a hunger for more pornography. Given a choice, perhaps the subjects would have preferred a Disney movie. All that can fairly be said is that some exposure reduced the arousal or shock value over time.

As with other studies, Zillman and Bryant noted that differences in the way males and females responded to the materials were "trivial statistically." This means that males and females were aroused in much the same way (something Russell and many other antiporn activists rarely bother to report) and that "massive prior exposure [to pornography] reduced aggressiveness sharply" in both sexes. Although the researchers were puzzled that after massive exposure to pornography, the research subjects were more likely to recommend shorter terms of imprisonment in a hypothetical rape trial—"rape is apparently considered a lesser offense" after exposure to porn—they added that in this too, "effects of massive exposure applied to males and females equally. The females' dispositions toward rape and its punishment were apparently just as much influenced as those of males."

Senn is one of the few enemies of porn who acknowledges that "studies of sexual arousal using both men and women have shown that sex differences in arousal to sexually explicit materials (no violent content) do not exist." Several studies, she admits, suggest "women are as aroused as men to pictures and written depictions of sex whether the content is affectional and romantic or not." In her own research, women's levels of anger and confusion dropped considerably on successive viewings of a slide show of violent and nonviolent pornography.

Senn calls this "affective desensitization" and worries that "lessened anger might reduce the chance of social responses." But why presume that the initial response is the more "true" one? A simpler explanation would be that the shock value dissipated, the women got used to the unfamiliar material, and they felt less personally threatened and could evaluate it more objectively. Their initial response could be likened to the fear and anxiety we feel toward the unknown—strangers from the other side of the globe, for instance—and what Senn calls "affective desensitization" could be more accurately termed "increased understanding and comfort" such as we experience once we have met and talked with strangers from China or the Congo. How many of us reacted with puzzlement and unease—even fear—the first time we heard about sex itself?

Rather than read too much into gender roles or pornography's influence, I would suggest that the ready response of males and females to pornography in these studies is yet another confirmation that college students may be more suggestible—because they are less sexually experienced and mature—than older people.

Despite the holes in their logic, the opponents of pornography often admit that their minds are simply made up. Kathleen Barry writes: "I submit that the causal connections between pornography and sexual violence are perfectly evident. We do not need to follow individual men out of specific pornographic theaters and witness them raping the first woman they see to realize as women what impact pornography has on our lives. We need only appeal to our common sense." Ray Wyre, who treats child sex abusers, says simply, "I don't know how many men actually have fantasies and don't put them into practice. But *I don't care about that* [emphasis added]. What I do know is the more they masturbate to pornography, the more likely they will be to put their fantasy into practice." With that reasoning, one should lobby to have all the fans of murder mysteries and true crime stories locked away before they are inspired to do some harm based on all the fantasy homicides and historic mayhem they read about. The most laughable analogies are fostered by MacKinnon: in at least two of her books, she suggests showing pornography to a man is like "saying 'kill' to a trained attack dog. . . ."

The theory that "porn causes people to be violent" is pretty suspect, Kathleen Barry's notion of common sense notwithstanding. If it were true that the more pornography a man sees, the more likely he is to commit violence, then older men would be more violent: Like radiation poisoning, the cumulative effect of repeated exposures to pornography eventually would kick in as their lives continued. But according to the FBI's *Uniform Crime Reports*, the largest concentration of men arrested for forcible rape is between the ages of 16 and 24. Sixty-one percent of the offenders are under the age of 25. As Susan Brownmiller writes, "The typical American perpetrator of forcible rape is little more than an aggressive, hostile youth who chooses to do violence to women," not a man who has seen years of pornography and finally snapped under the weight of it.

In all the books and essays against pornography I have read, I'm not sure I have ever seen the word "testosterone," or some form of the verb "to mature." Yet falling levels of testosterone, coupled with experience, increased understanding of the effects of one's actions on others, and a personal investment in one's relationships and career, all surely play a bigger role in one's propensity for violence of any kind than how many pictures of naked women one has seen.

And if antiporn commentators have been wrong about what men have been feeling, what might they have gotten wrong about what men have been seeing?

The Public Debate:

What Did Everyone Get Wrong About Pornography?

Since they have never consulted men for their perspectives, critics of pornography naturally missed quite a bit of the picture when they tried to describe what men think and feel as they use it. But what about pornography itself? How does the "message" of porn as constructed by its enemies compare to what the men say they see?

The Primary Tenets of Antipornography Theory

Opponents of pornography have constructed a theory of porn that rests on the concepts of objectification, subordination, degradation, and hatred of women.

Objectification. In the opening essay of *Take Back the Night*, Diana Russell and Laura Lederer assert, "even the most banal pornography objectifies women's bodies." By this they mean that "women are not seen as human beings but things." As British theorist Catherine Itzin puts it, women are "reduced to their sexual body parts, completely dehumanized, pieces of meat. . . ."

Crusaders often overstate the case. Dorchen Leidholdt told the Meese Commission "we rarely see the woman's face" in pornography, which is plainly not true. Whether during fellatio or any other sex act, men in my survey said they liked to see the woman's face, because her genuine enjoyment and excitement were important to them. Susan Lurie writes: "In pornography woman's body (and especially her genitals) is displayed as a dehumanized object to be exposed, manipulated, and, often enough, mutilated." This would be news to the men in my survey, few of whom described seeing anything like mutilation, let alone wanting to.

Opponents of pornography often use the word "dehumanizing." Pornography removes the humanity from women and makes them objects, the argument goes. Susan Griffin writes that the pornographic female "spreads apart her thighs and stares into the camera. Her tongue licks her lips. Her eyes reflect back nothing: she is not human. . . . at each turn of her body, at each face or curvature exposed, we see nothing. For there is no person there." Griffin lays on the dead metaphors: the woman "shows her goods," she is "like a piece of furniture," and the camera "produces an image of a thing." But this is open to interpretation. Do men really see what Griffin sees, let alone desire it?

According to many of the men in my survey, the answer is no. When men described what they liked in pornography, not a few said they liked to see a woman enjoying herself. They liked to see a spark of emotion and intelligence. They did not like dumb or selfish women and men. They did not like to look at people who "weren't into it"—in other words, people who behaved like objects. How would they know, if they couldn't see the woman's face? The fact that some men sought videos and magazines that featured a particular model or actress suggests they keyed into something personal, however tenuous or illusory, and that the performer mattered as well as the sex acts. Alan Soble, a professor of philosophy, notes that eye contact between the model and the viewer is often staged in photos and videos, which is a kind of communication—"the expression and recognition of intentions." He describes the interchange thus:

> The model who poses and licks her lips knows how the photographs are to be used, and she acts in that way in order to arouse the viewer. The viewer, in turn, knows that the model is acting in order to arouse, recognizes her intention to arouse, and is aroused by recognizing her intention to arouse. Despite the time and space between the two people, the model also appreciates that the viewer's recognition of her intention to arouse will contribute to his arousal, and she knows this while she is acting so as to arouse.

Men in my survey confirmed Soble's hypothesis. They appreciated the eye contact, which made the women seem a little more human, not less. One man said, "Just the eye contact is crucial, and the sense that the woman is there, is involved and into it." Said another, "I like to see women give a look that says 'I want you.' If their eyes are closed, that doesn't arouse me as much."

Objectification theory tends to overlook the extent to which we objectify people in other media. When our eye is drawn to an ad for a beer or automobile because a pretty woman is also in the picture, she has been objectified—both by the ad agency and by us. Canadian philosophy professor F.M. Christensen observes that "a little girl's doll represents real people as passive objects to be used and manipulated," as do "posters of pop stars that women pin up, or even photographs of loved ones. . . ."

When Dworkin asserts that "Objectification, in fact and in consequence, is never trivial," she is simply wrong. If objectification is a process that occurs in our heads when we look at someone (or a picture of someone)—seeing and making a snap judgment about that person without complete information about his or her nature—then we objectify other people many times a day. When we accord automatic respect to someone in a white lab coat or someone who steps up to a lectern, we have objectified that person. When we shy away from an unkempt character on the street, this is an act of objectification. On further investigation, the person in the white coat may be an actor or an escapee from a mental institution, and the street person is actually Howard Hughes or the Messiah; the point is that our initial act of objectification does not freeze the person in stone now and forever—we can respond to further input and continuously modify our judgments.

Soble observes that people regularly "dehumanize" one another for casual sex in a one-night stand, but it is a mutual transaction, so some forms of dehumanization must be, in his words, "morally permissible." I do nothing wrong, he suggests, if I fail to smile or say anything to a ticket-taker at the theater—and thereby treat the person like a ticket-taking machine—but there are limits: I cannot therefore step on her foot or cough in his face.

Antiporn analyses also neglect the issue of context. *This* means *that*, and *only* that, their arguments run. Nudity means loss of power (rather than an attempt to impress and evoke awe), the male gaze can only be degrading and acquisitive (rather than admiring and respectful), and women who enjoy performing fellatio and being squirted with ejaculate (let alone simply posing naked for men) must be deluded, brainwashed, and coerced.

At one point, Dworkin defines objectification in a more strict sexual sense: "the fixed response to the form of another that has as its inevitable consequence erection. . . ." But this too is inaccurate. Some men in my survey found *Playboy* nudes arousing in that sense, while others regarded the pictorials more as art. Some men masturbated every time they looked at pornography; others did not. The response was not "fixed" at all.

Enacting to arouse cannot be dehumanizing in itself, otherwise we would have to outlaw cosmetics, low-cut blouses, slit skirts, dancing, and other practices that once were reproved by Victorians and continue to be in certain Islamic nations. "Until the day women's bodies are not used to sell cars, cosmetics are not a necessity to the success of a woman's image, and we are not humiliated and tortured for men's pleasure, women will have no rights," MacKinnon declares. The idea that women have no rights is hyperbole, of course, as is the implication that women are routinely coerced into dressing provocatively. Note how casually MacKinnon equates having to wear cosmetics with being tortured. This statement appears in a book whose cover photograph shows the author wearing earrings. Is this a demonstration that even Mac-Kinnon cannot escape the tyranny of social objectification of women? (One also wonders whether the healthy glow of her skin was enhanced by makeup: Did MacKinnon choose this herself, was she merely encouraged to look more attractive, or did Harvard University Press coerce her into donning rouge by threatening to hold up publication of her book if she didn't?)

At one point MacKinnon calls objectification a result of objectivity, and says the process of objectification separates "the stance from which the world is known" from "the world that is apprehended." In other words, "to look at the world objectively is to objectify it." She adds that "this is the male standpoint socially." Ironically, no one in the pornography debate speaks with more "objectivity"—heavy use of the passive voice, with a crushing pseudo-scientific certainty about everything, especially how men think—than MacKinnon. In essays like "Not a Moral Issue," she argues strenuously against "the objective stance" and claims to speak on behalf of what women "know," yet MacKinnon never shows any sign of having read Nancy Friday, Tuppy Owens, or Avedon Carol, and she feels free to make wholesale objective declarations about what men think and feel without ever quoting any men except porn researchers who support her position—and the occasional convicted rapist.

I would argue that, in fact, sexual objectification entails just the *opposite* of "being objective": The viewer too closely identifies his or her own desires with those of the viewed. He presumes that what he sees accords perfectly with his values and desires—that the person he looks at feels the same way he does. That is both the charm and the danger of objectification. Men undoubtedly do this with the fantasy women in pornography . . . but Dworkin and MacKinnon do the same, in their own way, with pornography and the men who enjoy it.

As Ann Snitow remarks, "Not even in my most utopian dreams can I imagine a state in which one recognizes all others as fully as one recognizes oneself (if one can even claim to recognize oneself, roundly, fully, without fragmentation). . . . the antipornography campaign introduces misleading goals into our struggle when it intimates that in a feminist world we will never objectify anyone, never take the part for the whole. . . ."

Subordination. Another charge leveled at pornography is that it depicts, celebrates, and reinforces the subordination of women. Canadian feminist Susan Cole asserts, "rarely will a person encounter sexually explicit materials featuring adults that are not records of sexual subordination." As examples, she cites a spectrum from assault and torture to the coercion of poverty, and the subtler conditioning that teaches women that being a sex object should be every woman's dream. "Where there is no sexual subordination, there is no pornography," Cole concludes. Female subordination inevitably means male domination. As Irene Diamond explains, "Pornography is primarily a medium for expressing norms about male power and domination, thereby functioning as a social control mechanism for keeping women in a subordinate status."

Exhibit One for the antipornography activists is Linda Lovelace, the star of the top-grossing pornographic film of all time, *Deep Throat*. References to Lovelace and her story, related autobiographically in the book *Ordeal* (and a ghastly tale it is), are nearly as plentiful in antipornography polemics as those to snuff. For two and a half years, she was raped, beaten, threatened with a gun, prostituted, forced to perform in a video with a dog, and made to simulate lovemaking with other women on film and off though it gave her no pleasure. When MacKinnon declares that "Women are known to be brutally coerced into pornographic performances," Lovelace is her *only* example.

The problem with using Linda Lovelace as proof is that she was beaten and prostituted long before she had anything to do with appearing in pornography. She was an abused wife: It was her husband Chuck Traynor who did all these things to her. The celebrated bruises that can be seen on her legs in the movie were left there by her spouse, not pornographers. And he would have done most of the abuse—the beatings, the rapes, the humiliation, the pimping—whether she ever appeared in porn or not.

In fact, as some commentators have noted, Lovelace states in her book that working on *Deep Throat* provided some of the first happy and relaxed moments of her marriage. "Something was happening to me, something strange," Lovelace writes of the first day of filming. "It had to do with the fact that no one was treating me like garbage. And maybe it was just the chemistry of being part of a group. For the first time in many months, I was thrown in with other people, other people who weren't perverted and threatening." (Remember, these are porn actors and filmmakers she is referring to here.)

Although no one came to her aid when her husband beat her up, and they continued to make use of her performance for the movie, she could tell even at the time that no one approved of his treatment of her. Her book strongly suggests that if she had not appeared in *Deep Throat* and thereby become a minor celebrity known to many other people, she would have remained an unknown, abused wife and perhaps never gotten away from Traynor alive. Pornography did not put her in that mess; it helped her to get out of it, and may have saved her life.

Ordeal also offers portraits of many women in the sex industry who do not appear to be under any duress, and of men who treat female sex workers with consideration. Several girls willingly joined Traynor's pimping operation. Lovelace describes "Melody" as a very intelligent madame of her own sex business—she "always carried a book to read with her, even on jobs" and "she was smart, way too smart to ever become one of Chuck's girls." "Kitty" was a "tough and independent" 20-year-old who, when she learned that Linda was prostituting against her will, said, "I think that's terrible. I don't think anyone should *have* to do anything." Rob and Cathy were a married couple who starred in pornographic films together, by choice as far as Lovelace could see.

Andrea True, a costar in *Deep Throat II*, is said to be "very intelligent, a college graduate, and much too smart to be doing what she did for a living." During the filming, True unionized the actors. "For most of them, an eight-hour day was a big step up."

When Traynor tried to get Linda work at a New York brothel run by a woman named Milka, the madame asked her friend Martin to test the new woman out. In private, Linda began to cry, so Martin eased away and asked, "You don't really want to do this?" She acknowledged it was true, and he responded, "You're not into this kind of thing; you shouldn't be doing it." Back with Milka and Traynor, Martin praised Linda to the skies so her husband/pimp would not be suspicious, yet somehow conveyed to the madame that "something was not quite right here."

Even a 16-year-old runaway who casually agreed to prostitute for Traynor for a while told him off when he tried to get her to have sex with Linda for his enjoyment. "Whoa right there!" she yelled as Traynor put Linda's hand on her breast when "Ginger" was dozing off; "You think I'm supposed to give you some free entertainment? Jesus Christ, stop being such a creep and let me get some sleep." Later, when he started to tell Ginger how to wash a car, she left. "I certainly did respect her," Lovelace writes. "There she was, still a kid, no bigger than a splinter, and she was able to just walk away." None of the antiporn feminists who use Lovelace as an emblem has acknowledged any of these counter-examples to their case.

Ordeal is a story of spousal abuse, not pornography. That *Deep Throat* came to symbolize the battle between First Amendment speech rights versus women's rights was a consequence of authorities trying to shut it down, and antiporn feminists pretending that Lovelace had been abused solely to make pornography. MacKinnon complains that the film "is protected speech" even though *Ordeal* "makes clear that the film documents crimes, acts that violate laws in all fifty states." Perhaps it does, but the video of the Rodney King beating and the Fox network cop shows depict actual crimes too, and we do not prosecute the people who made or broadcast them. MacKinnon tries to pretend that the ordeal of Linda Lovelace is somehow every woman's story: "It is what men experience *as* our sexuality. What connects Linda's ordeal and the success of *Deep Throat* with the situation of all women is the force they are based on." Somehow I doubt MacKinnon means to imply her life has been one of unmitigated humiliation and coercion.

There are several basic problems with the subordination argument. For one thing, women in pornography are often assertive and sexually aggressive. Sex appears to be their idea: They tug at men's clothing, move into position, and initiate various sex acts. Rarely does anyone have to tell them what to do. These women are not acting the way opponents of pornography say they do, nor are they acting like women often do in public life.

And viewers like this. Several in my survey talked admiringly of "dominant women," "woman on top" sex, and females taking control. As many heterosexual men said they would like to see a woman anally penetrate a man as those who said they liked to see anal sex with a man penetrating a woman. "Seeing a straight man penetrated by a straight woman with a dildo would be exciting and different for a change," said one. If this is the case, how can Irene Diamond claim porn functions as a "social control mechanism for keeping women in a subordinate status"?

Louise Kaplan, a psychotherapist who is no friend of pornography, offers an interpretation at odds with the standard antiporn line. True, she believes "sadomasochistic sexual fantasies [with the woman in the submissive position] make up the bulk of pornographic reading materials and films"—although it is hard to imagine how this could be when so many magazines depict nude females alone or together without any men around. More provocatively, Kaplan asserts that men "unconsciously identify with the person in the submissive (feminine) position. The unconscious aim, as always, is to express yet disguise, even if barely, the man's wishes to be a submissive, denigrated female."

There may be something to this; now and then, men in my survey talked about identifying with the women, even in all-women scenarios. Kaplan's interpretation adds a piquant twist, but it overlooks the fact (and this is the second major problem with the "crime" of female subordination in pornography) that so many men are shown in submissive positions. Women sometimes tower over the males; fetish videos portray men bound and tied, even being whipped or stepped on by females. Confronted by such evidence, opponents of pornography cling to the "subordination of women" theory by shifting the definition: ". . . even when men are being subordinated, they are being treated like women," Cole insists. But why are *women* treating them "like women"?

The truth of the matter is, when you are in the submissive role, things are "done to" you; you get to lie back and concentrate on the sensations rather than have to run the show. When you are in the submissive position, the other person is taking more responsibility for the success or failure of the sex; whatever "doesn't work" is not your fault. Even what *does* work is not your fault, which is a convenient excuse if you have mixed feelings about it. This has been suggested as the reason behind women's historic rape fantasies. In the fantasy of being taken by someone who is so overpowered by desire for you, because of his lust or your beauty (preferably both), you make him responsible for whatever happens—for good or ill. It's not your fault if anyone gets hurt, or (god forbid) you actually enjoy yourself. Interestingly, when Nancy Friday did a follow-up book about women's sex fantasies nearly twenty years after *My Secret Garden*, she found a much lower incidence of the "faceless ravisher," which suggests that younger generations of women may be taking greater psychic responsibility for their sexual desires.

Sex workers and therapists know the truth of the matter. "In general I'd say it's nine to one that men want to *be* dominated," says Barbara, an escort worker in Britain:

> When you think, "What is the ideal girl that the client wants?" you might think: someone who is pretty, sweet, and submissive. And yet in actual fact, if you play that role with clients, nine times out of ten you won't see them again. Clients genuinely don't like submissive women. They want women who have spunk and who have a sense of humour. They don't just want you to roll over and put your legs up in the air. They want that spark, to get the repartee going. They really like it when you criticize them.

In a sense, the antiporn feminists are right: Men want to be in control of the encounter in order to fulfill their desires. But the antiporn analysis offers a superficial reading of the nature of power and control. In sexual exchanges between mutually consenting parties—which is the case in most sexual relationships, paid or free, as well as in pornography—it's often the one who is tied up, the one who is struck, the one who appears to be on the bottom, whose needs are primarily being served.

The flip side of "female subordination" is "male domination," also referred to as "male power and privilege." Pornography is supposed to depict and express the utter social, economic, political, and sexual power of men. Writes Kappeler, "The pornographic scenario . . . can be read and understood only in the context of a society based on the very same plot: the sadistic act of sex and violence, the power and domination of men, and their sexual subordination of women." In their discussion of the appeal of "lesbian" pornography, however, a number of men in my survey specifically said they liked the sense of equality and gentleness between two women making love. Others spoke of equality between the sexes as appealing, even necessary, to their own pleasure. Apparently those men were not being turned on by the dominance that opponents of pornography see in it.

Isn't it just as likely that pornography reflects male desire, frustration, and powerlessness as it does male power and privilege? Is it not possible that all this emphasis on penis size and staying power is in fact wish fulfillment—a fantasy of how sexual reality could be, ought to be . . . *because it isn't?* Sara Diamond thinks so: "I believe that in terms of unconscious messages, much pornography is ultimately about men's fears: of inadequacy, of being controlled by women emotionally and sexually through dependency, of losing power." She has a point, but why are women often shown taking control of the sexual encounter in pornography? Why do women in porn initiate sex acts? Pornographic females are willing and take the initiative because women often do not in real life. Pornographic organs stay erect as long as necessary—and even longer—because they sometimes don't when we want them to in life . . . especially when we are young.

I think most people intuitively understand this, even if they don't realize it. Women who have no interest in porn or actively dislike it tend to regard men who use it as pathetic. Why would they do this if porn depicts "the reality of male power and privilege"? If pornography really expressed the power and privilege of its viewers, most women would be clamoring to see porn with naked men in it, because then the women would be in the power position. Yet when women do see nude males, they often feel silly or embarrassed. Far from expressing the power and privilege most men "actually" possess in society, porn more likely expresses what the viewer feels he lacks or is missing out on . . . and that's why even ignorant and unsympathetic women regard masculine interest in porn as pathetic rather than a threat.

What sort of man most routinely shows disrespect toward women, and speaks of women coarsely, and draws pictures of female privates on bathroom walls? Usually a young, unformed male—one who does not enjoy great knowledge of women or power in the social or business world. Laura Kipnis theorizes that pornography is about transgression: mapping the borders of culture's decorum and stepping over them. Naturally, teens who are searching for identity—straining at adult-hood—try to locate and sometimes transgress those boundaries, whether it's through smoking cigarettes, sneaking alcohol, learning to drive as soon as possible, or looking at pornography (as well as experimenting with sex itself). This is not a reflection of their personal power, but their relative powerlessness. Says Camille Paglia:

> The dominance of woman's image in pornography is not about the sub-ordination of women—it's the opposite. It's about male anxiety. It's about the male mind trying to confront and take control of this enormous, mysterious power of female sexuality.

A man longs to know what a woman looks like when she is willing, when she wants to do everything he desires, because too often he does not have that experience in real life. This is no different from the longing that drives women to romance novels, where the heroes are unreal (or at least atypical) mirrors of feminine desires. When men fantasize in their heads, they often recall their past, most memorable sexual experiences, not just the ones they wish would happen. Part of the appeal of pornography is that it reproduces the feeling of one's greatest sexual experiences, when you knew for certain the other person wanted you and everything happened as it should. It merely substitutes a lovely stranger as the other player.

Degradation. A third charge against pornography is that it is degrading to women. To be objectified, Susan Griffin says, reduced to mere matter, is itself humiliating and degrading: "degradation is the central experience of pornography." We have already seen how objectification is in fact a common and harmless part of life. But there are also specific sex acts which, various commentators argue, degrade women and are intended to do so.

Diana Russell writes: "Degrading sexual behavior refers to sexual conduct that is humiliating, insulting, disrespectful, for example, urinating or defecating on a woman, ejaculating in her face, treating her as sexually dirty or inferior, depicting her as slavishly taking orders from men and eager to engage in whatever sex acts a man wants, calling her insulting names while engaging in sex, such as bitch, cunt, nigger, whore." That would seem to cover it, but . . . humiliating, insulting, and disrespectful according to whom? Everyone? Or just some people?

Most men in my survey would object to someone treating a woman as sexually dirty or inferior, too. One can hardly accuse them of reveling in the degradation of women when so many of them said they disliked or were positively revolted by cum shots, facials, violence (if they had seen any), close-ups of genitals and spread labia, S/M, anal sex, and urination and defecation during sex—all the things antiporn feminists attack. Fortunately, they also said they rarely saw most of this in pornography, where women's bodies and sexual pleasure are sought, worshipped, and praised. Women in pornography don't often take orders from men, because they understand them completely, know what they want, do what they want, and themselves want what men want. That this is unrealistic—a fantasy—is precisely the point. Few men expect this of a real woman; they go to pornography to enjoy the pretense. As for urination and defecation, few of us might find that to our taste, but what is Russell to make of the fact that men in pornography are on the receiving end of these acts too? Is that just as degrading? Or does it redress the power imbalance between the sexes? Should men be protected from enjoying—or at least exploring—activities that are in poor taste?

"Facial cum shots" or "facials" are a staple of certain brands of pornography, and one may also find footage of ejaculations on breasts or backsides, in hair, and other parts of women's anatomy. Like most antiporn commentators, Russell seems unable to comprehend that a woman could enjoy this. Susan Cole is a surprising exception when she faults Canadian law for its presumption on the matter: "But ejaculating onto a woman's body does not have to be degrading. It *could* also be a method of birth control." One of the men in the survey who enjoyed such images acknowledged his discomfort with them:

> [The appeal to me is] something I've never been able to explain to myself. It seems like such a demeaning thing, and I generally can't stand that kind of thing. It's just the kind of thing that feminists point to when they say porn demeans women, and it's an act I'd find slightly harder to defend against the claim (although it's still done of their own free will). I mean, what could be more degrading than spooging on someone's face? As far as I know, I don't enjoy any other acts that are even remotely similar—I have no interest in bondage, submission, or any of the other, more overtly "power-related" kinks. I always like sex to be an act between equal partners, something both share and enjoy with neither in control other than momentarily, and even then only to perform something the other likes. So while the "meaning" behind the act (power, control, subservience, submission) disgusts me, the act itself turns me on. Facials have an appeal I can't deny. It must be something deeply psychological of which I'm not aware.

Perhaps to read facial cum shots as inherently degrading may be unfair to male experience. It imposes women's feelings on men. In the typical "facial cum shot," the woman is rarely coerced or restrained. In fact, she rushes to position eagerly; she *invites* the event. She almost never looks as if she is suffering or upset by the result; often, she smiles approvingly or continues to make orgasmic sounds as if getting semen on her face is a thrilling experience. She savors the semen, lets it run out of her mouth, down her chin, and over her chest. She may look up gratefully into the man's face, or smile at the viewer. She may take the slowly deflating penis in her mouth again, and smear the semen all over it with her lips. If degradation and humiliation were the viewer's goal, wouldn't his pleasure be heightened by expressions of fear, disgust, and distaste on the woman's face, resistance on her part, and the necessity of holding her down? If pornography is an expression of raw male power and violence, how come there is so little evidence of it in these "disgusting" tableaux?

A 38-year-old man, married fifteen years, who said he liked "close-up shots of women giving head, and especially cum shots on their faces and breasts," added a critical caveat: "For a scene to be erotic at all, it must feature a woman's face, and it helps if she's expressing genuine enjoyment or excitement." A 27-year-old single man was even more explicit:

> I like "facials," for example—where the man ejaculates onto the woman's face. Not because it's humiliating, or out of any sense of power, but because (I think) it indicates enjoyment on the part of the woman. I don't think "Take that, bitch!" or anything remotely harsh.

In other words, the woman's acceptance and enjoyment is crucial for at least some of the men who liked to see facial cum shots.

I would suggest that "facials" in pornography are one of the ultimate expressions of a woman's acceptance—her celebration—of male sexuality and orgasm. For some men there may in fact *be* a lingering feeling of shame or dirtiness associated with semen, whether they were raised in a repressive, sex-phobic household or not. As we grew up, orgasms and the resulting mess were something men had to hide, to clean up, to remove all trace of in the home. (Bill Cosby has a humorous routine in which he expresses grateful and innocent amazement that his son began to do his own laundry—specifically, the sheets on his bed—in early adolescence.) Even in a long-term, loving relationship, one has the "problem" of how to mop up the goop, or who's going to lie on the wet spot. If not sinful or shameful, at the very least ejaculate is *inconvenient*, which may explain why pornography attempts to give it a positive, even magical value.

Thus, when a woman smiles and invites the explosion on her face—the part of her that gets the most public attention, the portion she assiduously washes and paints for presentation to the world—it may be the ultimate "I love you," or at least "you're okay, fella," for the man who has had to hide, clean up, and dispose of his semen most of his life. Although she does not specifically address "facials," Nancy Friday suggests men indeed search for this kind of approval and acceptance for their organ and its products:

> I know they exist, but in my twenty-five years of research I have never come across a man who had sexual fantasies of exposing himself. But mention the erotic dream of a woman who loves looking at his penis, inhaling the aroma, tasting the semen that spurts from it, followed by the final benediction, swallowing it! Well, hundreds of thousands of happy male eyes light up around the world. She accepts me! that fantasy says, she loves that deepest, sweetest part of me that women have taught me is repugnant, so vile that it makes them turn away from it and me, for we are interchangeable, inseparable, me and this penis with its magic fluid that most women, alas, want only for procreation.

Unfortunately, ignorance and training make many women loathe the notion of intimate contact with either. Friday parodies this feminine rejection ("and as for enjoying men's sticky semen jettisoning all over us—their 'homage'—please, take that ugly thing away!"), and concludes about men who look at nude women:

> Seeing only degradation in the eyes of men who masturbate while look-ing at women's bare breasts and genitals, angry feminists miss the point altogether. "The uninitiated think that men look at naked ladies to dis-parage them, or that the women hate the men and only do it to make a buck," says [Friday's psychologist friend] Richard Robertiello, who used to frequent burlesque theaters. "But it's a love fest. We men worship. These women see the adoration in the guys' eyes. The men think the women are goddesses for letting them look. Their wives don't care enough to show them their bodies. These women live out the guy's suppressed dreams of exhibitionism."
>
> "No catcalls?" I asked him.
>
> "The few times that happened, the men were so disapproved of by the rest of the audience, they were thrown out of the theater. The stripper/audi-ence relationship is a love affair, maybe even more important than a sex affair."

Hatred of Women. What underlies the drive to objectify, dominate, and degrade women, the argument goes, is undoubtedly hatred of them. For critics of pornography, it's an easy step from the first three to the fourth. "Most women hate pornography; all pornography hates women," Dworkin and MacKinnon declare in a coauthored essay. "What looks like love and romance in the liberal view looks a lot like hatred and tor-ture in the feminist view," says MacKinnon. And from psychoanalyst Kaplan comes the assertion that pornography is inspired by "uncon-scious hostility . . . a fear and hatred of the female body."

Actually, few of the men in this survey said what goes on in most pornography "looks like love and romance," though many said they would like to see more of that incorporated. If all pornography featured images like the ones Kaplan describes ("Labia are pierced. Breasts are lassoed . . . Nipples are pinched . . . Buttocks are branded . . . The genitals of prepubescent girls are licked by dogs"), one might think she had a point. However, Kaplan isn't describing the pornography most of the men in my survey routinely looked at.

If the critics' reading of the images and "message" of pornography with regard to objectification, domination, and degradation is inaccurate, then their claim that consumers of porn are motivated by hatred of women has to be suspect too.

Admittedly, some men are motivated by hatred of women. Sweet quotes one from a BBC radio show who said pornography "made me contemptuous of women and it also made me feel inadequate." This is not accurate: pornography did not *make* him do or believe anything; these are messages he *took* from it while other men and women might derive very different ones—just as the Bible has incited some people to violence and others to peacemaking. Sweet does not cite any other factors in the man's life that could have contributed to his attitudes, but I would bet there were some.

Consider the messages that men in this survey reported from their exposures to pornography. "Even at that age I began to appreciate the beauty of women, and I found nude women to be even more beautiful," a man said of his reaction to nudes in men's magazines at age 12. When they talked about what they liked in pornography, many men said "the incredible beauty of the women." One man thought the male performers should show more gratitude and consideration for the females. A literature professor stalked out of the theater when Jamie Gillis was portrayed raping a woman.

None of this sounds like hatred. Anxiety, sometimes. And fear—of women, of failure at sex, of not knowing what to do—perhaps. When they feel these feelings, men may go to pornography not to stoke them, not to build up hatred, but to allay them. To feel good about women. To worship their beauty. To imagine what it's like to have one want you. To pretend that sex is not so mysterious and complicated after all.

If such is the case, then theories about men and pornography need a serious and extensive overhaul.

Toward a New Theory
of Men and Pornography

It is inarguable that men have suppressed women and women's voices in a variety of ways—sometimes forcibly, more often through economic pressure and the planting of self-limiting doubts and fears. But few have noted the silences imposed on men: how men's tenderness, our peaceful side, our vulnerabilities have been ignored, devalued, and systematically bred out of us. We were given language to describe strength in terms of physical achievement, victory in terms of sports and war, manhood in terms of violence; but we did not learn—nor did we often seek—a language to describe strength in terms of patience, victory in terms of conquering fear (of intimacy, for example), manhood in terms of loving a child, a sibling, a parent, a spouse.

This silence about men's experience has been especially pronounced with regard to our experience of pornography. In the last 25 years, nearly all the substantive discussion has come from women, who have marched in the streets, testified before commissions, and published dozens upon dozens of books, pro and con, on the subject. But where could one find the voices of men?

The only language we were given to describe our experience of porn was denial or confession: We hid or we expressed shame. In the past, we were cowed by the stated morality of our mothers and fathers, the community, and our religions. Now the fierce disapproval of anti-pornography feminism has been added to the mix. All these factors denied a portion of our experience and the validity of at least some of our feelings, needs, and curiosities.

If the foes of pornography have been so wrong about men and erotic materials, what was missing? The comments of the men in my survey offer some clues.

Curiosity. Men look at pornography out of curiosity and a desire to enhance their fantasies. They want to see how women—and other men—experience sex (or appear to), what turns them on, what they are willing to try. In real life, it is ill-mannered to stare at others, even when they're fully clothed and not indulging in sexual behavior. The most interesting square foot on the street is another person's face, yet any time we encounter a stranger we allow ourselves only a glance and then look quickly away.

We hunger to know more about how other people look and act, but to look for any more than a few seconds tends to make both watcher and watched feel uncomfortable. With pornography, we may indulge our curiosity at length, and gaze steadily at other people being sexually intimate without fear of intrusion or embarrassment.

The Play of Fantasy. Much as the antipornography critique would contend that pornography offers a road map to action, many men in my survey said they simply liked to watch and had absolutely no intention of enacting what they saw, any more than fans of thriller movies want to fire an Uzi or engage in high-speed car chases. True crime and detective novel fans read about countless incidents of violence and murder, yet we never assume they pose a threat to society. Why should fans of pornography be regarded any differently?

The Pleasure of Surrender. Contrary to the notions of male power, domination, and force, pornography that shows men and women together often depicts them as equal participants, even men as passive recipients of sexual action.

In our relatively touch-starved culture, we have few opportunities to experience pleasurable physical contact with a stranger. No wonder porn stories and videos often start from everyday contacts with hairdressers, office workers, dental hygienists, and nurses, and amplify them into sexual encounters. This is a kind of wish-fulfillment—of daydreaming—because it doesn't happen in reality, for the most part. Nor do most viewers actively expect it to.

The act of looking at pornography itself constitutes a form of surrender. Fans of the genre allow images and stories to act upon them, inspiring physical and emotional responses that seem almost involuntary, and yet the images are chosen by the viewer, in a way that experiences in life often cannot be.

The Importance of Women's Pleasure. Time and again, the men in my survey said it was crucial to them that the women in pornography appeared to want to be doing what they were doing, and to enjoy it. Whether the performer was actually appearing in the porn due to coercion or economic difficulties was a different question. What mattered was that viewers sought to be convinced she was not. If that was the case, then coercion was probably not the primary turn-on, otherwise the woman's discomfort and fear would be more evident. If porn were nothing more than a simple demonstration of male power and the fulfillment of male desires, then what the women wanted or felt would be irrelevant. Pornography would indeed consist largely of violence, pain, and humiliation, as its critics assert. But it is not such a demonstration, and for the most part it does not involve such content.

Appreciation of Women's Beauty. If you look for the words that turn up most often in the men's remarks, you won't see humiliation, degradation, power, or their like; you see pleasure, fantasy, and beauty. Especially the beauty of women. Many women simply do not understand how beautiful men think they are, and how many ways we appreciate their beauty.

It may be some part of a woman's physical being that attracts a man's eye: the way she has done her hair or the way it falls and bounces; the way she has chosen her clothing to present herself, the way it falls lazily across the contours of her body or grips her curves; the lines of her torso, the length and smoothness of her legs, the delicate purity and wistfulness of the nape of her neck, the beguiling shape and bounce of her breasts, the equally heart-stopping globes of her derrière and its rolling grind as she walks. Each of these pieces forms a portion of a woman's entire physical presence, but any one of them alone can be beautiful.

A woman's beauty also lies in how she carries herself and the way she walks, the alert darting or penetrating glance of her eyes, the authority or grace of her hand movements, the way her face lights up when she smiles (and how readily and often it does) . . . all the subtle gestures and behaviors that suggest a woman is relaxed, healthy, self-confident, happy, and pleased with herself and with the world.

"I knew that when a man looks at a successful, satisfied woman, he may notice her age, but he feels her energy-life—and he wants some of it for himself," writes Nancy Friday. "But to insist today that men only want to be with, live with, and sleep with young women is to say that men are impervious to the glamour of intelligence, sophistication, economic power, and, yes, sexual initiative in the hands of a woman who knows what she owns."

One of Isabel Allende's heroines demonstrates this same understanding when she says, "As I approached my seventeenth year, I grew to my full height and my face became the face I have today. I stopped examining myself in the mirror to compare myself to the perfect bodies of movies and magazines; I decided I was beautiful—for the sim-

ple reason that I wanted to be. And then never gave the matter a second thought."

Women who constantly second-guess and worry about their physical appearance automatically diminish their own beauty. Many men
would take the company of a plain but lively and outspoken woman
who meets your gaze over that of a tight-lipped porcelain goddess who
rarely smiles and avoids looking back at you, as if to show a little life
would be to shatter her appearance.

Notice how men preen and strut, how their backs straighten and
their stride increases, when a lovely woman comes into view. This
effect is not merely a mating signal; men truly *feel good* when they see
a beautiful woman, whether or not she ever notices them or acknowledges them with a smile.

Why is male appreciation of women's beauty in all its variety such a
mystery to so many women? Partly because men have so few methods
of letting women know. We don't know how to do it gracefully and
respectfully; and the social context (let alone the current legal climate
and obsession with avoiding sexual harassment) gives us little opportunity to do so. Even when we attempt to pay a stranger a sincere compliment, with no strings attached, there's no guarantee we won't see
fear and suspicion in her eyes anyway . . . and that hurts.

Also, I think that women regard male appreciation of feminine
beauty as some sort of either/or phenomenon: If you like this, then you
don't like that; if I glance at her, I think she's better than you. Some
men may indeed give the impression they are weeding through the
crowd for the perfect model, but many more of us, I think, have no
such agenda. We enjoy women in all their manifold gifts. Strong and
assertive is beautiful, but so is ultra-feminine and demure.

Few men have a particular ideal of feminine beauty, especially as
they mature and experience different women as actual sex and romantic partners. When a man is young and all he sees in mainstream advertising as well as *Playboy* is a fairly limited range of body types and
attitudes, it's easy to form a mental picture of what he thinks is the
acme of perfection. But as he grows older and experiences women as

lovers, friends, and colleagues, a man tends to appreciate variety, even contrasting qualities, within and between women.

He finds powerful, outspoken women sexy, and quiet, calm ones sexy too—in a different way. There are appealing aspects of pert, small women, breezy buxom women, and tall, poised women. Large breasts may be compelling, but small ones are delightful too. It seems ironic that we stereotype young men as hormone-driven machines that will go after anything in a skirt, when their standards of beauty tend to be much more narrow than those of older men who have a firmer idea of what they like and do not like in a woman . . . but can appreciate so many different kinds of beauty as well. Many older men have committed themselves to a particular woman, yet can enjoy the sight and company of so many more types of women than a young man would—many more, in fact, than the older man probably did himself when he was young. (Women who frown at the small-mindedness of young men would do well to remember all the pleasant, unexciting fellows to whom they wouldn't give the time of day—or at best, immediately filed in the "he could be only a friend" category—when they were younger.)

And men's appreciation of women's beauty in all its variety carries over, to some extent, to pornography. Opponents of porn harp on the superficial features of women in erotic magazines and videos, but as my chapter on what men like shows, masculine tastes run all over the map. A bisexual friend of mine who participated in the survey told me he preferred British porn magazines because they tend to feature a wider variety of shapes and sizes of women.

Some of pornography's biggest stars don't conform to the stereotypes. Hundreds of beautiful women pass through the pornographic video mill, but the ones who become most popular tend to have something else—a positive attitude, the convincing portrayal that they love men and enjoy sex—that puts them ahead of the crowd.

Neither Nina Hartley nor Ginger Lynn, two of the most popular performers in pornographic videos, was surpassingly gorgeous in her prime. In the case of Hartley, fans spoke of her perfect ass and great sexual technique. Undoubtedly Lynn's little-girl voice and "innocent" style accounted for much of her appeal. But in both cases, the fact that the women acted as if they truly enjoyed sex and the company of men played a major role in their popularity. It was their spirit, the way they carried themselves and went about the business of performing sex—with verve, skill, and gusto—that stood out for a lot of male viewers.

To hear the antipornography activists describe it, the women in pornography are interchangeable. The feminist left and the religious right take it for granted that it doesn't really matter who's framed in the camera lens as long as she has breasts and opens her legs. Theoretically, the male viewer shouldn't really care what a woman looks like, because it's her humiliation, submissiveness, and degradation that matter most.

If such were the case, then the men I talked to would not have expressed gratitude and wonder toward these women: gratitude to them for revealing themselves in all their splendor, and wonder at the prettiness and variety of their charms. If looking at pornography involved nothing more than the expression of male power and privilege, there would be nothing to feel grateful about. These men would simply be enjoying their due. But they are not. When they say, in effect, *Thank you for allowing me this look at your nude body,* men tacitly grant that the woman had a choice in the matter—and the men regard the choice she made as a gift.

Clearly, the notion that all men want is to see women degraded and humiliated—let alone physically abused—is utterly wrong. As the men in the survey attested, what the woman looks like matters a great deal to them, and if she looks like she's enjoying herself, she doesn't necessarily have to resemble the models in *Vogue* and *Cosmopolitan* (who are only a little less naked, after all). Men like redheads, or small breasts, or ethnic features, or self-confidence, or assertiveness, or hundreds of other things that have nothing to do with either an artificial standard of feminine beauty or faceless degradation.

Sometimes, what captures a viewer's fancy is something infinitely intangible. After completing the survey, one man sent me a long follow-up note about an experience he felt was relevant:

After I sent [my answers] to you, I thought of one other thing. I was going to put it in originally, but it didn't seem to fit with any of the questions, and it seems so nebulous. When I was around 20 or so, I came across this one picture. I was at a friend's house, and I think it was in an old picture frame or something, an old piece of crap that he didn't care about. It was a small, oval picture, I recall, in a cheap wooden frame. It looked fairly old. But I was so struck by the photo that I asked him if I could have it, and he said he didn't care. What was it that struck me so? I really wish I could say. It was a woman, nude, sitting on a chair. Due to her hairstyle and the photographic technique I placed it perhaps somewhere in the 70s. You might know the "atmosphere" the photos in *Playboy* and *Penthouse* had in those days—a lot softer, more groovy and dreamy and surreal. They used a lot of filters on the cameras, especially Guccione in *Penthouse*. But I think it was the look on her face. Vaguely pensive, vaguely sad. She was pretty, of course, and had a nice body, but it wasn't just her figure. There was something about the picture that just really attracted me, turned me on sexually and emotionally. I lost it long ago, but thinking back, I guess what I liked so much about it—a plain old, garden-variety shot that could have come from any one of a million men's magazines—was that it not only captured what she looked like, [but also] the essence of a moment in time, a pretty young woman lost in thought, unconscious that anyone was looking at her. I felt like I had gotten a peek into her bedroom and seen her when she was by herself, not posed, no camera around—perhaps paused in the middle of dressing or undressing. Like a good novel or painting, just a few simple things created a whole atmosphere. I fantasized a lot about the picture, but not sexually. I thought it might be a rainy day, and she was pausing to listen to the peaceful sound of the rain on the window, or maybe she was missing her lover, or thinking about a sad memory. It was the essential un-posed, candid, human nature of the shot that I liked, I think. It wasn't garden-variety voyeurism, it was like getting an intimately personal, poignant peek into someone's life as she paused, unconscious of the way her body might look. Her eyes were ever so slightly downcast, with a faraway look in them. The hazy filter the photographer had used had made it seem dreamlike and soft, not at all like the sharp-edged clarity of today's stuff. It was a halcyon atmosphere, a single moment frozen in time, the atmosphere perfectly captured even though probably no one but me ever noticed anything special about the picture—other than the person who framed it. I wanted to meet that person and ask them what they had seen in it, but the ownership was a complete mystery. I like to think that for that instant she had forgotten she was posing nude for some magazine, forgotten that the purpose of her being there was for horny men to ogle her while masturbating, and was remembering something from her life. It brought to my mind similar times in my life—sad, pensive, rainy Sunday afternoons when you just lounge around and reminisce about things gone by. She was the Mona Lisa of nudes, unknowingly captured by some dirtbag photographer for some nameless sleazy magazine. I could connect with her, sympathize with her mood, share her experience. If I had been there, I thought, I could have slipped up quietly behind her, returning from the shower in my bathrobe, and put my hands on her shoulders. She'd look up at me and smile a faint smile. I'd ask her what she'd been thinking about. "Oh, nothing," she'd say, unconvincingly. Then I'd smile down at her, take her chin in my hand, turn her face up to mine, and give her a tender kiss. I masturbated with that photo a lot even though it was only vaguely sexual and I had many, far more explicit photos available. Why? The answer is the difference between pornography and erotica, the difference between fucking and making love. Yes, I "use pornography," but I still know the difference between those things.

Until Andrea Dworkin or Catharine MacKinnon can account for an experience like this and incorporate it into their theories about what porn "does" to men, they will remain hopelessly ignorant about men and what pornography means to us. When men who look at pornography feel tenderness, vulnerability, affection, and gratitude (as well as desire and lust), to be told that what they feel is only a desire for power and the need to humiliate and degrade women is inaccurate and insulting. No wonder we have been loathe to speak up: What men have to say seems utterly and literally incomprehensible when put next to much of what has been said up to now.

With the publication of this book, I hope that more women will recognize the lies of antiporn ideology, and be more prepared to listen to their men. I hope we will all question the tendency of Congressmen, legislators, and prosecutors to assume they can elicit knee-jerk hysteria in the electorate simply by screaming, "we have to protect the children!" I also hope that men will be freed—will be able to free *themselves*—to speak about their true feelings and desires, and to meet their spouses and lovers on a more open and equal footing.

Notes

Introduction

pornography is the theory Robin Morgan, *The Word of a Woman: feminist dispatches, 1968-1992* (NY: Norton, 1992), 88.

more sexually real Catharine MacKinnon, *Only Words* (Cambridge, Mass.: Harvard University Press, 1993), 24.

censorship of pornography is unfeminist Lisa Palac, "How Dirty Pictures Changed My Life," in *Debating Political Correctness: pornography, sexual harassment, date rape and the politics of sexual equality,* Adele M. Stan, ed. (NY: Delta Books, 1995), 236-252.

pornography cannot be separated from art Camille Paglia, *Sexual Personae: art and decadence from Nefertiti to Emily Dickinson* (NY: Vintage Books, 1991), 24.

male insecurity . . . cloying self-pity Anne McClintock, "Gonad the Barbarian and the Venus Flytrap" in *Sex Exposed: sexuality and the pornography debate,* Lynne Segal and Mary McIntosh, eds. (New Brunswick, NJ: Rutgers University Press, 1993), 112, 113. McClintock is a professor of English and Women's Studies at the University of Wisconsin.

interesting but guilt-ridden Linda Williams, "Second Thoughts on *Hard Core*: American obscenity law and the scapegoating of deviance," in *Dirty Looks: women, pornography, power,* Pamela Church Gibson and Roma Gibson, eds., (London: British Film Institute, 1993), 60, note 14. Williams is a professor of Film and Rhetoric at the University of California at Berkeley.

flawed and unreliable Robert T. Michael, John H. Gagnon, Edward O. Laumann, and Gina Kolata, *Sex In America: a definitive survey* (Boston: Little, Brown & Co., 1994), 11.

Unveilings

studies of first exposure Technical Report of the U.S. Commission on Obscenity and Pornography, Vol. 1 Preliminary Studies, "College Students' Attitudes on Pornography" pp. 181-182; "Westchester College Students' Views on Pornography" pp. 185-1877; and "Study Finds Children Consuming Pornography," NFD Journal 11(2) (February 1987), 13-14, reported in *Sourcebook on Pornography,* Franklin Mark Osanka and Sara Lee Johann, eds. (Lexington, Mass.: Lexington Books, 1989), 19.

brief, intense affair with pornographic magazines Celia Barbour, "Looking At Pictures," *The New York Times,* 23 April, 1994.

The Appeal of "Lesbian" Pornography

does not document lesbian lovemaking Andrea Dworkin, *Pornography: men possessing women* (NY: Perigee, 1981), 46.

imaginary and distorted access Mariana Valverde and Lorna Weir, "Thrills, Chills and the 'Lesbian Threat' or, The Media, the State and Women's Sexuality," in *Women Against Censorship,* Varda Burstyn, ed. (Vancouver, BC: Douglas & McIntyre, 1985), 103.

Contrary to popular belief Laura Lederer, "Then and Now: an interview with a former pornography model," in *Take Back the Night: women on pornography* (NY: Morrow, 1980), 60, 61.

Lesbians and die-hard bisexuals Susie Bright, *Susie Sexpert's Lesbian Sex World* (Pittsburg, Penn.,: Cleis Press, 1990), 97-98.

Such a rude question Ibid., 99, 100.

The Image of Men

real man having real sex Michael S. Kimmel, ed., *Men Confront Pornography* (NY: Crown, 1990), 11-12.

regarding the matter of sex objects Phillip Lopate, "Renewing Sodom and Gomorrah," in Kimmel, 30.

Tits and ass flood our culture Lisa Palac in Stan, 250.

Hitler's Aryan Susan Griffin, *Pornography and Silence: culture's revenge against nature* (NY: Harper & Row, 1981), 161.

appreciate watching men subordinate women Susan G. Cole, *Pornography and the Sex Crisis* (Toronto, Ont.: Amanita, 1989), 32.

Male-supremacist sexuality John Stoltenberg, *Refusing to be a Man: essays on sex and justice* (Portland, Ore.: Breitenbush Books, 1989), 129.

How Men Use Pornography

Pornography is masturbation material MacKinnon, *OW*, 17; *empirical observation* MacKinnon, *OW*, 119, note 22.

Sharing Porn

Many men felt that romance novels The notion that romance novels are a form of pornography for women is not new. Helen Hazen devoted an entire book to the phenomenon, called *Endless Rapture: rape, romance and the female imagination* (NY: Scribner's, 1983).

Off the Beaten Track

breeders, raped for the pleasure Alice Walker, quoted in *Making Violence Sexy: feminist views on pornography*, Diana E.H. Russell, ed. (NY: Teachers College Press, 1993), 97.

animals that can be bred against their will Patricia Hill Collins, "Pornography and Black Women's Bodies," in Russell, *Making Violence Sexy*, 97.

She is punished in sex Dworkin, *Pornography: men possessing women*, 215.

Animal Sex among Black Women, Seductive Black Bitch cited in Russell, *MVS*, 170.

Public Policy

Look at any photo or film Gloria Steinem, "Erotica and Pornography: a clear and present difference," in *Take Back the Night*, 37.

The 75% Problem

"Three Daughters" Candida Royalle, "Porn in the U.S.A." interview by Anne McClintock, *Social Text* 37 (Winter 1993), 27.

65 to 70 percent Andrea Dworkin, testimony before the Attorney General's Commission on Pornography, Jan. 22, 1986, in *Pornography's Victims*, Phyllis Schlafly, ed. (Alton, Ill.: Pere Marquette Press, 1987), 239.

Dworkin raised the ante to 75 percent Andrea Dworkin, *Pornography: a practice of sex discrimination* (Minneapolis, MN: Organizing Against Pornography, 1986): 13, quoted in Catherine Itzin, "Pornography and the Social Construction of Sexual Inequality," in *Pornography: women, violence and civil liberties*, Catherine Itzin, ed. (Oxford: Oxford University Press, 1992), 66.

study by the Delancey Street Foundation Mimi H. Silbert and Ayala
M. Pines, "Pornography and Sexual Abuse of Women," Sex Roles,
10 (11/12), 1984.

less than 15 percent Gail Pheterson, "The Whore Stigma: female
dishonor and male unworthiness," Social Text 37, 61, note 8.

eighty percent of the American production United States. "Attorney
General's Commission on Pornography." Volume 1, 285.

The Public Debate: What Did Everyone Get Wrong About Men?

Men Cannot Separate Fact from Fantasy

Men believe what turns them on Catharine MacKinnon, Feminism
Unmodified: discourses on life and law (Cambridge, Mass.: Harvard
University Press, 1987), 11.

Deep Throat was a success Ibid., 129.

The experience of the (overwhelmingly) male audiences Ibid., 149.

Pornography is often more sexually compelling MacKinnon, OW, 24.

much like the moments in musicals Similarities in style and
techniques between hard-core porn videos and mainstream movie
musicals are a central theme in Linda Williams's anslysis of the
former in Hard Core: power, pleasure, and the "frenzy of the visible"
(Berkeley, Calif.: University of California Press, 1989). See
especially pp. 123-152.

there are real women in the pictures Cole, P&SC, 43.

telling a trained attack dog to "kill" MacKinnon, see notes to page 382 below.

the argument that consumers of pornography Russell, *MVS*, 137.

Edward Donnerstein's reputed comment MacKinnon, *FU*, 188.

copping out Russell, *MVS*, 151-166.

the pornographer . . . never admits to his hatred Griffin, 170.

the pornographic mind is identical ... to the Nazi mind Ibid., 193-4.

Women in Porn Represent All Women

Pornography purports to define MacKinnon, *Toward a Feminist Theory of the State* (Cambridge, Mass.: Harvard University Press, 1989), 209.

In the real world, real women are seen Cole, *P&SC*, 150.

has become all women Griffin, 112.

No matter what men may do Nancy Friday, *Men In Love: men's sexual fantasies, the triumph of love over rage* (NY: Laurel, 1980), 21-22.

Most of the fantasies in this book Ibid., 37-38.

hence the great popularity Ibid., 37.

In pornography books, magazines, and films Helen E. Longino, "Pornography, Oppression, and Freedom: a closer look," in *Take Back the Night*, 42.

pornography asserts that women have neither Susan Lurie, "Pornography and the Dread of Women: the male sexual dilemma," in *Take Back the Night,* 171.

Ordinary women wear makeup Griffin, 206.

teaches women, step-by-step Lisa Steele, "A Capital Idea: gendering in the mass media," in Burstyn, 72.

No one has shamed my body Naomi Wolf, *Promiscuities: the secret struggle for womanhood* (NY: Random House, 1997), 45.

Itty-bitty Titty Wolf, 46.

Any woman who has stolen a glance Cole, *P&SC,* 47.

Krafka and Cash studies reported by Alison King in *Bad Girls and Dirty Books: the challenge to reclaim feminism,* Alison Assiter and Avedon Carol, eds. (London: Pluto Press, 1993), 78.

Dimensions *and* Over 50 *magazines* Laura Kipnis, *Bound and Gagged: pornography and the politics of fantasy in America* (NY: Grove Press, 1996), 117, 165.

Readers feel short-changed Laura Lederer, "'Playboy Isn't Playing,' An Interview with Judith Bat-Ada" in *Take Back the Night,* 130-131. Bat-Ada is a professor of mass media and speech communications.

We spend our money MacKinnon, *FU,* 91.

Porn Shows What Men Want

Pornographers . . . know what to make Cole, *P&SC,* 42.

Pornography provides an answer MacKinnon, *Toward a Feminist Theory of the State*, xiii.

eroticizes the despised MacKinnon, *FU,* 53.

women feel compelled Ibid., 95.

Porn Teaches Men about Sex

young male adolescents Cole, *P&SC,* 68.

only form of sex 'education' Ibid., 47.

"It was an all-points bulletin search" Wolf, 97.

Porn remains about the only source Sara Diamond in Burstyn, 52.

young men do not find it hard Baker in Itzin, 130.

debriefing procedures Edna Einsiedel, "The Experimental Research Evidence: Effects of Pornography on the 'Average Individual'" in Itzin, 255.

The argument that pornography causes violent behavior Kipnis, 175.

Men Use Porn Only When They Are Unhappy

It is also not surprising Baker in Itzin, 134.

Of course, pornography can never meet the real need Ibid.

There is something very sad and desperate Ibid.

many men become obsessed with the size of their penises Ibid., 135.

Porn Is Addictive

These testimonies prove Schlafly, *Pornography's Victims*, 16.

many men are fully addicted Sweet in Itzin, 188.

2.25 million Baker in Itzin, 125-126.

Porn Consumers Steadily Progress to More Violent Material

There is a cycle of addiction Sweet in Itzin, 191.

More and more violence has become necessary MacKinnon, *FU*, 151.

There is almost no pornographic work Griffin, 47, 111.

Abuse is not caused Cole, *P&SC*, 18.

The depiction of rape Beverly LaHaye in Schlafly, viii.

hung by their breasts Itzin, 20.

fucked, tied up, spread-eagled Russell, *MVS*, 18.

electrodes being applied MacKinnon, *OW*, 59.

men shove bamboo Susan G. Cole, *Power Surge: sex, violence and pornography* (Toronto, Ont.: Second Story Press, 1995), 55, 81.

A woman, nearly naked Andrea Dworkin, *Letters From a War Zone: writings 1976-1989* (NY: Dutton, 1988), 199.

One reason pornography is incredibly dangerous Ray Wyre, "Pornography and Sexual Violence: working with sex offenders," in Itzin, 236.

Pornography sexualizes rape MacKinnon, *FU*, 171.

only 7.8% of women MacKinnon, *FU*, 6, 232-233.

Dietz, Elliott, Sears Itzin, 35-37.

detective magazine covers Bill Thompson, *Soft Core: moral crusades against pornography in Britain and America* (London: Cassell, 1994), 154.

more and more pornography is more and more violent MacKinnon, *OW*, 88.

increasingly violent in the past two decades Diana Russell and Karen Trocki, "Evidence of Harm," in *MVS*, 211. Senn study cited: Charlene Senn & Lorraine Radtke, "Women's evaluations of violent pornography: Relationships with previous experience and attitudes," unpublished 1985 manuscript.

Thompson on Malamuth and Spinner *Soft Core*, 154. Discusses N. Malamuth and E. Spinner, "A longitudinal content analysis of sexual violence in the best-selling erotica magazines," *Journal of Sex Research*, 16 (3), 1980, 226-237.

Palys study Russell, *MVS*, 124-125. Discusses T.S. Palys, "Testing the common wisdom: The social content of video pornography," *Canadian Psychology*, 27 (1), 1986, 22-35.

Scott and Cuvelier study Ibid., 154-155. Discusses J.E. Scott & S.J. Cuvelier, "Sexual violence in *Playboy* magazine, a longitudinal content analysis," *Journal of Sex Research,* 23 (4), 534-539.

Reading University study Ibid., 177-178.

sadomasochistic pornography and lynching Catharine MacKinnon, *Toward a Feminist Theory of the State,* xiii.

most couples who participate Louise J. Kaplan, *Female Perversions: the temptations of Emma Bovary* (NY: Doubleday, 1991), 28.

Many women recoil James Ridgeway and Sylvia Plachy, *Red Light: inside the sex industry* (NY: Powerhouse Books, 1996), 84.

The portrayal of men as sexual victims Dworkin, *Pornography: men possessing women,* 34.

Mistress Holly John Preston, *My Life as a Pornographer, and other indecent acts* (NY: Richard Kasak, 1993), 72-73.

20 males to each female Kaplan, 24-25.

Mistress Anastasia Ridgeway, 90.

Pornography reveals that male pleasure Dworkin, *Pornography: men possessing women,* 69.

liked the sex-and-dominance games Andrea Dworkin, *Life and Death: unapologetic writings on the continuing war against women* (NY: The Free Press, 1997), 7.

chopped-up fingers Beverly LaBelle, "*Snuff*—The Ultimate in Woman-Hating," in *Take Back the Night,* 274.

The actress is alive and well The New York Times, 10 March, 1976.

"snuff" exists as a genre Cole, P&SC, 19.

they kill or rape or torture John Douglas and Mark Olshaker, *Journey Into Darkness* (NY: Scribner, 1997), 29. Douglas was the model for the character of "Agent Jack Crawford" played by Scott Glenn in the movie *The Silence of the Lambs*.

home movies Ibid., 35.

In Los Angeles Griffin, 116.

came down the grapevine Lederer, "Then and Now," in *Take Back the Night*, 69.

are believed to be flourishing Aminatta Forna, "Pornography and Racism: sexualizing oppression and inciting hatred," in Itzin, 105-106.

In a notorious underground porn movie Mary Daly, *Gyn/Ecology* (Boston: Beacon Press, 1978), 215.

Information . . . is understandably hard to get MacKinnon, *FU*, 285, note 61.

the film was never found MacKinnon, *Toward*, 312, note 52. Also cited in *FU*, 285, note 61.

The intended consumer MacKinnon, *OW*, 35.

How many women's bodies Ibid., 22.

priced to make it available to Everyman Morgan, 87.

increasingly popular as videos in the American home Kappeler in Itzin, 97.

absolutely the ultimate Cole, *Power Surge*, 23.

a hoax Ibid., 53.

As far as anyone in the bureau knows Yaron Svoray, *Gods of Death: around the world, behind closed doors, operates an ultra-secret business of sex and death; one man hunts the truth about snuff films* (NY: Simon & Schuster, 1997), 146.

I've never seen one Ibid., 127.

Dutch police Ibid., 161.

There was no snuff porn industry Ibid., 130.

Blood sells Ibid., 296.

Porn Causes Men to be Violent

men believe ... that they have the right to rape Dworkin, *LFWZ*, 164.

Pacifist males Dworkin, *Pornography: men possessing women*, 52.

Clifford Olson Cole, *P&SC*, 45.

Barbra Schlifer Cole, *P&SC*, 99.

Paul Bernardo Cole, *PS*, 53.

Lawrence Singleton Griffin, 107.

bully, a thief, and a con artist Maclean's, 95:4, January 25, 1982, 21.

[Olson] raped by an uncle Saturday Night, v108, July/August 1993, 35.

[Bernardo's] violent tantrums . . . ran away Maclean's, v108, Sept. 11, 1995, 22.

[Bundy's mother] pretended to be his sister Ann Rule, The Stranger Beside Me (NY: Signet, 1989), 8-9.

swung cats by the tail Ibid., 467.

laid knives around her body Ibid., 469.

Bernardo learned at 16 Maclean's, Sept. 11, 1995, 22.

cousins teased him . . . third legal surname Rule, 9, 16; see also Elizabeth Kendall, The Phantom Prince: my life with Ted Bundy (Seattle: Madrona Publishers, 1981), 27.

Our research has shown John Douglas and Mark Olshaker, Mindhunter: inside the FBI's elite serial crime unit (NY: Scribner, 1995), 356.

I'm not going to tell you Douglas, Journey Into Darkness, 136.

the fairly strong consensus Alison King, "Mystery and Imagination: the Case of Pornography Effects Studies," in Assiter and Carol, 72-73.

Paul Tillich Rollo May, Paulus: reminiscences of a friendship (NY: Harper & Row, 1973) and Hannah Tillich, From Time to Time (NY: Stein & Day, 1973). In The Word of a Woman (pp. 87-88),

Robin Morgan bewails Tillich's infidelities and interest in pornography as discussed by his widow, but neglects to note that other women were writing him obscene letters and engaging in affairs with him. She also overlooks Hannah Tillich's affairs, and the fact that she had sex with Paul Tillich while she was engaged and then married to her first husband. Indeed, Morgan herself proudly details *her* affairs in such books as *The Anatomy of Freedom*, so it is difficult to see on what basis she can fault the man.

Louis Armstrong Lawrence Bergreen, *Louis Armstrong: an extravagant life* (NY: Broadway Books, 1997), 420, 463-464. Bergreen writes that Armstrong owned a collection of erotic movies when he was single and touring in the 1940s, and enjoyed written soft-core pornography—which he sometimes asked his wife Lucille and various friends to read and recite aloud.

Eugene Goossens In 1956 the distinguished conductor was threatened with prosecution, forced to resign as chief conductor of the Sydney Symphony Orchestra, and fled Australia in disgrace after Customs discovered pornographic photographs and films in his luggage on a return trip from England. See Carole Rosen, *The Goosens: a musical century* (Boston: Northeastern University Press, 1993).

M. Scott Peck "Playboy Interview," *Playboy,* March 1991, 62.

life on a sub Sherry Sontag and Christopher Drew, *Blind Man's Bluff: the untold story of American submarine espionage* (NY: Public Affairs, 1998), 207.

The fact of the matter is that most people who buy and read pornography Douglas, *Journey Into Darkness*, 136-137.

Kelley study King in Assiter & Carol, 77.

it is because . . . feminism has made them so Deborah Cameron and Elizabeth Frazer, "On the Question of Pornography and Sexual Violence: moving beyond cause and effect," in Itzin, 364.

appears to be feminist Ibid., 364-365.

I wish that I could believe his motives Rule, 495.

users force women they know Cole, P&SC, 62.

For some men Peter Baker, "Maintaining Male Power: why heterosexual men use pornography," in Itzin, 138.

On paper and in life MacKinnnon, *FU*, 155.

it is not the ideas in pornography MacKinnon, OW, 15.

Sooner or later, Ibid., 19.

murdering a young woman Ibid., 19.

1971 Donald Mosher study, Russell, *MVS*, 143.

Sex in America study re: proportion of virgins; Michael, Gagnon, Laumann, Kolata, 95. The figures are 1.0 percent for males and 4.6 percent for females in the 1930s, and 8.3 percent for males, 5.8 percent for females in the 1960s.

Senn study, Russell, *MVS*, 143. Discusses Charlene Senn, "Women's contact with male consumers: One link between pornography and women's experience of male violence," paper presented at the

Canadian Psychological Association Meetings, Quebec, June 1992.

Russell study regarding 14 percent asked to pose, 10 upset, in Russell and Trocki, 195.

Russell study concerning 24 percent of married women who had been raped, in Diana E.H. Russell, *Rape in Marriage* (NY: Macmillan, 1982), 84.

That is a lot of women MacKinnon, *FU,* 188.

"It was a proposition" Russell, *Rape in Marriage,* 84-85.

Cosmopolitan study in Itzin, 224-226.

Even Ted Bundy backed down Kendall, 76, and Rule, 157. Rule asserts the same thing happened between the two with regard to anal intercourse, but Kendall denies she ever allowed it.

It's too easy to get a skewed Jen Durbin, "Confessions of a Feminist Porn Teacher," in *Tales From the Clit,* Cherie Matrix, ed. (Edinburgh, Scotland and San Francisco, Calif.: AK Press, 1996), 53.

quote from man in Hite study Russell, *MVS,* 120; the quote is taken from Shere Hite, *The Hite Report on Male Sexuality* (NY: Knopf, 1981), p. 718.

Many men would not rape Hite, 731 ff.

not acted them out—yet Russell, *MVS,* 122.

feminist colleagues like Robin Morgan see Morgan, "The Politics of Sado-Masochistic Fantasies" in *Going Too Far* (NY: Random House, 1977), 227-240. Morgan sternly explains that the world of fantasy and the world of actual sex practices "are totally separate" for her (p. 234), at least in terms of sadomasochism, yet her assertions about men and porn fail to grant the same capability to men.

Hite's percentages are quite comparable MVS, 123.

having a desire to behave in a certain way Ibid., 123.

1984 Zillmann study quotes from Russell, *MVS*, 134, 135.

Russell on Zillmann, Ibid. Actual details from Dolf Zillmann & Jennings Bryant, "Recent Research on the Effects of Massive Exposure," in *Pornography and Sexual Aggression,* Neil Malamuth & Edward Donnerstein, eds. (Orlando, Fla.: Academic Press, 1984), 123.

massive prior exposure reduced aggressiveness sharply Ibid., 129-130.

effects of massive exposure applied to males and females equally Ibid., 133.

studies of sexual arousal Senn in Ibid., 185.

women are as aroused as men Ibid.

affective desensitization Ibid., 189.

I submit that the causal connections Kathleen Barry, "Beyond Pornography: from defensive politics to creating a vision," in *Take Back the Night,* 311.

I don't know how many Wyre in Itzin, 243.

saying "kill" to a trained attack dog MacKinnon, *OW,* 12; the same simile appears in *FU,* 156.

FBI Urban Crime Reports, *The typical American perpetrator* Susan Brownmiller, *Against Our Will: men, women and rape* (NY: Simon and Schuster, 1975), 176.

The Public Debate: What Did Everyone Get Wrong About Pornography?

Objectification

even the most banal pornography Diana E.H. Russell with Laura Lederer, "Questions We Get Asked Most Often," in *Take Back the Night,* 24.

reduced to their sexual body parts Itzin, 66.

we rarely see the woman's face Dorchan [sic] Leidholdt, testimony before the Attorney General's Commission on Pornography, June 19, 1985, in *Pornography's Victims,* 55.

In pornography woman's body Susan Lurie, "Pornography and the Dread of Women: the male sexual dilemma," in *Take Back the Night,* 159.

spreads apart her thighs Griffin, 36.

The model who poses Alan Soble, *Pornography: marxism, feminism, and the future of sexuality* (New Haven, Conn.: Yale University Press, 1986), 157.

a little girl's doll F.M. Christensen, *Pornography: the other side* (NY: Praeger, 1990), 27-28.

Objectification, in fact Dworkin, *Pornography: men possessing women,* 115.

ticket-taking machine Soble, 162.

the fixed response to the form of another Dworkin, *Pornography: men possessing women,* 113.

Until the day women's bodies MacKinnon, *FU,* 27-28.

the stance from which the world is known Ibid., 50.

Not even in my most utopian dreams Ann Snitow, "Retrenchment Versus Transformation: The Politics of the Antipornography Movement," in Burstyn, 116.

Subordination

rarely will a person encounter Susan Cole, *P&SC,* 23.

Where there is no sexual subordination Ibid., 24-25.

Pornography is primarily a medium Irene Diamond, "Pornography and Repression: a reconsideration of 'who' and 'what,'" in *Take Back the Night,* 188.

Something was happening to me Linda Lovelace with Mike McGrady, *Ordeal* (Secaucus, NJ: Citadel, 1980), 128-129.

"Melody" Ibid., 59.

"Kitty" Ibid., 70-71.

Rob and Cathy Ibid., 105-106.

Andrea True Ibid., 195.

Milka and Martin Ibid., 101-102.

I certainly did respect her Ibid., 141, 143.

the film documents crimes MacKinnon, *FU*, 129.

It is what men experience Ibid.

sadomasochistic sexual fantasies Kaplan, 28.

even when men are being subordinated Cole, *P&SC*, 161, note 5.

Interestingly, when Nancy Friday See *Women on Top: how real life has changed women's sexual fantasies* (NY: Simon & Schuster, 1991).

In general I'd say it's nine to one "Barbara," "It's a Pleasure Doing Business with You," in *Social Text* 37, 17.

The pornographic scenario Susanne Kappeler, "Pornography: the representation of power," in Itzin, 93.

I believe that in terms of unconscious messages Sara Diamond, "Pornography: image and reality," in Burstyn, 44.

pornography is about transgression This is a central theme of Kipnis's entire book, *Bound and Gagged*; but see, for example, page 164: ". . . [pornography]'s greatest pleasure is to locate each and every one of society's taboos, prohibitions, and proprieties and systematically transgress them, one by one."

dominance of woman's image Camille Paglia, "Woman as Goddess: Camille Paglia tours strip clubs," *Penthouse*, 26:2, October 1994, 132.

Degradation

degradation is the central experience Griffin, 47, 111.

Degrading sexual behavior Russell, MVS, 3.

But ejaculating onto a woman's body Cole, P&SC, 79.

his son began to do his own laundry Bill Cosby, *"Those of You with or Without Children, You'll Understand"* The David Geffen Company, 1986.

I know they exist Nancy Friday, *The Power of Beauty* (NY: HarperCollins, 1996), 452.

take that ugly thing away! Ibid., 456-457.

Seeing only degradation Ibid., 440-441.

Hatred of Women

Most women hate pornography Dworkin and MacKinnon, "Questions and Answers," in Russell, MVS, 89.

What looks like love and romance MacKinnon, FU, 149.

unconscious hostility Kaplan, 322

Labia are pierced, Ibid.

made me contemptuous of women Corinne Sweet, "Pornography and Addiction: a political issue," in Itzin, 180.

Toward A New Theory of Men and Pornography

I know that when a man looks Friday, *PB*, 481.

As I approached my seventeenth year Isabel Allende, *Eva Luna*, trans. Margaret Sayers Peden (NY: Knopf, 1988), 166-167.